Pfeiffer™

Training Older Workers and Learners

Maximizing the Workplace Performance of an Aging Workforce

JAMES L. MOSELEY and

JOAN CONWAY DESSINGER

BICENTENNIAL
1807
WILEY
2007
BICENTENNIAL

John Wiley & Sons, Inc.

Published by Pfeiffer
An Imprint of Wiley
989 Market Street, San Francisco, CA 94103-1741
www.pfeiffer.com

For additional copies/bulk purchases of this book in the U.S. please contact 800-274-4434.

Pfeiffer books and products are available through most bookstores. To contact Pfeiffer directly call our Customer Care Department within the U.S. at 800-274-4434, outside the U.S. at 317-572-3985, fax 317-572-4002, or visit www.pfeiffer.com.

Pfeiffer also publishes its books in a variety of electronic formats. Some content that appears in print may not be available in electronic books.

Library of Congress Cataloging-in-Publication Data

Moseley, James L. (James Lee), (date)
   Training older workers and learners : maximizing the workplace performance of an aging workforce / James L. Moseley and Joan Conway Dessinger.
      p. cm.
   Includes bibliographical references and index.
   ISBN-13: 978-0-7879-8117-4 (alk. paper)
   ISBN-10: 0-7879-8117-6 (alk. paper)
  1. Older people—Employment. 2. Employees—Training of. I. Dessinger, Joan Conway. II. Title.
   HD6279.M67 2007
   658.3'1240846—dc22

                                   2006027906

Acquiring Editor: Matthew Davis
Director of Development: Kathleen Dolan Davies
Production Editor: Justin Frahm
Editor: Kristi Hein
Manufacturing Supervisor: Becky Carreño
Editorial Assistant: Julie Rodriguez
Illustrations: Ralph Butler

Printed in the United States of America

Printing   10 9 8 7 6 5 4 3 2 1

About Pfeiffer

Pfeiffer serves the professional development and hands-on resource needs of training and human resource practitioners and gives them products to do their jobs better. We deliver proven ideas and solutions from experts in HR development and HR management, and we offer effective and customizable tools to improve workplace performance. From novice to seasoned professional, Pfeiffer is the source you can trust to make yourself and your organization more successful.

Essential Knowledge Pfeiffer produces insightful, practical, and comprehensive materials on topics that matter the most to training and HR professionals. Our Essential Knowledge resources translate the expertise of seasoned professionals into practical, how-to guidance on critical workplace issues and problems. These resources are supported by case studies, worksheets, and job aids and are frequently supplemented with CD-ROMs, Web sites, and other means of making the content easier to read, understand, and use.

Essential Tools Pfeiffer's Essential Tools resources save time and expense by offering proven, ready-to-use materials—including exercises, activities, games, instruments, and assessments—for use during a training or team-learning event. These resources are frequently offered in looseleaf or CD-ROM format to facilitate copying and customization of the material.

Pfeiffer also recognizes the remarkable power of new technologies in expanding the reach and effectiveness of training. While e-hype has often created whizbang solutions in search of a problem, we are dedicated to bringing convenience and enhancements to proven training solutions. All our e-tools comply with rigorous functionality standards. The most appropriate technology wrapped around essential content yields the perfect solution for today's on-the-go trainers and human resource professionals.

Essential resources for training and HR professionals

ABOUT THE INSTRUCTIONAL TECHNOLOGY AND TRAINING SERIES

INSTRUCTIONAL TECHNOLOGY & TRAINING SERIES

This comprehensive series responds to the rapidly changing training field by focusing on all forms of instructional and training technology—from the well-known to the emerging and state-of-the-art approaches. These books take a broad view of technology, which is viewed as systematized, practical knowledge that improves productivity. For many, such knowledge is typically equated with computer applications; however, we see it as also encompassing other nonmechanical strategies such as systematic design processes or new tactics for working with individuals and groups of learners.

The series is also based upon a recognition that the people working in the training community are a diverse group. They have a wide range of professional experience, expertise, and interests. Consequently, this series is dedicated to two distinct goals: helping those new to technology and training become familiar with basic principles and techniques, and helping those seasoned in the training field become familiar with cutting-edge practices. The books for both groups are rooted in solid research, but are still designed to help readers readily apply what they learn.

The Instructional Technology and Training Series is directed to persons working in many roles, including trainers and training managers, business leaders, instructional designers, instructional facilitators, and consultants. These books are also geared for practitioners who want to know how to apply technology to training and learning in practical, results-driven ways. Experts and leaders in the field who need to explore the more advanced, high-level practices that respond to the growing pressures and complexities of today's training environment will find indispensable tools and techniques in this groundbreaking series of books.

Rita C. Richey	Kent L. Gustafson
William J. Rothwell	M. David Merrill
Timothy W. Spannaus	Allison Rossett
Series Editors	*Advisory Board*

Confirmative Evaluation: Practical Strategies for Valuing
Continuous Improvement
Joan C. Dessinger and James L. Moseley

Instructional Engineering in Networked Environments
Gilbert Paquette

Learning to Solve Problems: An Instructional Design Guide
David H. Jonassen

To my friend Scott Pitts, who teaches by modeling behavior

To my stellar fencing friends Marek Petraszek, Justyna Konczalska, and Katarzyna Kuzniak, who teach by competitive spirit and ethical example

To my resident assistants Dennis Fiore, Andy Maggetti, Melanie Pezeshki, and Jasmine Singleton, who teach by sharing youthful enthusiasm

To my advisee Michael Nemer, who teaches by his devotion to and perseverance in academic and workplace pursuits

And to all my OWL friends who have shared their working lives and generational differences with me

I dedicate this book.

—JLM

To all the OWLS and WLP practitioners who dare to dream dreams of an ageless workplace

To my coauthor Jim Moseley—this was his vision quest, and I was happy to share it.

—JCD

CONTENTS

PART 1

Make Way for the OWLS

PART 2

OWLS in Transition

PART 3

Transforming OWLS

FIGURES, TABLES, AND PERFORMANCE SUPPORT TOOLS

Figures

BENEFITS STATEMENT

Today, employers around the globe are taking a closer look at how to train older worker-learners (OWLS). For years, adult educators have recognized that older learners may require learning events that are different in design and content from those provided for younger adult learners. In the workplace, OWLS may also need some assistance and accommodation to capitalize on their potential for amplifying the successful performance of their companies and organizations. *Training Older Workers and Learners: Maximizing Workplace Learning and Performance* offers a multidimensional picture of OWLS and suggests ways to analyze, select, design and develop, implement, and evaluate OWL-friendly training.

Flocks of older worker-learners (OWLS) are staying in the workplace or returning to it, and experts predict that this trend will continue well into the third decade of the twenty-first century. At the same time, the level of education and training required for the current and future workforce is increasing.

OWLS are like and yet not like the other adults who populate the workplace. Organizations and those who are tasked with improving organizational, team, and individual learning and performance need to become better acquainted with OWLS, learn why and how to value them, and discover how to help maximize the learning and performance of the OWLS in their workplace.

Audience

We have written *Training Older Workers and Learners: Maximizing the Workplace Performance of an Aging Workforce* for workplace learning and performance (WLP) practitioners who need and want to learn more about the OWLS in their workplace. Workplace learning and performance is "the integrated use of learning and other interventions for the purpose of improving individual and organizational performance" (Rothwell, Sanders, & Soper, 1999, p. xiii). WLP practitioners are active professionals from human resource development (HRD), instructional technology (IT), human performance technology (HPT), organizational development (OD), training, and other related fields. Students who are taking graduate-level courses in any of these fields and have some work experience in the fields will also benefit from this book.

WLP practitioners perform many roles—manager of WLP initiatives, analyst of human performance gaps, selector of learning and performance interventions, designer and developer of WLP interventions, implementer of WLP interventions, change leader, and evaluator of the effectiveness of WLP interventions (Rothwell et al., 1999).

WLP practitioners are also generalists. They know a little bit about a lot of different learning and performance interventions—and may know a lot about at least fifty different interventions, depending on their education, training, and experience (Hutchinson & Stein, 1997). However, it is impossible for WLP practitioners to have "sufficient depth of knowledge in all the necessary fields" (Spitzer, 1992, p. 118), so they rely on research, literature, and human expertise from a variety of fields to help them learn what, why, and how. This book will fill in some of the *what, why,* and *how* and refer them to other resources for more in-depth knowledge and know-how.

Goal and Objectives

The goal of this book is to help WLP practitioners maximize the workplace learning and performance of older worker-learners (OWLS), based on sound theory and best practice. The book will help WLP practitioners accomplish the following objectives:

- Identify the characteristics of OWLS as workers, as learners, and as retirees—or *not*
- Analyze the OWLS within a specific workplace

- Analyze workplace perceptions about OWLS

- Identify how theories and best practices in the field of adult learning apply to OWLS

- Recognize how cognitive, psychosocial, and physiological transitions affect the learning and performance of OWLS

- Recognize how learning styles and challenges affect the learning performance of OWLS

- Recognize how health, wellness, and leisure issues affect the learning performance of OWLS

- Apply knowledge about OWLS to the selection, design and development, implementation, and evaluation of training strategies

- Locate additional resources that will provide more in-depth knowledge and know-how about potential training strategies

- Collaborate with OWLS to manage, analyze, select, design and develop, implement, and evaluate OWL-friendly learning and performance interventions, and to initiate organizational change

Scope

Training Older Workers and Learners focuses on learning and performance in an aging workplace. The cast of characters includes companies and organizations, OWLS, younger worker-learners, and WLP practitioners. The main stage is the U.S. workplace; however, whenever possible reference is made to the global aging workplace.

Although the emphasis is on learning and training, the book will sometimes suggest nontraining interventions. More and more companies and organizations are recognizing that training may or may not be the solution to a performance problem. Training and development units within organizations are also beginning to go beyond training, taking a broader view of performance improvement.

How This Book Is Organized

This book is divided into three parts: Part One, Make Way for the OWLS; Part Two, OWLS in Transition; and Part Three, Transforming OWLS. The book progresses from knowledge to application. Parts One and Two focus on learning more about OWLS; Part Three is application-driven and includes a call to collaborate with OWLS to improve workplace learning and performance.

Each part begins with an introduction or advance organizer. The chapters each contain an introduction, a discussion of the topic, implications for workplace learning and performance, and action steps for WLP practitioners. The chapters may also include figures, tables, performance support tools (PST), and information on additional resources related to the chapter topic(s). A glossary, index, and complete reference list appear at the end of the book.

Part One: Make Way for the OWLS

Part One offers a broad view of OWLS as workers, as learners, and as retirees—or *not;* implications for workplace learning and performance; and action steps for finding out more about OWLS and their workplaces.

Chapter One—The OWLS Are Here. Learn about the aging global workplace and demographic shifts. Discover that OWLS may be older and younger than you think.

Chapter Two—OWLS as Workers. Find out why OWLS are in the workplace, how they impact the workplace, and how the workplace impacts them. Review some common workplace perceptions about OWLS as workers.

Chapter Three—OWLS as Retirees—Or Not. Learn more about the new face in the workplace—retirees. Read the stories of some OWLS who retired and returned and others who never left.

Chapter Four—OWLS as Learners. Examine major research, theory, and practice on *later life learners* (another term for OWLS). Investigate six major perceptions about OWLS as learners.

Part Two: OWLS in Transition

Part Two describes the transitions that OWLS go through as they continue the search for wisdom, knowledge, self, function, and well-being that they began in childhood.

Chapter Five—OWLS in Search of Wisdom: Cognitive Development. Discover how age-related changes may affect how OWLS think and remember. Be amazed at the potential of multiple intelligences.

Chapter Six—OWLS in Search of Knowledge: Learning Styles and Challenges. Learning can be just a matter of style, or it can be a major challenge for OWLS. Delve into the learning style preferences of OWLS. Learn how to translate the alphabet soup of learning challenges that follow OWLS from playground to workplace.

Chapter Seven—OWLS in Search of Self: Psychosocial Transitions. For years psychologists and sociologists have studied the passage from childhood to adulthood. Explore the various ages, tasks, and stages of OWLhood. Look into the generation gap that may challenge the aging workplace.

Chapter Eight—OWLS in Search of Function: Physiological Development. Learn about the normal, age-related changes that occur over the lifespan of OWLS. Find out what can be done to accommodate OWLS in the workplace.

Chapter Nine—OWLS in Search of Well-Being: Health, Wellness, and Leisure. Solve the equation: health + wellness + leisure = well-being. Discover the link between well-being and maximized learning and performance.

Part Three: Transforming OWLS

Part Three is designed to help WLP practitioners analyze, select, design and develop, implement, and evaluate training strategies that will transform both OWLS and organizations into high-level learners and performers.

Chapter Ten—OWLS in Action: Sharing Experience and Motivation. Review the basic principles and practices of action learning. Decide whether OWLS have both the experience and the creativity to become action learners.

Chapter Eleven—OWLS on Teams: Collaborating to Learn. Discover the benefits of team versus individual learning. Explore ways to encourage OWLS to join the team and actively participate in team learning activities.

Chapter Twelve—OWLS on the Job: Learning with the Workflow. Learn how to help OWLS go with the flow when it comes to workflow learning strategies like just-in-time (JIT) or on-the-job (OJT) training. Check out how mentoring and coaching may encourage OWLS to share their experience and know-how with other workers.

Chapter Thirteen—Live OWLS: Learning in the Classroom. Classroom learning may or may not be just-in-time, but it definitely is real-time learning. Find ways that you can make learning sizzle for the OWLS in the classroom.

Chapter Fourteen—Virtual OWLS: Computerized, On the Web, At a Distance, Digitized. Today OWLS need to be computerized, on the web, at a distance, and digitized. Find out why OWLS may like or dislike virtual learning. Discover how to make virtual learning technology more user-friendly and accessible to OWLS.

Chapter Fifteen—Collaborating with OWLS. Learn that the best way to analyze, select, design and develop, implement, and evaluate training interventions that meet the needs of the OWLS and are OWL-friendly is to ask an OWL. Find out how to build a business case for collaborating with OWLS to discover their learning needs and find ways to accommodate their learning styles and challenges.

How to Use This Book

The reader should begin with Part One for a broad view of OWLS as workers, as learners, and as retirees—or *not*. Continue on to Part Two to discover more in-depth knowledge about OWLS. Part Two follows OWLS as they transition through cognitive development; changes in learning styles and challenges; physiological development; psychosocial development; and health, wellness, and leisure in search of wisdom, learning, self, function, and well-being.

Part Three is about specific strategies for training OWLS. The reader may read all the chapters in Part Three or concentrate on the one(s) that meet his or her immediate needs. Even readers who do skip a chapter or two should read Chapter Fifteen on collaborating with OWLS, to ensure that training interventions are OWL-driven and OWL-friendly.

Some Final Thoughts

The amount of literature on OWLS is staggering. Trying to winnow the wheat from the chaff was even more staggering. We had to ask ourselves, over and over, "Is this relevant to OWLS as learners and performers?" More often than not the answer was a resounding Yes. We made most of our decisions based on our experiences as WLP practitioners—and as OWLS.

We also struggled not to appear to stereotype OWLS or younger worker-learners. Joan and I are very similar yet very different OWLS. We both enjoy research and writing, teaching, consulting with organizations to improve workplace learning and performance, going to the theatre, walking, traveling, and gourmet dining. However, I am at one end of the technology continuum and Joan is at the other. I prefer face-to-face or telephone contact and writing or editing with a pen; Joan prefers emails or texting and says her handwriting has totally disintegrated through lack of practice—she writes and edits directly on the computer.

We hope this dichotomy has helped us avoid stereotyping either OWLS or younger worker-learners. You will note that when we discuss OWLness we use phrases and words like "some OWLS." We also use "may" or "could" when we suggest learning and performance strategies.

One note of caution: this book will *not* give step-by-step recipes for training OWLS—OWLS are too diverse and the catalog of possible training strategies is too broad to be covered in one book. It *will* provide background information on OWLS and suggest implications for workplace learning and performance and action steps that WLP practitioners can take to help OWLS succeed in the workplace.

WLP practitioners need to know their audience—and there is a lot to know about OWLS. They also need to be able to help OWLS grow and flourish in the workplace—and there are a lot of opportunities for OWLS to soar. We'd like to think that the sky's the limit, and we hope our readers will think the same when they have finished this book.

James L. Moseley, Ed.D., CPT
Wayne State University
Detroit, Michigan
January, 2007

Joan Conway Dessinger, Ed.D., CPT
The Lake Group
St. Clair Shores, Michigan
January, 2007

ACKNOWLEDGMENTS

Researcher and librarian Ruth Wilson, who scoured the databases looking for OWLS.

Special subject matter researchers Nancy Hastings, Peter Lichtenberg, Kate MacKenzie, Jennifer Mendez, Lynn Miller-Wietecha, and Joyce Wilkins.

OWLS who shared their stories with us.

Matt Davis, Kathleen Dolan Davies, Jeffrey Leeson, Justin Frahm, and all the editors and reviewers at Pfeiffer/Wiley.

Kristi Hein, for her insightful edits.

Series editors William Rothwell, Rita Richey, and Tim Spannaus, with a special thank-you to Bill Rothwell, who also wrote Appendix 4.1 on workplace learner competencies for Chapter Four.

Ralph Butler, for his striking OWL illustrations.

And our favorite caricaturist, Mark Siermaczeski, who made sure we did not take ourselves too seriously.

Part One will explore aging workplaces, demographic shifts, and OWLS as workers, as learners, and as retirees—or not. There are four chapters in Part One:

After we introduce the twenty-first-century aging global workplace, we draw a three-dimensional picture of the OWLS who inhabit that workplace. We draw each dimension based on research, theory, and practice, and we begin to build a foundation for educating and training OWLS. We end each chapter with the implications for workplace learning and performance (WLP) and suggestions for action steps that WLP practitioners can take to help their organizations learn more about the OWLS in their workplace.

1

The OWLS Are Here

I walked away from the corporate world at 57 . . . spent two happy years traveling, sailing, and volunteering . . . earned a second Master's degree in Human Resource Development at 59 while consulting with one of industry's best employers of mature workers. At 64 I'm still consulting and showing HRD departments how to capture the spirit of the mature worker and maximize the mature worker's potential. I love what I'm doing and don't anticipate retiring as long as my health remains constant . . . I just enjoy life and learning new things . . . I often wonder what I'll be doing when I'm 80.

Kenneth, age sixty-four, senior consultant

OLDER WORKER-LEARNERS (OWLS) like Kenneth are here— and they're here to stay. At age sixty-four, he is on the cusp of two demographic groups: (1) the age sixty-five-plus group, which is becoming the fastest-growing segment of the U.S. workforce and will steadily increase through 2030, and (2) the age twenty through sixty-four group, which is predicted to steadily decline through 2030 (Allier & Kolosh, 2005; *Reimagining America,* 2005). This puts Kenneth right in the middle of two major workplace trends—the aging or graying of the workplace and the demographic shift that will disturb the balance of the global workforce.

This chapter will discuss these two trends and establish the age span of the OWLS who are at the heart of the trends. The chapter will also suggest how workplace learning and performance (WLP) practitioners can use their competencies as analysts and change agents to assess the aging of their workplaces and make recommendations for action.

Workplace Trends

It is the same throughout the working world. The global workplace is aging and demographics are shifting. OWLS are getting younger—and older. And they are an integral part of a workplace that is undergoing other dramatic changes as well. We know of the growing use of information technology; offshoring, outsourcing, and rightsizing; contingent employment; performance pressures; life and work balance, and other pressing issues. Trends like these will continue to define work in the future (O'Toole & Lawler III, 2006).

The Global Workplace Is Aging

The total number of OWLS in the U.S. workplace began to rise around 1990 (Callahan, Kiker, & Cross, 2003); nine years later the *Monthly Labor Review* reported that over forty million OWLS were actively participating in the workforce, an increase from 1990 of 30 percent (Fullerton, 1999). Looking into the future, the U.S. Department of Labor predicts that 51 percent of the U.S. workforce in 2010 will be OWLS ("Labor Force Predictions," 2004), and the *Monthly Labor Review* forecasts that the number of OWLS will rise to nearly seventy million by 2015 (Fullerton, 1999).

The aging of the workforce is not limited to the United States. Literature from and about European and Asia Pacific workforces reports a similar increase of OWLS (Leven, 2004; Lesser, Farrell, & Payne, 2004; "Briefing Sheet," 2005; Lesser, Hausmann, & Feuerpeil, 2005). Currently, in most European Union (EU) countries the number of OWLS is relatively small; however, EU governments have agreed to introduce laws, regulations, and policies to encourage

- OWLS to stay in, enter, or reenter the workplace
- Organizations to introduce policies that "enhance the position and chances of older workers" and help OWLS "stay healthy, productive, motivated, and involved" (*Age,* 2006, n.p.)

In Asia, China will begin to see an aging workforce around 2040 and South Korea will encounter an aging workforce by 2050 (Lesser, Farrell, & Payne, 2004). The governments of South Korea and Japan are both anticipating their aging workforce and establishing legislation and policies to encourage OWLS to stay in the workplace.

However, there is more than just aging going on. Global demographers are predicting a concurrent demographic shift from a balanced workforce of older and younger workers to an imbalanced workplace in which OWLS predominate. For example, half of Japan's population is over age 41. According to Charles Leven, Chair of the AARP Board of Directors: "I am told it is Japan's destiny to have the oldest, working-age population of any member country of the Organization for Economic Cooperation and Development (OECD)" (Leven, 2004, n.p.).

Demographics Are Shifting

The results of shifting demographics will be felt in the workplace of industrialized nations throughout the world, including Asia-Pacific, Canada, Europe, and the United States. For example, over the next two decades the fifty-through-sixty-four age group of European Union (EU) workers will *increase* by 25 percent, whereas the twenty-through-twenty-nine age group will *decrease* by 20 percent (Lesser, Farrell, & Payne, 2004). In the United States, the Employment Policy Foundation predicts that when the baby boomers begin to turn age sixty-five in 2011, available jobs could outnumber available workers by 4.3 million (Hall, 2005). As the number of people in the age sixty-five-plus population increases, the number of people in the age twenty-through-sixty-four population will decline, and there will be fewer U.S. workers to replace those who are retiring.

Business, industry, and service sectors with a large proportion of OWLS will be particularly affected by the shifting demographics. The manufacturing sector estimates it may need as many as ten million new skilled workers by 2020, "partially to replace aging workers who represent a large portion of the 14 million people currently employed in the sector" (Maher, 2005). The oil and utilities industries also anticipate problems filling the vacancies anticipated from massive retirements.

In the government sector, the U.S. Library of Congress employs four thousand people and is considered to have a mature workforce; for example, "70 percent of its librarians (the single largest group of its employees) are age 50 or older" (Joyce, 2005). The Library could need to replace more than half of its librarians within the next fifteen years.

To compound the problem, another demographic shift is occurring—a shift in the age span of OWLS. Once upon a time people became OWLS in their sixties. Then the social phenomenon called *the culture of youth* occurred and OWLS became younger . . . and older.

OWLS Are Getting Younger . . . and Older

When we first began to research this book we thought OWLS were men and women age fifty through seventy who actively participate in the workforce as workers and learners. Then we read Hale's 1990 book *The Older Worker.* Hale defined *older* as fifty through seventy; however, she also admitted: "There is widespread variation in how *older* is defined in law, theories, surveys, studies, and the popular press and media. *Older* can be a label attached to anyone from forty to seventy and beyond" (p. 2). And that started our quest for the real age span of OWLS.

The more we read, the more we expanded our thinking, until we finally settled on an age span of forty and older. This age span encompasses those both younger and older than in our original assessment. Research on life and workplace trends, the normal aging process, and the influence of perceptions from the workplace all confirm that the age span of OWLS is expanding—OWLS are getting younger and older.

OWLS Are Getting Younger

There is no consensus in the global literature regarding when a worker-learner becomes an OWL; however, there is a general consensus that OWLS are getting younger. In the United States, the American Association of Retired Persons (AARP) 2002 national survey on work and careers included workers age forty-five (*Staying Ahead of the Curve,* 2002); the U.S. Department of Labor labels worker as *old* at age forty-five; and the U.S. Congress states that age discrimination laws are applicable at age forty.

In the United Kingdom (UK), Metcalf and Thompson (1990) and Arrowsmith & McGoldrick (1996) found that many managers consider forty-year-old workers as *older,* and a few managers even responded that thirty-year-old workers are older.

Some of the literature speculates as to *why* OWLS are getting younger. Mostly it is a matter of perception—impressions, attitudes, or understandings based on observation or thought that may or may not be true. For example, Stein & Rocco (2001) suggest that U.S. workers are perceived as OWLS at age forty because that is when they begin to think about retirement and organizations begin to view them as less productive and more useful as mentors to younger workers. The perception is that job skills peak and then plateau or decline at age forty; yet, for many OWLS, skills and interests just keep expanding.

Arrowsmith & McGoldrick (1996) suggest that the UK managers who think OWLS become OWLS at age thirty or forty may have been influenced by the workers' attitude toward life. The authors do not specify which attitudes are indicative of older workers; however, Chapters Two and Four of this book discuss some common attitudes and characteristics that the workplace attributes to OWLS as workers and learners.

Perceptions of being *older* may also be triggered by the normal age-related physical changes that begin around age forty. A worker *may* begin to show wrinkles and gray hair. Changes in vision, hearing, and so forth *may* begin to affect how the worker learns or performs. However, improvements in health, nutrition, and overall physical and mental well-being *may* also diminish or postpone the effects of physical aging and help to explain why OWLS are getting older (see Chapter Eight).

OWLS Are Getting Older

There is less controversy surrounding the upper groups of OWLS. AARP's survey *Staying Ahead of the Curve* (2002) surveyed OWLS as old as age seventy-four—well beyond the traditional retirement age of sixty-five. *Experience Works,* a national organization that supports and honors older workers, reports that more and more OWLS age eighty to one hundred-plus are actively participating in the U.S. workplace, and many of them are full-time OWLS ("The Search Is On," 2006). From a global perspective, an increasing number of Japanese men and women are working until they are age ninety to one hundred (Watanabe, 2005).

The reasons why OWLS are getting older are more of a reality than a perception. We have already mentioned that life trends toward better health, increased fitness levels, and longer life expectancy extend both the length of time an OWL can live—the lifespan—and the length of time an OWL can be able to work—the workspan. Workplace trends such as the shift from physical to nonphysical job demands (see Chapter Two) and the need to retain or rehire older workers also allow OWLS to stay active in the workforce beyond the traditional retirement age. Workplace accommodations such as flexible work schedules, telecommuting, and consulting opportunities can extend the working life of OWLS indefinitely.

OWLS Span Five Age Groups

There are more than sixty years of separation between younger and older OWLS. The forty-plus span we have discussed previously is so broad that the picture is out of focus unless we break down the age span into smaller age groups. We decided to use traditional descriptive terms found in the research literature (Neugarten, 1936; Neikrug, Ronen, & Glanz, 1995) to help us categorize the age span of OWLS:

Young OWLS—age forty through fifty-four

Mid-Old OWLS—age fifty-five through sixty-four

Old OWLS—age sixty-five through seventy-four

Old-Old OWLS—seventy-five through eighty-four

Oldest OWLS—eighty-five-plus

Table 1.1 presents a statistical snapshot of Young to Oldest OWLS here in the United States. There were some slight differences between the age spans we use in our categories and the age spans used in the various studies. We have only reported statistics that begin with the age group or do not deviate more than one or two years from the age group.

Table 1.1. OWLS Here and There—A Global Snapshot.

OWL Age Span	U.S. Workplace Statistics
Young OWLS Age forty through fifty-four	There were approximately forty million Young OWLS in the workplace in 2002 (U.S. Bureau of Labor Statistics, 2002).
Mid-Old OWLS Age fifty-five through sixty-four	There were 18.8 million Mid-Old OWLS in the U.S. in 2002 (U.S. Bureau of Labor Statistics, 2002). The Social Security Administration reports that OWLS age fifty-five-plus are the fastest-growing segment of the U.S. working population and will remain the predominant segment through 2010 (Allier & Kolosh, 2005; *Staying Ahead of the Curve*, 2002; "Turning Boomers into Boomerangs," 2006).

(Continued)

Table 1.1. OWLS Here and There—A Global Snapshot, *Continued.*

OWL Age Span	U.S. Workplace Statistics
Old OWLS Age sixty-five through seventy-four	There were 3.3 million Old OWLS in 2002 (U.S. Bureau of Labor Statistics, 2002). OWLS age sixty-five-plus will become the fastest-growing segment from 2010 to 2030: they will increase from thirty-nine million to seventy million (Allier & Kolosh, 2005; Wellner, 2002).
Old-Old OWLS Age seventy-five through eighty-four	Seventy percent of men seventy-five-plus are supporting themselves and their spouses (Atchley, 1991).
Oldest OWLS Age eighty-five-plus	There were nearly a million Oldest OWLS in 2002 (U.S. Bureau of Labor Statistics, 2002). All of the past *America's Oldest Worker Award* winners have been 100 years or older and working almost full time ("The Search Is On," 2006).

The largest segment of the global OWL population is currently age fifty-five-plus. In 2015, the demographics will shift slightly. As Young Owls become Old OWLS, the largest, fastest-growing group of OWLS will be age sixty-five-plus. The sixty-five-plus group will continue to grow through 2030.

Implications for Workplace Learning and Performance

WLP practitioners and their organizations need to accept that "demography is destiny when it comes to improving workplace learning and performance" (Woodwell, 2004, p. 9). Whether OWLS are forty or one hundred, Young, Oldest, or in between, they are working and will continue to work well into the twenty-first century. The very presence of large numbers of OWLS challenges existing workplace learning and performance policies, procedures, and practices. The fact that OWLS may be irreplaceable adds to the challenge.

Organizations need to recognize how shifting demographics may affect their success and survival. They need to adapt to a potential imbalance between younger and older workers. They need to look at the demographics and turn a challenge into an opportunity. If current demographic patterns persist, there will be more OWLS in the workplace and fewer younger workers available to replace the OWLS who do retire or to meet increased customer needs for products or services. Researchers such as Aaron, Bosworth, and Burtless (1989) and Johnson (2004) suggest that increasing employment among older adults could relieve the demographic pressures in the workplace; however, it takes a combination of awareness and action to maximize the learning and performance potential of OWLS in the workplace. The *ASTD Trends Watch* also suggests that organizations should hire more OWLS, work hard at retaining OWLS, and expand education and training efforts to meet the needs of OWLS—especially their need for continuing training in new technologies: ". . . success in the knowledge economy will depend to an unprecedented degree on workers' skills and their willingness to learn, not on whether they are young or old, male or female, black or white" (Woodwell, 2004, p. 21).

Finding the key to successful hiring, retention, and training of OWLS is not easy. OWLS "defy stereotyping" (Roberson, 2003, p. 5). The large age span of OWLS—sixty years or four generations—makes it almost impossible to establish "OWLness"; yet WLP practitioners need to become aware of the totality of OWLness and how to adapt workplace learning and performance initiatives to OWLS of all ages and stages.

The Key: Awareness + Action

To make the most of the aging workplace, organizations need to be aware of the degree to which their specific workplace is influenced by the presence of OWLS and to actively pursue learning and performance interventions as required. On a global level, the EU and countries like Japan and South Korea are currently funding projects to create jobs, training, and wage support for OWLS over the next decade (Lesser, Farrell, & Payne, 2004). In the United States, a 2002 survey by DBM, a global human resources firm, found that 61 percent of the companies were aware of the demographic shift; however, only 45 percent were actively strategizing how to retain, hire or rehire, or train or retrain OWLS (McIntire, 2005).

A 2003 study by the Society of Human Resource Management (SHRM), National Older Worker Career Center (NOWCC), and Center for Economic Development (CED) also found that while 28 percent of large U.S. employers in the study planned to set up programs to attract and retrain OWLS, less than 50 percent provided training to upgrade the skills of OWLS (*SHRM Trends,* 2003). WLP practitioners are in a unique position to help their organizations integrate awareness with action.

WLP Practitioners Can Help

WLP practitioners come from many disciplines—training, human resources, quality, human performance technology, and so forth. They are champions or advocates of learning and performance and masters of practical workplace-based learning and performance interventions and change strategies. They perform many roles—manager, analyst, intervention selector, intervention designer and developer, intervention implementer, change leader, and evaluator—and each role represents a group of competencies—analytical, business, interpersonal, leadership, technical, and technological

(Rothwell, Sanders, & Soper, 1999; Van Tiem, Moseley, & Dessinger, 2001).

Action Steps for WLP Practitioners

WLP practitioners need to become analysts and change leaders if they want to help their organizations integrate awareness with action. The associated competencies they will need to achieve success include data analysis, work environment analysis, identification of critical business issues, negotiation, communication, relationship building, diversity awareness, and visioning. The last section of this chapter suggests how to use these roles and related competencies to build awareness and recommend action. Meanwhile, here are some up-front action steps to help prepare WLP practitioners and their organizations for a potential influx of OWLS.

1. Learn more about the new American workplace—major themes, changes, and consequences to the American worker.

   Read *The New American Workplace* (O'Toole & Lawler III, 2006).

2. Add to your analysis toolbox.

   Read *Organizational Surveys: Tools for Assessment and Change* (Kraut, 1996).

3. Design and implement an organizational audit to determine whether the organization is aging and in danger of becoming demographically unbalanced.

   You can plan, design, and develop the audit; collect existing data and interview or survey members of the organization; analyze the data; draw conclusions; and make recommendations for next steps. Go to Performance Support Tool (PST) 1.1, How to Perform a Preliminary Organizational Audit at the end of the Action Steps. The PST will provide you with guidelines for conducting an audit, including questions to ask, formats to use for data collection and analysis, and so forth.

4. Learn more about roles and competencies for WLP practitioners.

   Read *ASTD Models for Workplace Learning and Performance* (Rothwell, Sanders, & Soper, 1999).

5. Learn more about OWLS as workers.

   Chapter Two, OWLS as Workers, discusses work-related characteristics attributed to OWLS. The chapter also provides a PST for how to discover what people within an organization really think or feel about OWLS as workers.

PST 1.1. How to Perform a Preliminary Organizational Audit.

Purpose: To help you conduct a preliminary audit of your organization to assess the current situation and determine whether your workplace is aging and whether shifting demographics will impact the organization.

Instructions:

1. Collect the information.

   Collect existing data about the current situation in your industry and in your organization from the research and professional literature on older workers, industry reports, and human resource (HR) or other organizational records. The *Sample Data Sheet* that follows suggests the type of information you could collect about your organization. Customize the *Sample Data Sheet* so it is specific to your organization.

   You may also want to collect information and opinions from people in your organization about older workers. Interview or survey executives, human resource practitioners, managers or supervisors, workers, customers, and OWLS. Use the sample survey: *What Do You Think About the Aging Workforce?* at the end of this audit or customize the survey for your organization. The survey can also be used as an interview guide.

2. Quantify and record the information.

   Use frequency counts or percentages to quantify the quantitative data collected during the audit. Record and summarize comments and other qualitative data. You can use the *Sample Data Sheet*, spreadsheets, or a blank survey form to record the results.

   Here is an example of how to quantify the data:

   a. Total the number of the respondents to this survey.

   b. Total the number of respondents by classification—executives, managers, and so forth.

   c. Total the number of respondents by classification and age group (20–29, 30–39, 40–64, and so forth).

   d. Calculate the percentage of the total number of respondents who selected each response to each item or perception.

   e. Calculate the percentage of the respondents within a classification—executives, managers, and so forth—who selected each response to each item or perception.

f. Calculate the percentage in each classification who selected each response to each item or perception by age group (20–29, 30–39, 40–64, and so forth).

g. Calculate the percentage of the total number of respondents who selected each response by age group.

h. Other . . .

The following is an example of how to record results after you have quantified the data.

Sample Data Record:

2. Should our organization offer the same training or retraining opportunities to older workers that we offer to younger workers?	Yes	No	Not Sure
Executives	20%	69%	11%
Managers	50%	45%	5%

3. Analyze the data.

Here are some analysis questions you can use to analyze the demographic and perception data you have collected and quantified or summarized:

Sample Analysis Questions: Demographics

• What percentage of our total workforce is made up of OWLS?

• What percentage of our OWL population is in each age group: Young, Mid-Old, and so forth?

• What age group or groups of OWLS is most heavily represented in our workplace?

• What age group or groups of OWLS is represented in *each* of our divisions, departments, jobs, and so forth?

• What specific divisions, departments, jobs, and so forth have the highest and lowest percentages of OWLS?

• Other . . .

Sample Analysis Questions: Perceptions

• How did each group—executives, managers, and so forth—respond to each question in the perception section?

PST 1.1. How to Perform a Preliminary Organizational Audit, *Continued.*

- Are the responses to each question from the different groups aligned with each other?

- How did each age group—Young to Oldest—respond to each question in the perception section?

- Are the responses from the different age groups aligned with each other?

- Are the responses from the different age groups aligned with the responses from OWLS?

- Other . . .

4. Draw conclusions.

   Interpret what the results mean to the organization; make deductions based on the audit results. Here are some examples:

   Sample Conclusions:

   - Currently, we *are/are not* an aging workplace.

   - We *do/do not* need to plan a strategy for maximizing the workplace learning and performance of our OWLS.

   - The following divisions, departments, and so forth are most affected by the aging of the workforce . . .

   - Our organization *is/will be* faced with an imbalance between OWLS and younger replacement workers.

   - We *do/do not* need to plan how to: *retain, hire or rehire, or train or retrain* OWLS.

   - Reports indicate that our industry *will/will not* be affected by shifting demographics.

   - Reports indicate that the global workplace in which we function *will/will not* be affected by shifting demographics.

   - Other . . .

5. Make recommendations for action.

   Encourage the organization to act, based on the results of the audit. If the organization is aging or will be affected by shifting demographics, suggest that it will be necessary to collect and analyze more information. For example, suggest that the organization continue by analyzing how the organization perceives its OWLS as workers and learners (see Chapters Two and Four). Another recommendation might be to investigate existing retention, hiring, training, retraining, and career development policies, procedures, and practices for OWLS.

6. Communicate the results.

   Build awareness and, if action is required, begin to gain support for a change initiative that will maximize the performance of the OWLS and the organization. Share the process and the results of the audit with the people who provided you with the data and anyone else in the organization who needs to know—especially anyone whose support you will need if you decide to recommend further action steps. Send an email or fax report; print the results in a newsletter; discuss the results at meetings, information briefings, and brown bag lunches; and so forth.

Sample Data Sheet:

Sample Data Sheet (for use by WLP practitioner)

Is our workplace affected by the aging trend?

1. Total number of people employed in this organization	_____ Total number
2. Total number of OWLS employed in this organization	_____ Total number
3. Number of OWLS in each age group	___ 40–54 ___ 55–64 ___ 65–74 ___ 75–84 ___ 85+

	Location	# OWLS
4. Total number of OWLS in each division, department, job description, and so forth. *Note: Use a spreadsheet to collect all this data; attach it to the data sheet.*	**Division** **Department** **Job title**	

Sample Data Sheet (for use by WLP practitioner), *Continued.*

	Location	Age	#
5. Number of OWLS in each age group by division, department, and so forth. *Note: Use a spreadsheet to collect all this data; attach it to the data sheet.*	**Division** **Department** **Job title**		
6. Evidence that our organization is or is not aging (comparison of past and present workforce, future workforce predictions, and so forth)	Our organization is/is not aging. *Attach an executive summary and supporting documentation.*		
7. Evidence that our business or industry sector is or is not aging	Our sector is/is not aging. *Attach an executive summary and supporting documentation.*		
8. Evidence that the global workplace in which we function is or is not aging	The global workplace in which we function is/is not aging. *Attach an executive summary and supporting documentation.*		
9. Other . . .			

Sample Data Sheet (for use by WLP practitioner), *Continued.*

Is our workplace affected by shifting demographics?

10. Total number of OWLS who could retire in x year. *Note: You may want to do a projection (3 years, 5 years, and so forth) depending on available data. You may need to use and attach a spreadsheet for this.*	____Total number in (year) ____

11. Total number of OWLS who could retire from specific divisions, departments, and so forth in x year. *Note: You may want to do a projection (3 years, 5 years, and so forth) depending on available data. You may need to use and attach a spreadsheet.*		# OWLS in (year)
	Location	
	Division	
	Department	
	Job Title	

12. Total number of OWLS the organization will need to replace in x year. *Note: You may want to do a projection (3 years, 5 years, and so forth) depending on available data. You may need to use and attach a spreadsheet.*	____ Total number in ____ (year) ____

13. Total number of OWLS the organization will need to replace in specific divisions, departments, job titles, and so forth in x year. *Note: You may want to do a projection (3 years, 5 years, and so forth) depending on available data. You may need to use and attach a spreadsheet.*		# OWLS in (year)
	Location	
	Division	
	Department	
	Job Title	

Sample Data Sheet (for use by WLP practitioner), *Continued*.

14. Evidence that our organization *is or is not* at risk due to shifting demographics and the pending imbalance between older and younger workers	Our organization *is/is not* at risk. *Attach an executive summary and supporting documentation.*
15. Evidence that our business or industry sector *is or is not* at risk due to shifting demographics and the pending imbalance between older and younger workers	Our business or industry sector *is/is not* at risk. *Attach an executive summary and supporting documentation.*
16. Evidence that the global market in which we function *is or is not* at risk due to shifting demographics and the pending imbalance between older and younger workers	The global market in which we function *is/is not* at risk. *Attach an executive summary and supporting documentation.*
17. Evidence that we *do or do not* include strategies for addressing the issues of the aging workplace in our strategic plans	We *do/do not* include strategies addressing the issues of aging. *Attach an executive summary and supporting documentation.*
18. Other	

PST 1.1. How to Perform a Preliminary Organizational Audit, *Continued.*

Sample Survey

Title: What Do *You* Think About the Aging Workforce?

Purpose: To find out whether the people in our organization think that our organization is an "aging workplace." We plan to use the information from this survey to _____ *[What will the organization do with the survey results? How will the respondents benefit if they complete the survey?]*

Instructions: Please read each statement and check (✓) your *immediate* response.

If you want to add a statement or make a comment, please write it in the *Comment* box at the end of the survey.

This is an anonymous survey; however, to help us interpret the results we are asking you to provide us with some general information about yourself.

D1. Check (✓) the statement that best describes your work relationship with OWLS in this organization:

☐ a. As an executive I work directly and indirectly with OWLS.

☐ b. I hire OWLS.

☐ c. I manage or supervise OWLS.

☐ d. I train OWLS.

☐ e. I work directly with OWLS.

☐ f. I am a customer of OWLS.

☐ g. Other . . . (please explain)

D2. Check (✓) the age group that best describes you:

☐ a. Under age 20

☐ b. Age 20–29

☐ c. Age 30–39

☐ d. Age 40–54

☐ e. Age 55–64

☐ f. Age 65–74

☐ g. Age 75–84

☐ h. Age 85+

Thank you for your help. Please read each of the following questions and check (✓) the item that best describes how you would answer.

1. At what age do you think a worker becomes older?	☐ 40 ☐ 45 ☐ 50 ☐ 55 ☐ 60 ☐ 65 ☐ Other ____
2. What do you think is the maximum age at which a person can actively participate in our workplace?	☐ 65 ☐ 70 ☐ 75 ☐ 80 ☐ 85 ☐ 90 ☐ 95 ☐ 100 ☐ Other ____
3. Is our organization aging?	☐ Yes ☐ No ☐ Not sure
a. If Yes, will it continue to age over the next two decades?	☐ Yes ☐ No ☐ Not sure
b. If No, will it begin to age over the next two decades?	☐ Yes ☐ No ☐ Not sure
4. Is our organization aware of the effects of aging on our workplace?	☐ Yes ☐ No ☐ Not sure

PST 1.1. How to Perform a Preliminary Organizational Audit, *Continued*.

5. Are we or will we be faced with a shortage of younger workers in the future?	☐ Yes ☐ No ☐ Not sure
6. Does our organization retain, rehire, or hire older workers?	☐ Yes ☐ No ☐ Not sure
7. Should our organization retain, rehire, or hire older workers?	☐ Yes ☐ No ☐ Not sure
8. Does our organization offer the same training or retraining opportunities to older workers that we offer to younger workers?	☐ Yes ☐ No ☐ Not sure
9. Should our organization offer the same training or retraining opportunities to older workers that we offer to younger workers?	☐ Yes ☐ No ☐ Not sure
Comment. . .	

2

OWLS as Workers

I still have dreams about sewing kimonos, but I can't anymore.

Seamstress Kura Ikeba, who retired in 2001 at
age ninety-nine (as cited in Watanabe, 2005)

I N CHAPTER ONE we established that OWLS are older worker-
learners aged forty-plus who will become a larger and larger component of
the U.S. and the global workplace well into the twenty-first century. We also
established that OWLS in some workplaces may become irreplaceable as the
number of available younger workers decline. Some European Union (EU)
and Asia-Pacific countries are gearing up to meet the challenges of the aging
workplace; however, few U.S. organizations are developing strategic plans to
retain, hire or rehire, or train or retrain OWLS.

This chapter will continue the discussion of OWLS in the workplace by
focusing on OWLS as workers. The chapter will begin by discussing why
OWLS work and how OWLS as workers are perceived in the workplace.
Then the chapter will describe how the presence of OWLS impacts the workplace and how the workplace impacts OWLS. The chapter will end with

implications for workplace learning and performance and action steps for WLP practitioners, including a sample audit instrument that the practitioners can use to identify perceptions in their organization about OWLS as workers.

Why OWLS Work

People in the United States and around the world are living longer and working longer. Ramsey (2003) reports that United States OWLS stay in the workforce beyond the traditional retirement age for two major reasons: they need to work or they want to work.

People Live Longer

Roberson (2003, p. 3) feels that increased life expectancy is "the most significant demographic change" in the United States. Today the average life expectancy in the United States is approximately age 77.6, and many adults expect to live another twenty to twenty-five years beyond their sixtieth birthday. Even adults who have not led lives dedicated to health and fitness can often improve their lifespan significantly when they quit smoking, improve their diet, or start exercising.

Globally, an increasing number of adults are living to 100 and beyond; for example, Japan has approximately 23,000 people who are in the 100-plus age group, and it is predicted that the number will reach one million by 2050. Some people in their nineties still work in Japan (Lesser, Farrell, & Payne, 2004).

People Work Longer

More and more of the aging population will continue to be an increasingly integral part of the twenty-first century workplace. AARP (*Staying Ahead of the Curve,* 2002) predicts that between 2002 and 2012 the number of workers aged fifty-five-plus will increase by more than ten million workers. As the number of OWLS increases, the difference between the number of men and women in the workplace is declining. Men will continue to be the majority in the workplace; however, working women aged fifty-five-plus will account for 53 percent of the growth (*America's Changing Workforce,* 2003).

One reason people are working longer may be that with fewer physical demands on the job and better health, more workers are now able to delay retirement and work until older ages (Crimmins, Reynolds, & Saito, 1999). Two other reasons are that people have no choice, they need to work; or, people want to work because they like working.

Some Need to Work. There are several economic reasons why OWLS need to work. The projected population shift includes an increasing number of elderly and dependent children who need to be supported and will compound the pressures on working adults, forcing OWLS to stay in the workforce beyond the current retirement age (Findsen, 2005). In addition, 70 percent of men aged seventy-five and older are still supporting themselves and their spouses (Atchley, 1991).

Changes in Social Security also make it necessary for OWLS to work longer before they can become eligible for full benefits. The increasing cost of retirement brought about by changes in pension plans and medical benefits is also driving OWLS to stay in the workforce.

Some Want to Work. OWLS are mentally younger, physically more fit, and healthier than ever before. "There's a new feisty attitude among men and women in their 50s, 60s, 70s and even beyond. They don't feel old in the sense their grandparents were old. They don't feel burned out or used-up" (Ramsey, 2003, p. 9).

Many OWLS are not ready to retire at age sixty-five, let alone take an early retirement. They either prefer to continue working in their present field or organization, or they may want to make a career change. Wanting to work is one of the unique characteristics of Boomer OWLS who were born between 1946 and 1964 (*America's Changing Workforce,* 2003).

Even this early in the discussion of OWLS as workers, it is evident that OWLS are not all alike. OWLS do not all work for the same reason. Their motivation for being in the workplace affects how they learn and perform, how they view themselves, and how the workplace views them.

Workplace Perceptions About OWLS

According to the literature, there are many perceptions or stereotypes attributed to OWLS as workers. When the perceptions are negative it may be the result of attitudes toward aging: "There is a fear of aging, and it perpetuates discrimination and negative self-images among older people" ("Test your attitudes," 2006, n.p.).

All OWLS Are Not Alike

In Chapter One we established that OWLS' ages span sixty years—from ages forty to one hundred, or even older—and five age groups—Young OWLS, Mid-Old OWLS, Old OWLS, Old-Old OWLS, and Oldest OWLS. There are great differences between a forty-year-old Young OWL and an eighty-five-year-old Oldest OWL.

Even within the various age groups of OWLS there are differences related to normal physical aging; physiological and psychosocial transitions; generational differences: individual approaches to health, wellness, and leisure; and so forth. (See Part Two for more details.) Any or all of these differences may have a significant impact on how an individual OWL is perceived in the workplace.

There are five positive perceptions about OWLS as workers that, while they cannot be generalized to all OWLS, are most frequently found in the literature. OWLS as workers are perceived to be wise, experienced, educated, work-oriented, and self-directed. On the negative side, OWLS as workers are most frequently perceived as unhealthy, unwilling or unable to adapt to change, and unskilled or obsolete.

Some Perceptions About OWLS Are Positive

Ramsey (2003) believes that OWLS can balance any lack of energy, strength, or stamina with a combination of wisdom, experience, and know-how—that almost inseparable combination of knowledge and skill.

Wise. Wisdom is defined as "excellent judgment and advice about important and uncertain matters of life" (Baltes, 1993, p. 586.) Hooyman & Kiyak (1999) say that "wisdom is a combination of experience, introspection, reflection, intuition, and empathy . . . qualities that are honed over many years . . ." (p. 149) and that are frequently found in OWLS.

Experienced. Experience is the sum total of an individual's repertoire of knowledge and skills derived from past actions and perceptions. OWLS bring three types of experience to the workplace:

- Situation experience—OWLS use their repertoire of responses to past situations to define present situations

- Interaction experience—OWLS use past interactions with a variety of persons to develop their individual styles of interacting

- Self-experience—OWLS see themselves from others' points of view and integrate this awareness with past memories

Most employers of OWLS agree that OWLS bring a whole lifetime of experience and know-how to the workplace and the organization. For example, in an SHRM study 79 percent of the employers cited *invaluable experience* as a perceived advantage of retaining and hiring OWLS (Grossman, 2003). Certainly, younger workers may have any one of these skills; however, integration of these skills in people's interactions with their external worlds requires the maturity and wisdom of OWLS (Hooyman & Kiyak, 1999).

Educated. Approximately 70 percent of the OWLS in the year 2000 U.S. workplace had a high school diploma, over 15 percent had at least a bachelor's degree, and their average level of education has increased annually (Bolch, 2000). More recently, diversity consultant Grace Odums reported that 23 percent of Boomer OWLS possess a bachelor's degree and "baby boomers have more formal education than any generation in history" (Odums, 2006, p. 35).

Work Oriented. Boomer OWLS—Young and Mid-Old OWLS born between 1946 and 1964—epitomize the work-oriented OWL. Approximately 80 percent of the Boomer OWLS in an AARP survey plan to and want to continue working beyond retirement (*America's Changing Workforce*, 2003; Ramsey, 2003). The SHRM study previously cited also reported that 69 percent of the employers listed a strong work ethic as an advantage of hiring or retaining OWLS (Grossman, 2003).

Self-Directed. The literature also refers to OWLS as self-directed or self-starters. For example, Mid-Old OWLS aged fifty-plus make up 40 percent of the self-employed, and approximately one-third of the self-employed workers surveyed did not begin working for themselves until age fifty or later ("Self Employment," 2005). Despite the entrepreneurial spirit of OWLS, employers report that OWLS are able to accept authority, cooperate with others, and make independent decisions, depending on the situation (*America's Changing Workforce,* 2003).

Other Positives. In addition to wisdom, experience, self-directedness, and work-orientation, employers who responded to an ASTD survey cited the following positive qualities of the OWLS in their workforce: stability, loyalty, low turnover, strong work ethic, wide contact base, less mobility, and less safety exposure (*America's Changing Workforce,* 2003). In a similar survey, employers reported that they hire OWLS because they have traits that younger employees lack: OWLS are dependable, hard-working, loyal, and adaptable, take pride in their accomplishments, and are less apt to "do" politics (Ramsey, 2003). Other advantages of hiring and retaining OWLS include their willingness to work nontraditional schedules, ability to serve as mentors, and reliability (Grossman, 2003).

See the sidebar for a national positive—a whole week dedicated to OWLS.

 A WEEK FOR OWLS ONLY

National Employ Older Workers Week was initiated by the American Legion after World War II. It is set aside to encourage activities that recognize the important participation of older workers in the American labor market. The U.S. Administration on Aging and the U.S. Department of Labor are among the sponsors.

The activities include an award ceremony honoring the most outstanding OWLS in the United States. Most of those honored are aged eighty to one hundred. All are actively participating in the workforce.

Some Perceptions About OWLS Are Negative

Employers also reported some characteristics that are *disadvantages* when hiring or retaining OWLS. In the SHRM study, 53 percent of the employers listed lack of technical expertise as a disadvantage, 36 percent cited increased expenses due to health care needs, and 28 percent cited lack of flexibility or an inability to accept new ways of working (Grossman, 2003).

In the EU, "the stereotypic image of older workers is that they are slow, unmotivated, often ill, and cannot learn new things. Even though these images do not hold for most older workers, many people, including the older workers themselves, believe them and act accordingly" (*Age,* 2006, n.p.). A review of studies from Canada, Europe, and the United States indicated that OWLS "face a number of systemic barriers to obtaining re-employment and training which younger individuals may not face, including skills that are no longer in demand, less education, lack of mobility, lack of job-search experience and negative stereotyping by employers" ("Older Worker," 1999, n.p.).

Whether the characteristics attributed to OWLS as workers are positive or negative, myths or realities, the bottom line is that OWLS can and do impact the workplace. How they impact it depends on the perceptions of the people who populate that workplace and the OWLS themselves.

Impact of OWLS on the Workplace

OWLS could ease the predicted labor shortages that threaten the well-being of the now and future global economy. OWLS also have characteristics of loyalty and a work ethic that can benefit the whole workplace, and even the global economy; they are "mature, conscientious, have admirable work qualities, and communicate well with clients" (Hodson & Sullivan, 2002). And they can help the bottom line.

The eight public companies who made AARP's list of the *Best Employers for Workers Over 50* are also strong performers in the stock market. According to an analyst from T. Rowe Price, "a company that's good to OWLS is probably good to all its employees, which can lower turnover and boost productivity" (Wild, 2004, p. 16).

Employing experienced OWLS also eases the need for replacement workers and makes it possible to reduce per-capita output, maintain or increase living standards, and help ensure that the global economy will continue to grow and prosper (Grossman, 2003; Johnson, 2004). Retaining, rehiring, or hiring OWLS can also reduce retirement benefit claims and help support the world's increasingly aging populations.

Impact of the Workplace on OWLS

Even OWLS who are wise, experienced, self-directed, and work-oriented are often challenged by the changing nature of the workplace—restructuring, reduction, and the movement away from paternalism. Age bias and age discrimination; the big BOP—Burnout, Obsolescence, and Plateauing—and changing job demands also impact how OWLS function in the workplace. Figure 2.1 illustrates how these factors create a "gray ceiling" that can keep OWLS from achieving their potential.

Workplace Changes Focus on OWLS

In the midst of demographic change, the very nature of the U.S. workplace is also changing. Sicker (1993) discussed three trends that are especially hard on workers over the age of forty: corporate restructuring, workforce reduction, and loss of corporate paternalism.

Restructuring. Corporate restructuring and down- or rightsizing tend to focus on eliminating middle management and other positions populated by age forty-plus workers who then lose their jobs. Workforce reduction eliminates full-time jobs and gives rise to the contingent workforce: part-time, contract, or self-employed workers who earn less than full-time workers and do not receive benefits.

Reductions. Both voluntary and involuntary reductions result in job loss, lower wages, and loss of benefits, and could jeopardize worker pensions. Voluntary reductions can benefit working mothers and retirees, who may prefer part-time or flex-time work, especially if their benefits are covered by a spouse, pension plan, or Social Security.

Figure 2.1. It Isn't Always Easy for OWLS to Soar.

Restructuring   Reductions   Nonpaternalism   Big BOP   Age Bias   Job Demands

Nonpaternalism. Then there is corporate paternalism, or the lack thereof. Paternalism was a favored corporate policy until the early 1980s—and one that is within the experience of many Old to Oldest OWLS. It is being replaced by a move away from taking corporate responsibility for the welfare of employees to a trend toward offering jobs rather than careers. Writers like Thomas Friedman are calling for a humanistic replacement for paternalism—*lifetime employability* (see the sidebar for a brief explanation). Lifetime employability would require a strong workplace learning and performance support system to help OWLS help themselves.

TOWARD LIFETIME EMPLOYABILITY

Thomas Friedman (2005) addresses paternalism in his bestseller *The World Is Flat*. After discussing ten economic, political, and technological forces that have converged to flatten the globe, Friedman suggests that to compete in a flat world the concept of *lifetime employment* will need to be replaced by the concept of *lifetime employability* in which governments partner with companies to give workers of all ages the "tools" they need to keep them employable. In Friedman's scenario the individual worker becomes more and more responsible for "managing his or her own career, risks, and economic security . . ." (p. 284).

Age Bias and Discrimination. Age bias is global, and when it is institutionalized it leads to age discrimination. In the UK, one source explained: "you have only five years in the workplace—ages 35–40—when you're free of age bias. Otherwise you're seen as too young or too old" ("The Wonder Years," 2004). Ramsey (2003) reports that despite the passage of the Age Discrimination in Employment Act (ADEA) in the United States, the number of workers between ages forty-five and seventy-five who were laid off, fired, or refused jobs because of their age rose to 4 percent in 2002 and is still rising.

The Big BOP. Allen (1993) lists three negative career-related characteristics that are attributed to OWLS: burnout, obsolescence, and plateauing:

- OWLS are burned out—they are emotionally and physically exhausted from the stress of keeping up with the demands of their career.

- OWLS are obsolete—their skills are outdated, and they can no longer meet the demands of their career.

- OWLS have reached a career plateau—they are no longer *promotable;* they are at the end of their careers with nowhere to go.

"For many, the notion that older people have had their day and should make room for the next generation is deeply ingrained" (Grossman, 2003). In fact, Beigel (2001) calls this a "Depression-era attitude" and stresses that today's workplace needs both older *and* younger workers (Beigel, 2001). On the side of the OWLS, Ramsey (2003) reports that most OWLS think of themselves as a *will be* rather than a *has been* and just want to be employed.

Changing Job Demands. Changing job demands may help or hinder an OWL on the job. Johnson (2004) measured recent trends in job demands at older ages by comparing self-reported job characteristics among older workers in 1992 and 2002. Johnson gathered data for the study from the *Health and Retirement Study (HRS),* a nationally representative survey of older Americans conducted by the University of Michigan for the National Institute on Aging. He divided his findings into physical and nonphysical job demands.

When Crimmins, Reynolds, and Saito (1999) studied the workplace in the 1990s, they suggested that, based on fewer physical work demands and better health, more workers are now able to delay retirement and work until older ages. However, Johnson (2004) reported that between 1992 and 2002 reduction in physical job demands was limited to jobs that required physical effort only *some of the time.* In the Johnson study, nearly one in five workers age fifty-five through sixty reported that their jobs *almost always* required substantial physical effort.

Based on his findings, Johnson suggests that despite recent overall declines in the physical demands of work and the potential improvements in the capacity to work at older ages, physical job demands still remain an overwhelming concern for many OWLS.

Nonphysical Job Demands. Johnson's study also found that although only a minority of OWLS work in physically demanding jobs, OWLS must cope with potentially stressful nonphysical demands on the job. A majority of the OWLS reported that their jobs *always* required potentially stressful activities—such as concentrating intensely, dealing with people, or working with computers—as well as good eyesight. In addition, approximately one out of five OWLS *strongly agreed* that their jobs involve a lot of stress, and about one out of six *strongly agreed* that their jobs are more difficult now than they were in the past.

In summary, Johnson discovered evidence that the demands of nonphysical jobs performed by OWLS has increased significantly during the past decade. Although OWLS are now better-educated and healthier than they were only a few years ago, both physical and nonphysical job demands may lead some to work-related stress and early retirement, giving rise to the perception that OWLS are unwilling or unable to perform or are burned-out and less motivated than younger workers.

Implications for Workplace Learning and Performance

OWLS "defy stereotyping" (Roberson, 2003); it is impossible to establish just one set of characteristics or perceptions that fits all OWLS. As an age group, OWLS in any given workplace may span up to sixty years and three generations. OWLS are not all alike; nurture and nature intervene over the years to create OWLS in multiple images. The changing nature of the workplace and changing job demands also affect how OWLS act in and react to the workplace.

OWLS may be long-time employees, midlife career changers, displaced workers, or retirees returning to their old or a new workplace. When workplace perceptions are positive, OWLS are viewed as wise, experienced, work-oriented, self-directed workers—a benefit to their workplace. When workplace perceptions are negative, OWLS may be perceived as inflexible, obsolete, unwilling or unable to perform, or burned out. Faced with negative perceptions, OWLS begin to feel stressed, isolated, unvalued, held back, or marginalized. Myths turn into realities, and OWLS are fired or retired—there is no perceived benefit to retaining or hiring them.

Organizations often fail to recognize and deal with negative perceptions about OWLS as workers and their impact both on the OWLS and on workplace learning and performance. For example, a 2003 study by the Conference Board reported a "startling difference" between the perceptions of OWLS and the perceptions of 150 HR executives: "In fact, significant numbers of HR executives seemed oblivious to the concerns expressed by older workers" (Grossman, 2003, n.p.).

While OWLS are busy becoming younger in body and spirit, organizations that do not have a positive perception of OWLS may institute policies, processes, procedures, and practices that are equally busy "aging" their OWLS. For example, OWLS are the first to go when the organizations rightsize or downsize; OWLS are encouraged to take early retirement to make way for younger workers; and OWLS are offered fewer training opportunities than younger workers (Bolch, 2000).

There is another side to the training issue. The sidebar tells how one international corporation actually used too much training to force Emily and other OWLS to retire. In this case Emily and another company turned out to be the winners.

EMILY

Emily worked for a large international corporation as a legal secretary. At the age of fifty-two she was removed from her position as secretary to the vice president in charge of real estate development and reassigned to a corporate "holding pen for fifty-somethings." Emily, whose former position was highly interactive and visible, now spent her work time sitting in a carrel and interfacing with a computer. Her new job was to complete computer-based training courses on all the new computer programs that the company might want to integrate into their enterprise resource program (ERP) system "someday." She was never reassigned to a department and never used any of the skills she was learning. At age fifty-five she took an early retirement and went to work for another organization that valued her knowledge, experience, and work ethic . . . and especially her extensive computer training!

Action Steps for WLP Practitioners

Now that you know more about OWLS as workers you will be able to add the role of champion to your repertoire as a WLP practitioner. Here are some suggested action steps that combine the roles of champion, analyst, and change agent.

1. Discover more about OWLS as workers by exploring the concept of OWLS as retirees—or not.

   Chapter Three represents a cornucopia of hope. It is all about OWLS who retire from the workplace, OWLS who stay in the workplace, and OWLS who retire and flock back into the workplace. It also discusses workplace retention of human capital and knowledge capital.

   You will realize that retirement is no longer perceived as a negative ending or passage through life—there are no longer any traditional retirement years. PST 3.1 will guide you through an engaging way to survey whether your organization has a workplace-wide culture of retaining OWLS and knowledge. You will explore strategies you could suggest for retaining, rehiring, or hiring OWLS.

2. Become a champion of OWLS as workers.

   As natural champions or advocates of workplace learning and performance, you, the WLP practitioner, are in a unique position to make your organization more aware of the positive benefits that wise, experienced, work-oriented, self-directed OWLS can bring to workplace learning and performance. For example, OWLS can mentor younger worker-learners; share troubleshooting or problem-solving heuristics from their past experience; and model a work ethic that includes reliability and flexibility.

3. Help your organization identify and adjust workplace perceptions about OWLS as workers.

> Workplace perceptions may or may not match reality. As an analyst, you can help your organizations identify how their workplace perceives OWLS as workers. As a change agent, you can share survey material, statistics, or success stories from the literature to support a positive view of OWLS as workers and help your organizations turn negative perceptions into positive perceptions.

> PST 2.1, How to Audit Workplace Perceptions About OWLS as Workers, will guide you through an audit process that will help identify existing perceptions. The purpose of the audit is to assess the perceptions of executives, managers or supervisors, coworkers, customers, and the OWLS themselves about the work-related characteristics of the OWLS in this workplace. You can also use PST 2.1 to identify why the OWLS are in the workforce.

> You can conduct the audit now or together with an audit of perceptions about OWLS as learners (see PST 4.1 at the end of Chapter Four). Use the sample survey that follows as a guide and add or delete items as needed. Distribute the survey electronically or virtually. You can also use the survey as an interview guide.

PST 2.1. How to Audit Workplace Perceptions About OWLS as Workers.

Purpose: To design and develop a survey that will identify what people in the organization really think about older worker-learners (OWLS).

Instructions: Customize the sample survey that follows so it will meet the needs of your organization.

1. Collect the data.

   Use the sample survey at the end of the PST instructions to collect data on workplace perceptions about OWLS as workers. You can use the sample survey as is or customize it for your organization.

   Distribute the surveys to everyone in the company or do a random sampling. Use electronic resources such as the company intranet, distribute printed copies at staff meetings, fax copies to subsidiaries, and so forth. Be sure the surveys contain clear directions for when and how to return the completed surveys.

2. Quantify the data.

   Use raw data, frequency counts, or percentages to quantify the data collected during the survey. Suggestions for quantifying the results include the following:

   - Total the number of the respondents to this survey.
   - Total the number of respondents by classification—executives, managers, and so forth.
   - Total the number of respondents by classification and age group (20–29, 30–39, 40–64, and so forth).
   - Calculate the percentage of the total number of respondents who selected each response to each item or perception.
   - Calculate the percentage of the respondents within a classification—executives, managers, and so forth—who selected each response to each item or perception.

Sample Data Record:

2. OWLS are as productive as younger workers, given the same skill levels and training	Myth	Reality	Not Sure
Executives	20%	69%	11%
Managers	50%	45%	5%

- Calculate the percentage of each classification who selected each response to each item or perception by age group (20–29, 30–39, 40–64, and so forth).

- Calculate the percentage of the total number of respondents who selected each response by age group.

3. Analyze the data.

   Use the following sample analysis questions to analyze the data.

   - What perceptions about OWLS are listed as realities by 50 percent or more of the total number of respondents?

   - What perceptions about OWLS are listed as realities by 50 percent or more of the total number of respondents in each classification (executives, manager, and so forth)?

   - What perceptions about OWLS as workers were listed as realities by 50 percent or more of *each* age group (20–29, 30–39, 40–64, and so forth) within *each* respondent classification?

   - Which perceptions of the individual respondent classifications were aligned with each other? (Example of alignment: More than 50 percent of all the respondents agreed that OWLS are as productive as younger workers given the same skill levels and training. Example of misalignment: More than 50 percent of the managers, coworkers, customers, trainers, and OWLS and less than 50 percent of the executives and human resource staff felt that OWLS are as productive as younger workers, given the same skill levels and training.)

   - What perceptions are aligned by age group? (Example: More than 50 percent of the respondents in the age groups 65 and older feel that OWLS are as productive as younger workers given the same skill levels and training; less than 50 percent of the respondents in the 20–29 age groups agree.)

   - Other . . .

4. Draw conclusions.

   Summarize what the results mean to the organization. Draw conclusions or make deductions based on the audit results. Use the sample conclusions as a guide.

   Sample Conclusions:

   - Currently, we *do/do not* have a positive perception of OWLS as workers.

   - *We do/do not* need to plan a strategy for developing a more positive perception of our OWLS as workers.

- The following classifications are *more/less* positive than others . . .

- Our organization is *aligned/not aligned* in its perception of OWLS as workers (*specify areas of alignment and/or misalignment—topics, classifications, age groups*).

- Other . . .

5. Make recommendations.

    Encourage the organization to act based on the results of the audit. Use the sample recommendations that follow as a guide.

    Sample Recommendations:

    - If you did not wait to combine this audit with the survey at the end of Chapter Three, suggest that the organization should continue by analyzing how the organization perceives its OWLS as learners.

    - Suggest that it is also time to start collecting and analyzing existing information about the current policies, procedures, and practices related to OWLS; for example, training, retirement, and health and safety initiatives.

6. Communicate the results.

    Begin to build awareness and, if action is required, begin to gain support for a change initiative that will maximize the performance of the OWLS and the organization.

    Share the process and the results of the audit with the people who provided you with the data and anyone else in the organization who needs to know—especially anyone whose support you will need if you decide to recommend further action steps.

    Send an email or fax report; print the results in a newsletter; discuss the results at meetings, information briefings, brown bag lunches; and so forth.

Sample Survey

Title: What do you think about OWLS as workers?

Purpose: The purpose of this survey is to find out what people in our organization really think about older worker-learners (OWLS) aged forty-plus.

Benefits to the Respondents: We plan to use the information from this survey to
_____ (Note: The respondents will want to know how the organization will use the results of the audit and how it will benefit them.)

PST 2.1. How to Audit Workplace Perceptions About OWLS as Workers, *Continued*.

Demographic Information: This is an anonymous survey; however, to help us interpret the results we are asking you to provide us with the following information before you begin the next part of the survey.

A. Please check (✓) *one* statement that best describes your work relationship with older worker-learners (OWLS) in the workplace:

☐ 1 I am an executive with this organization.

☐ 2 I work in Human Resources and I interview and hire OWLS; administer benefit and retirement plans; and so forth.

☐ 3 I manage or supervise OWLS.

☐ 4 I train OWLS.

☐ 5 I work with OWLS.

☐ 6 I am a customer of OWLS.

☐ 7 Other . . . (please explain)

B. Please check (✓) the age group that best describes you:

☐ 8 Under age 20

☐ 9 Age 20–29

☐ 10 Age 30–39

☐ 11 Age 40–54

☐ 12 Age 55–64

☐ 13 Age 65–74

☐ 14 Age 75–84

☐ 15 Age 85+

C. Please check (✓) *one* statement that best describes why you are working:

☐ 16 I am working because I want to work.

☐ 17 I work working because I need to work.

☐ 18 Other . . .

Thank you for your help. Please continue with the survey.

The topics and statements in the following table were taken from the literature on OWLS. Please read each statement and check (✓) the column to the right that best describes your *immediate* reaction to the statement. If you want to add a statement or make a comment on the topic, please do so in the Comment box at the end of each topic.

PST 2.1. How to Audit Workplace Perceptions About OWLS as Workers, *Continued.*

Topic: Productivity	Myth	Reality	Not Sure
1. OWLS are less productive than younger workers, given the same skill levels and training.			
2. OWLS are as productive as younger workers, given the same skill levels and training.			
3. OWLS are more productive than younger workers, given the same skill levels and training.			
4. For most occupations, the productivity levels of OWLS remain stable with age.			
5. For most occupations, the productivity levels of OWLS can even increase with age.			
6. OWLS begin to hit a career plateau around age forty.			
7. OWLS begin to become obsolescent around age forty.			
Comment . . .			

Topic: Medical Benefits	Myth	Reality	Not Sure
8. OWLS raise the cost of medical benefits.			
9. Workers who are parents of young children use the most medical benefits.			
10. Many OWLS work part-time and do not receive employee benefits.			
Comment . . .			

PST 2.1. How to Audit Workplace Perceptions About OWLS as Workers, *Continued.*

Topic: Attitude toward Work	Myth	Reality	Not Sure
11. Many OWLS have a positive work ethic.			
12. OWLS are willing to work overtime.			
13. OWLS are willing to work flexible schedules.			
14. It is important to OWLS to "do the job right."			
15. OWLS from the baby boomer generation prefer to work rather than retire.			
16. OWLS value the chance to contribute.			
17. OWLS prefer not to work; they lose interest and motivation.			
18. OWLS thrive on hard work.			
19. OWLS tend to become burned out.			
20. OWLS work because they want to work.			
21. OWLS work because they need to work.			
Comment . . .			

Topic: Absenteeism	Myth	Reality	Not Sure
22. OWLS seldom miss work for personal reasons other than legitimate illness.			
23. OWLS have higher absentee rates than younger workers.			
24. Absenteeism among OWLS is lower than it is among younger workers.			
Comment . . .			

Topic: Change	Myth	Reality	Not Sure
25. OWLS adapt to change if it benefits the organization.			
26. OWLS are inflexible.			
27. Adaptability is unrelated to age.			
28. OWLS are set in their ways.			
29. OWLS are flexible if they see the benefit to themselves.			
30. Rightsizing or downsizing and reductions impact OWLS.			
Comment . . .			

Topic: Basic Skills	Myth	Reality	Not Sure
31. OWLS lack basic skills.			
32. OWLS may appear to lack basic skills because they tend to first apply techniques that have worked in the past.			
33. OWLS tend not to develop their technical skills.			
34. OWLS may just lack the vocabulary to express their knowledge and experience as it applies to new technology.			
Comment . . .			

Topic: Conflict	Myth	Reality	Not Sure
35. People do not become more difficult to work with as they age.			
36. OWLS tend to be more satisfied with their work and their coworkers.			
37. OWLS conflict with younger workers.			
38. Workers age sixty-five-plus have the highest job satisfaction rate of any age group.			
Comment . . .			

Topic: Health and Wellness	Myth	Reality	Not Sure
39. Health is a major issue with OWLS.			
40. OWLS who are highly active at work have better health.			
41. OWLS age sixty-five-plus take fewer days off for health reasons than younger workers.			
42. Enforced idleness at work can lead to poor health.			
43. Work is stressful for OWLS.			
44. Ability to cope with stress is a factor of personal characteristics and past experience, not age.			
45. OWLS experience less stress on the job.			
46. OWLS have fewer incidences of admission to psychiatric institutions.			
Comment . . .			

Topic: Safety	Myth	Reality	Not Sure
47. OWLS appreciate their limitations and are more safety conscious than younger workers.			
48. OWLS have more accidents on the job.			
49. OWLS have more experience, so they avoid situations where accidents occur, and they "expect the unexpected."			
Comment . . .			

Topic: Turnover	Myth	Reality	Not Sure
50. OWLS leave the job.			
51. OWLS have a lower turnover rate than younger workers.			
52. OWLS stay with employers who are loyal to and listen to their employees.			
Comment . . .			

Topic: General	Myth	Reality	Not Sure
53. OWLS take jobs away from younger workers.			
54. Our organization needs older and younger workers to succeed in the marketplace.			
Comment . . .			

3

OWLS as Retirees—
or *Not*

Me, retire? You've got to be kidding. I don't intend to retire. What
will I do? I don't have any hobbies. My wife is deceased. My kids live
in three different states. I will work till they carry me out. Retirement
is a dirty word.

Lucasz, age seventy-eight, safety engineer

THIS IS NOT YOUR GRANDFATHER'S or father's retirement. "Boomers approach retirement as a work style not as a lifestyle"
(Smith & Clurman in *Rocking the Ages,* as cited in Woodwell, 2004, p. 14).
Even Oldest OWLS like Lucasz are making work a "lifestyle." Both the times
and the terms are changing.

The twenty-first century has put a whole new face—and body—to the
concept and reality of retirement. It is no longer a time to abruptly depart
from the workplace or give up a job or vocation in favor of leisure; " . . .
retirement is not a time when human beings have reached the end of their
useful working life . . ." (Jarvis, 2001, pp. 84, 95).

This chapter is all about the newest faces that you and other WLP practitioners will meet on your way to improving workplace learning and performance. The faces belong to Mid-Old to Oldest OWLS who do not plan to retire or who retired, then later return to the workplace. The chapter provides WLP practitioners with the kind of information required to expand their role as information gatherer, analyst, change leader, and champion of learning and performance for Mid-Old to Oldest OWLS.

After an overview of retirement then and now, the chapter will present new insights from the literature and the workplace about OWLS as retirees— or *not*. Whether OWLS retire or not, their decisions will have an impact on how and how well organizations retain their human and knowledge capital and avoid "brain drain." The chapter will end with action steps that you can take to help your organization maximize learning and performance, whether OWLS retire—or not.

Retirement—Evolution and Revolution

There has been both an evolution and a quiet revolution in the history of retirement. Retirement has evolved from an event to a transition. As the workplace began to age, larger and larger numbers of OWLS stopped talking about "when I retire" and began proclaiming "Why should I retire?" or "How could I retire?"

That Was Then

A wall plaque in a London, England, store reminds us that once upon a time the concept of retirement was relatively simple: retirement was a time when you "stopped living at work and started working at living." It was a time when friends, relatives, and work associates asked, "What are you going to *do* when you retire?" and the answer was, "I'm going to throw away my watch" or "do some traveling" or "go fishing" and the like.

Hardy (2002) traces the history of retirement and notes that by the end of the twentieth century a combination of Social Security and pension plans made retirement possible for millions of adults who were still young and healthy enough to enjoy it. Of course there were always OWLS who liked or needed to work and were in an organization or sector that did not force them to retire at age sixty-five. Arthur is one example (see sidebar).

ARTHUR

In the early 1970s Arthur retired from the research and development department of a small natural gas company at age seventy-five. He was in good health and he loved his work, but he felt his time had come to draw his monthly Social Security and pension checks. He rejoined the company as a volunteer mentor in the company's speakers bureau. Most of his efforts were directed to working with the external communities surrounding the natural gas company. Because of his knowledge and expertise, he became the voice of the company and a recognized name in the communities. He also mentored knowledgeable, yet novice speakers. He was an active mentor and company spokesperson until his death at the age of eighty-five.

In 1978, Congress passed the Age Discrimination in Employment Amendments (ADEA) that eliminated mandatory retirement before age seventy and "encouraged the development of retraining programs for older workers in business and industry" (Peterson, 1985, p. 11). The programs helped expand the career alternatives for OWLS who wanted to seek new careers or prepare for second and third careers (Sheppard & Fisher, 1985). When the vision and the reality of retirement changed, Sheppard and Fisher (1985) also predicted a steady increase in the number of older persons who would continue to work beyond age sixty-five.

This Is Now

Today "some people retire and leave, and others retire and stay" (Blank & Slipp, 1994, p. 131), and even the very concept of retirement is changing again. Retirement has evolved from an event to a transition: "The abrupt transition from work to retirement has begun to lengthen into a process of anticipation, bridge jobs, intermittent part-time work, and eventual withdrawal" (Hardy, 2002). According to Hardy, three categories of retirees began to develop in the latter part of the twentieth century: working retirees; multiple retirees, who have retired from more than one job; and partial retirees. The sidebar *Here's Emily—Again!* is a real-life example of the transitioning retiree.

HERE'S EMILY—AGAIN!

Over the past twenty-nine years Emily has transitioned from worker to working retiree to multiple retiree to part-time retiree. In Chapter Two you read how she was forced to retire and accept a reduced pension after eighteen years as a legal secretary in the law department of an international corporation. She then went to work as a full-time legal secretary for a large law firm and after ten years retired from that job with another pension. Emily recently "retired" to Florida, where she is now employed part time as an administrative assistant in a land development company.

There are many reasons why today's OWLS may retire—or *not*. Some OWLS are tired of working. They want to travel, to engage in community service, to develop their green thumb for gardening, to have fun with their grandchildren, or to pursue a host of other productive "nonwork" activities. Or they might just want to read books, sit in the sun, go fishing, and play cards with their friends.

Other OWLS are faced with economic issues that make it impossible to retire; for example, potential decreases in Social Security benefits; increases in the eligibility age for benefits; the need to develop personal retirement plans to subsidize or replace benefits; the need to support a dependent child or aging parent. Still other OWLS like to work and want to keep working. Or there are OWLS—like Sophia—who both want and need to work (see sidebar).

SOPHIA

Sophia is still working as an inner-city high school biology teacher at age eighty-two. She loves teaching, and she needs the income; however, there is more to the story.

Sophia left the school system to move to another state when her husband's company relocated him. He had to take a pay cut when they relocated, so she took her money out of the school retirement system to cover relocation and living expenses. When her husband died, Sophia returned to her original school district; she was fifty-four years old and entered the system as a new employee. In two more years she will qualify for full retirement benefits. This time she plans to retire for good.

New Faces in the Workplace

So now our workplace is populated with OWLS who stay, OWLS who retire, OWLS who retire and are rehired, and new OWLS who are hired to fill the vacancies left when other OWLS retire or younger workers leave. Figure 3.1 illustrates the cycle for four OWLS in the workplace.

Whoooo Are the Retirees-or-Not?

Some Old to Oldest OWLS age sixty-five-plus are in the workplace because they elected to stay in the same organizations and maybe even in the same jobs they held before the issue of retirement arose. Other Old, Old-Old, and Oldest OWLS needed—or wanted—to try something new or change careers or just plain get a job.

OWLS who are white-collar or blue-collar knowledge workers who have specialized skills and responsibilities may be able to work at the same job indefinitely. Others may need to find a new job because the performance of their job or profession could be affected by normal physical aging processes or health problems (Hodson & Sullivan, 2002). The sidebar on Ralph gives an example of a man who worries that his gradual physical losses may jeopardize his remaining vibrant in the workplace.

Figure 3.1. A Tale of Four OWLS.

Once upon a time there were four OWLS—Mac, Marie, Myrtle, and Mark. Mac, Marie, and Myrtle worked for Company A; they were all hired on the same day. Mark decided to work for Company B instead. At age sixty-five and seven months they all met at Mark's retirement party.

Mac said "I'm retiring and going fishing."

Mary said "I'm retiring and going back to work; Company A wants to rehire me part time"

Myrtle said: "I'm *not* retiring; I'm staying here"

Mark said, "I'm retired from Company B and now Company A wants to hire me to replace Mac".

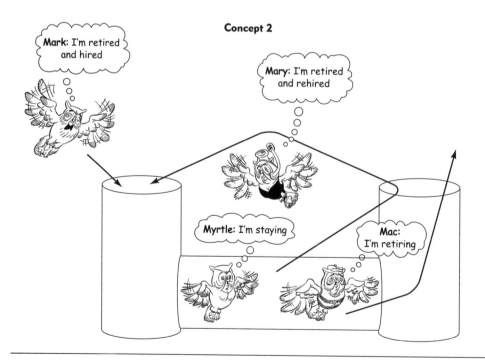

RALPH

Ralph is a Mid-Old OWL and an airline pilot for a major airline. He gets regular physicals and retrains regularly. At age fifty-six, he is concerned about potential safety risks due to gradual deterioration of his vision, hearing, and reflexes.

OWLS who want or need to continue working after retirement have another layer of options to explore: they can choose full-time or part-time work or self-employment or volunteer service.

Full-Time OWLS. The traditional nine-to-five or day-or-night-shift type of employment may still suit the needs of Young or Mid-Old OWLS, especially those who decide to retire early. OWLS choose early retirement options for a variety of reasons: job buyout, health concerns, caregiving, desire to spend quality time with family and friends or travel, and unstated credible pursuits. Many of these same people, however, are too young to collect Social Security. They often find they have too much free time, so they return to full-time paid employment. The sidebar story about Scott is a good example.

SCOTT'S STORY

Scott retired at age fifty after thirty years as a successful elementary school teacher and reading consultant. For two years he occupied his time with taking care of an aging parent, some travel, and an occasional substitute teaching position. When caregiving ended with the death of his parent, he found he had time on his hands. His friends were still in the workplace and he felt he was too young to live in retirement. So Scott returned to full-time employment as a director of grant support for a school district. He works thirty hours per week. Scott says: "I enjoy being back in the workforce . . . there's a significant difference between working because you have to and working because you want to." He approaches life now with a whole new attitude and perspective.

The new Social Security laws also make it possible for retirees age sixty-five-plus to work full time without jeopardizing their benefits (although the Social Security benefits are subject to income tax if total income exceeds a particular amount). However, full-time work may become a less desirable option for many OWLS, as cost-cutting organizations seek alternatives to corporate funding of health benefits or pension plans or both.

Part-Time OWLS. Some OWLS may like the option of working part time, so they can pursue leisure activities or even explore new career or educational opportunities. Job sharing, flex time, flex place, phased retirement, and contracting of OWLS as consultants are just some of the options open to organizations who want to develop alternatives to full-time paid employment. The crucial element for most OWLS is they have a safety net; that benefits such as health care, vacation time, sick days, and so forth will still be there for them; and that they will not lose their pensions or accrued benefits.

LEN

Len, who is an active and healthy Old OWL of seventy, is truly transitioning into retirement. He is a teacher whose employer allows him to stretch retirement over three years. He works four months each year at half salary with full pension and full health care benefits. He enjoys traveling, occasional casino visits, and writing. His part-time paid employment affords the luxury of discretionary time, keeps his mind intellectually sharp, and provides the best of both worlds. Len considers himself "lucky to be so blessed."

Self-Employed OWLS. WLP practitioners frequently run into self-employed OWLS. They are the vendors hired to develop a computer-based training (CBT), the trainers who deliver the new management training program, the evaluators who do a return on investment (ROI) analysis of the latest training program. Self-employed OWLS are also found throughout organizations, mingling with the "regular" employees on a daily basis, hired in or hired back to consult or do project work or provide basic services like word processing or specialized machine maintenance.

There are actual and potential self-employed OWLS in the workplace. Actual self-employed OWLS like Paula, whose story is in the sidebar, frequently work on-site with marketing teams. Potential self-employed OWLS are regular workers with an entrepreneurial spirit who are practicing for the day when they will go out on their own. They are the risk-taking self-starter OWLS, the self-directed learners, the visionaries.

The statistics indicate that self-employment is a viable option or second career for a wide range of OWLS. Young OWLS in the forty-five-to-fifty-four age range make up the "fastest growing group of entrepreneurs in the nation" (Kroll, 2004). OWLS aged fifty-plus, which includes Young-Oldest OWLS, make up 40 percent of the self-employed workers in the United States ("Self Employment," 2004).

PAULA AND TONY

Paula has always preferred contract to full-time work. Some twenty years ago she started her own small marketing firm, and at age sixty-nine both she and her company are still going strong. Paula's husband, Tony, took an early retirement and never looked back. Whenever he asks her "Isn't it time yet?" Paula's response is "Never." She truly believes that entrepreneurship is ageless.

Volunteer OWLS. Volunteering is another work option for OWLS to consider. "Some companies recognize volunteerism as a vital and fulfilling part of their retirees' lives, as well as good common-sense public relations for the company" (Dychtwald & Flower, 1989, p. 167).

Some of these companies encourage volunteer employees and retirees to help with company-subsidized community programs or activities. For example,

when Marshall Fields–Detroit sponsored a weekend of free public music per-
formances in various venues throughout the city, they used volunteer employees, and retirees volunteered to help plan and staff the weekend's activities.

Other organizations incorporate volunteerism into their culture. The Principal Financial Group of Des Moines, Iowa, works with managers and other
senior-level employees to set up temporary transfer opportunities so the
employees can work at local offices of charities such as the United Way ("Best
Practices," 2004). Other organizations, like Electronic Data Services (EDS),
make it possible for employees to combine a leave of absence and vacation time
to perform volunteer work with local, national, or international programs.

Implications for Workplace Learning and Performance

The average retirement age has been falling over most of the past century, and
even though the trend seems to have leveled off and even reversed in recent
years, it has caused a problem that could threaten the overall health of the
nation and the world (Johnson, 2004). When OWLS retire, the knowledge
and skills they possess often retire with them—it's all part of the "brain drain"
that the workplace is talking and writing about.

When OWLS Retire, the Workplace Brain Drains

In today's corporate world, organizational success is increasingly dependent
on knowledge held by employees. Knowledge is "actionable information";
that is, accessible when and where it is needed and written in a meaningful
context (Tiwana, 2002). Organizations, especially high-tech ones or ones in
which individuals think for a living, are especially vulnerable to brain drain
(Gomez-Mejia, Balkin, & Cardy, 2001; Davenport, 2005).

By virtue of their experience, seniority, and know-how, OWLS are knowledge workers who create, distribute, and apply knowledge. They differ from
other employees in their autonomy, motivations, and attitudes. Their work
tends to be unstructured and they often use experience-based heuristics or
rules of thumb to solve problems (Davenport, 2005). When an OWL retires,
the corporate brain drains. The sidebar lists some of the statistics that indicate the scale of the problem.

OWLS AND THE BRAIN DRAIN

The predictions are dire. When the exodus of the Boomer OWLS is in full swing around 2010, about 50 percent of the population could retire from the workforce, leaving "gaping holes in institutional memory and experience" (Kramer, 2004); causing a "hemorrhage of corporate insight" (Lesser, Hausmann, Feuerpeil, 2005, p. 6); and creating "a brain drain of daunting proportions" (Harris, 2005, p. 44).

"[T]he coming talent crisis is a 'global, cross industry threat,' skills and experience will begin to disappear from the job market as soon as 2008" (Kaplan-Leiserson, 2005, p. 12).

Nineteen percent of the workforce holding executive, administrative, and managerial positions in the United States are Boomer OWLS who will begin to retire by 2008 ("The Global Human Capital Study," 2002).

Organizations Can Cause and Cure Brain Drain

Some experts say that the current situation is a perfect storm. A combination of factors have come together to create it; for example, lack of investment in senior talent and the decline in the number of Generation Xers who are ready, willing, or able to replace retiring baby boomers ("The Perfect Storm," 2005).

Causes of Brain Drain. Organizational policies such as downsizing, rightsizing, early retirement, or forced retirement all contribute to the perfect storm, and they are all policies generated by organizations to shrink the size of their workforces. Whether the brain drain concept is a perfect storm or just a "shower" (Concelman & Burns, 2006, p. 51), these policies target OWLS and siphon know-how, know-who, know-what, know-where, know-why, and know-when from an organization—a costly result of a cost-saving effort (DeLong, 2004). According to Jarvis (2001, p. 89), these policies may save money initially; however, in the long term the organizations who implement these policies without a sound knowledge-management strategy tend to lose more than they gain, because they will

- Lose the knowledge and skills gained by workers over the course of their total experience

- Lose the ability to pass on to new workers the knowledge and skills acquired by older workers

- Send a message that older workers are not valued

The lack of retention policies for keeping OWLS in the workplace is still another cause of brain drain. The Global Human Capital Study 2002 reported that of more than three hundred chief human resources officers (CHROs) surveyed, only one-third of the CHROs' leadership teams were rewarded based on "growing" key staff within the organization, and less than a third were evaluated on the retention of key staff ("The Global Human Capital Study," 2002). Three years later, The Global Human Capital Study 2005 found a proactive approach to retaining key personnel is still not a priority for a majority of the organizations surveyed ("The Global Human Capital Study," 2005).

Solutions for Brain Drain. Organizations are also part of the solution to brain drain. One of the factors that can be controlled is the number of OWLS who remain in the workforce (Allier & Kolosh, 2005). Grossman (2003) and others suggest that predicted labor shortages can be countered by hiring and retaining OWLS. However, Grossman warns: "[M]any older employees feel they aren't being given a fair shake. And the primary federal tool for protecting them—the Age Discrimination in Employment Act (ADEA), which bars discrimination against those who are 40 and older—doesn't seem to be helping their cause" (n.p.).

Organizations who do not already have one need to develop a "culture of retention"—values, norms, and practices for keeping both OWLS and knowledge in the workplace. They also need to use both WLP practitioners and OWLS to help them manage past and current workplace knowledge.

Action Steps for WLP Practitioners

To institutionalize a culture of retention, organizations must invest time and money to ensure they have well-planned and executed policies, procedures, and practices to retain and maintain OWLS as knowledge resources and managers—and you can help them achieve this. Just polish up your roles as information gatherer, analyst, and change leader; add your roles as performance improvement intervention selector, designer, developer, implementer, and evaluator, and take action:

1. Analyze your organization's culture of retention.

   As an information gatherer, analyst, and change leader, you have already built awareness of (1) your organization's status as an aging workplace, (2) the perceptions within the organization regarding OWLS as workers and learners, and (3) the value-added benefits that OWLS bring to your workplace. Now it's time to gather and analyze information about your organization's culture of retention—to learn whether your organization values and supports the retention of OWLS in the workplace. Use PST 3.1 as a guide for analyzing your organization.

2. Help your organization retain OWLS who want to stay in your workplace.

   As a WLP practitioner, you may be asked to help your organization select, design, develop, implement, or evaluate performance improvement interventions for retaining OWLS in the workplace. Because the ultimate goal is to keep OWLS in the workforce, you may also be asked to suggest or help develop strategies for rehiring retired OWLS or hiring OWLS from other organizations. The interventions may involve training—or they may not. Here are some strategies you could suggest for retaining, rehiring, or hiring OWLS:

   • Encourage your organization to develop a culture of retention that includes well-planned and executed policies, processes, procedures, and practices for career management, phased retirement, training and retraining, and succession planning (DeLong, 2004).

- Help your organization create new ways of encouraging older employees to stay in the workplace longer. Research and suggest ideas for flexible work schedules, less-than-full-time assignments, and mentoring opportunities (Stetson, 2006, p. 12).

- Create a program that integrates both returning and new OWLS into the organization through the use of training and nontraining performance improvement interventions.

3. Encourage your organization to rehire OWLS who retire.

   - Help your organization establish a formal program to recruit, rehire, and manage retirees as consultants or part-time employees.

   - Help your organization create and maintain an informal database of potential retiree resources for managers and others to call upon as needed. The database could include links between retirees who interacted with each other in crucial areas and might be able to regenerate lost knowledge.

   - Suggest the "alumni concept" to help retirees stay connected to the organization through informal networks, social events, and so forth.

4. Encourage your organization to hire external OWLS.

   - Suggest that your organization could establish and maintain a database of OWLS who have retired within your business or industry sector and are experts in a particular field or process.

   - As an alternative, find out if your organization can access an existing database maintained by a professional organization in the field.

   - Encourage your organization to link up with a professional organization or advocacy group. The sidebar illustrates what happened when AARP and Home Depot linked forces.

HOME DEPOT LINKS WITH AARP TO RECRUIT OWLS
In 2004, Home Depot and the American Association for Retired Persons
(AARP), an advocacy group for both OWLS and retirees, teamed up to recruit
OWLS. Within two months more than 7,500 people applied for jobs at Home
Depot through the AARP Web site and more than 5,400 were accepted into
the pool of qualified applicants. Some of the applicants were OWLS who had
been downsized or were otherwise displaced workers; others were retirees
("AARP/Home Depot," 2004).

---

5 . Help your organization utilize OWLS to capture and retain knowl-
    edge capital.

   Wise organizations understand that OWLS can help them capture
   and retain knowledge within the organization. The goal is to capture both rule-based knowledge and tacit or know-how knowledge
   before OWLS retire permanently. A blended approach is best in
   order to ensure that both rule-based knowledge and know-how
   knowledge is captured and retained by the organization.

   • Suggest that when it comes to implicit or tacit know-how—
     also called heuristics or "rules of thumb" or "flying by the
     seat of your pants"—storytelling, mentoring, and communi-
     ties of practice can help transform these types of knowledge
     into practical solutions to existing problems. OWLS can also
     model how they integrate past and current knowledge and
     experience to troubleshoot and solve problems. Offer train-
     ing programs to provide OWLS with the skills they need to
     use these strategies for maximum advantage.

   • Encourage your organization to initiate and support the in-
     tegration of knowledge sharing practices into the daily work
     environment (DeLong, 2004). The practices could include

audio- or videotaped interviews or debriefing sessions, training, documentation, storytelling, mentoring, or informal online or real-time networks, such as communities of practice. Documentation and interviewing could capture knowledge for current or future use; documentation and training would be useful for the direct transfer of explicit or rule-based knowledge.

- Encourage OWLS to serve as knowledge champions. Since corporate knowledge is highly cross-functional, champions from different functional areas can help define vision and serve as catalysts in generating knowledge and connecting knowledge with present and future initiatives and projects. The presence of OWLS in a knowledge management system can be a cohesive force in supporting the infrastructure of both application and transfer of knowledge (Tiwana, 2002).

6. Learn more about retention interventions and retirement.

For more information on nontraining interventions for retaining OWLS and their knowledge—such as mentoring, retirement planning, hiring and rehiring, succession planning, organizational values, and so forth—read *Performance Improvement Interventions: Enhancing People, Processes, and Organizations Through Performance Technology* by Van Tiem, Moseley, and Dessinger (2001). This book includes a four-phase intervention selection process and the *Intervention Selection Tool,* a PST that can guide you through the selection process.

For information about the coming shortage of skills and talent, the needs and capabilities of mature workers, and the changing retirement picture, read *Workforce Crisis: How to Beat the Coming Shortage of Skills and Talent* (Dychtwald, Erikson, & Morison, 2006). The book's perspective covers three cohort groups ranging in age from 18–55+.

7. Learn more about OWLS as learners.

"All humans are learners—and workers learn every day" (Cross & O'Driscoll, 2005, p. 32). Chapter Four describes OWLS as lifelong adult learners and includes an audit instrument to help identify the characteristics of OWLS as learners.

PST 3.1. Guide to Analyzing the Culture of Retention in Your Workplace.

Purpose: To determine (1) whether there is a workplace-wide culture of retention for OWLS; (2) whether the culture includes hiring, rehiring, and training OWLS; and (3) whether the culture is enabled by policies, processes, procedures, or practices that are planned, normed, practiced, valued, and supported.

Definition of Terms:

- Policies—definite statements of the philosophy or purpose of the organization in regards to OWLS and/or knowledge management

- Processes—planned action over time

- Procedures—established or correct steps that ultimately determine a course of action

- Practices—actual performance of the established or correct policies, processes, or procedures

- Planned—the policies, processes, procedures, or practices were intentionally designed

- Normed—performance or quality standards have been set for the policies, processes, procedures, or practices

- Valued—the organization values the policies, processes, procedures, or practices

- Supported—the organization supports the policies, processes, procedures, or practices with time, money, and people

Instructions:

A. Use existing documents, interviews, surveys, focus groups, and so forth to answer the following questions:

- Are there policies, processes, procedures, or practices in place to **retain** OWLS in the workplace?

- Are there policies, processes, procedures, or practices in place to **rehire** OWLS after they retire?

- Are there policies, processes, procedures, or practices in place to **hire** OWLS?

- Are there policies, processes, procedures, or practices in place to **train or retrain** OWLS?

- Are existing policies, processes, procedures, or practices planned, normed, practiced, valued, and supported?

B. Quantify your findings using percentages, frequency counts, and so forth.

C. Use the definitions provided above to analyze your findings and check (✓) all the appropriate responses in the following table.

1. Retaining OWLS

   a. There are planned   ☐ policies   ☐ processes   ☐ procedures   ☐ practices.

   b. There are normed   ☐ policies   ☐ processes   ☐ procedures   ☐ practices.

   c. OWL retention   ☐ policies   ☐ processes   ☐ procedures   ☐ practices are practiced.

   d. OWL retention   ☐ policies   ☐ processes   ☐ procedures   ☐ practices are valued.

   e. OWL retention   ☐ policies   ☐ processes   ☐ procedures   ☐ practices are supported.

   f. There are no   ☐ policies   ☐ processes   ☐ procedures   ☐ practices to retain OWLS.

   g. Not sure about   ☐ policies   ☐ processes   ☐ procedures   ☐ practices to retain OWLS.

2. Rehiring OWLS after they retire

   a. There are planned   ☐ policies   ☐ processes   ☐ procedures   ☐ practices.

   b. There are normed   ☐ policies   ☐ processes   ☐ procedures   ☐ practices.

   c. OWL rehiring   ☐ policies   ☐ processes   ☐ procedures   ☐ practices are practiced.

   d. OWL rehiring   ☐ policies   ☐ processes   ☐ procedures   ☐ practices are valued.

   e. OWL rehiring   ☐ policies   ☐ processes   ☐ procedures   ☐ practices are supported.

   f. There are no   ☐ policies   ☐ processes   ☐ procedures   ☐ practices to rehire OWLS.

   g. Not sure about   ☐ policies   ☐ processes   ☐ procedures   ☐ practices to rehire OWLS.

3. Hiring OWLS

   a. There are planned ☐ policies ☐ processes ☐ procedures ☐ practices.

   b. There are normed ☐ policies ☐ processes ☐ procedures ☐ practices.

   c. OWL hiring ☐ policies ☐ processes ☐ procedures ☐ practices are practiced.

   d. OWL hiring ☐ policies ☐ processes ☐ procedures ☐ practices are valued.

   e. OWL hiring ☐ policies ☐ processes ☐ procedures ☐ practices are supported.

   f. There are no ☐ policies ☐ processes ☐ procedures ☐ practices to hire OWLS.

   g. Not sure about ☐ policies ☐ processes ☐ procedures ☐ practices to hire OWLS.

4. Training or retraining OWLS

   a. There are planned ☐ policies ☐ processes ☐ procedures ☐ practices.

   b. There are normed ☐ policies ☐ processes ☐ procedures ☐ practices.

   c. OWL training ☐ policies ☐ processes ☐ procedures ☐ practices are practiced.

   d. OWL training ☐ policies ☐ processes ☐ procedures ☐ practices are valued.

   e. OWL training ☐ policies ☐ processes ☐ procedures ☐ practices are supported.

   f. There are no ☐ policies ☐ processes ☐ procedures ☐ practices to train OWLS.

   g. Not sure about ☐ policies ☐ processes ☐ procedures ☐ practices to train OWLS.

D. Make recommendations to your organization to:

Maintain the existing culture of retention as it relates to ☐ retaining ☐ rehiring ☐ hiring ☐ training or retraining

Improve the existing culture of retention, specifically as it relates to ☐ retaining ☐ rehiring ☐ hiring ☐ training or retraining

Initiate a culture of retention that includes ☐ retaining ☐ rehiring ☐ hiring ☐ training or retraining

E. If you want to obtain a more complete picture of your organization's knowledge management strategies and learn whether your workplace values the role of OWLS in knowledge management, then follow the same process to answer the questions in the following table.

---

1. Does your organization systematically capture existing and new knowledge?

   a. There are planned ☐ policies ☐ processes ☐ procedures ☐ practices.

   b. There are normed ☐ policies ☐ processes ☐ procedures ☐ practices.

   c. Knowledge capture ☐ policies ☐ processes ☐ procedures ☐ practices are practiced.

   d. Knowledge capture ☐ policies ☐ processes ☐ procedures ☐ practices are valued.

   e. Knowledge capture ☐ policies ☐ processes ☐ procedures ☐ practices are supported.

   f. There are no ☐ policies ☐ processes ☐ procedures ☐ practices to capture knowledge.

   g. Not sure about ☐ policies ☐ processes ☐ procedures ☐ practices to capture knowledge.

2. How does your organization systematically store existing and new knowledge?

   a. There are planned ☐ policies ☐ processes ☐ procedures ☐ practices.

   b. There are normed ☐ policies ☐ processes ☐ procedures ☐ practices.

   c. Knowledge storage ☐ policies ☐ processes ☐ procedures ☐ practices are practiced.

    d. Knowledge storage   ☐ policies   ☐ processes   ☐ procedures   ☐ practices are valued.

    e. Knowledge storage   ☐ policies   ☐ processes   ☐ procedures   ☐ practices are supported.

    f. There are no   ☐ policies   ☐ processes   ☐ procedures   ☐ practices to store knowledge.

    g. Not sure about   ☐ policies   ☐ processes   ☐ procedures   ☐ practices to store knowledge.

3. How does your organization systematically maintain existing and new knowledge?

    a. There are planned   ☐ policies   ☐ processes   ☐ procedures   ☐ practices.

    b. There are normed   ☐ policies   ☐ processes   ☐ procedures   ☐ practices.

    c. Knowledge maintenance   ☐ policies   ☐ processes   ☐ procedures ☐ practices are practiced.

    d. Knowledge maintenance   ☐ policies   ☐ processes   ☐ procedures ☐ practices are valued.

    e. Knowledge maintenance   ☐ policies   ☐ processes   ☐ procedures ☐ practices are supported.

    f. There are no   ☐ policies   ☐ processes   ☐ procedures   ☐ practices to maintain knowledge.

    g. Not sure about   ☐ policies   ☐ processes   ☐ procedures   ☐ practices to maintain knowledge.

4. How does your organization systematically retrieve existing and new knowledge?

    a. There are planned   ☐ policies   ☐ processes   ☐ procedures   ☐ practices.

    b. There are normed   ☐ policies   ☐ processes   ☐ procedures   ☐ practices.

    c. Knowledge retrieval   ☐ policies   ☐ processes   ☐ procedures   ☐ practices are practiced.

    d. Knowledge retrieval   ☐ policies   ☐ processes   ☐ procedures   ☐ practices are valued.

    e. Knowledge retrieval   ☐ policies   ☐ processes   ☐ procedures   ☐ practices are supported.

f. There are no ☐ policies ☐ processes ☐ procedures ☐ practices to retrieve knowledge.

g. Not sure about ☐ policies ☐ processes ☐ procedures ☐ practices to retrieve knowledge.

5. How does your organization systematically use existing and new knowledge?

a. There are planned ☐ policies ☐ processes ☐ procedures ☐ practices.

b. There are normed ☐ policies ☐ processes ☐ procedures ☐ practices.

c. Knowledge usage ☐ policies ☐ processes ☐ procedures ☐ practices are practiced.

d. Knowledge usage ☐ policies ☐ processes ☐ procedures ☐ practices are valued.

e. Knowledge usage ☐ policies ☐ processes ☐ procedures ☐ practices are supported.

f. There are no ☐ policies ☐ processes ☐ procedures ☐ practices to use knowledge.

g. Not sure about ☐ policies ☐ processes ☐ procedures ☐ practices to use knowledge.

6. Do OWLS help the organization manage knowledge?

a. OWLS help capture ☐ existing knowledge ☐ new knowledge.
☐ OWLS do not help capture knowledge.   ☐ Not sure

b. OWLS help store ☐ existing knowledge ☐ new knowledge.
☐ OWLS do not help store knowledge.   ☐ Not sure

c. OWLS help maintain ☐ existing knowledge ☐ new knowledge.
☐ OWLS do not help maintain knowledge.   ☐ Not sure

d. OWLS help retrieve ☐ existing knowledge ☐ new knowledge.
☐ OWLS do not help OWLS retrieve knowledge.   ☐ Not sure

e. OWLS help the organization to effectively use ☐ existing knowledge
☐ new knowledge.   ☐ OWLS do not help organization to effectively use knowledge.   ☐ Not sure

4

OWLS as Learners

Just as I exercise my body by walking every day, I also exercise my mind.
I work crossword puzzles, read the paper and even try to keep up with my
former profession by reading professional journals. You've got to keep your
mind active as you age.

Sally B., professor emerita, who retired at age sixty-eight

THE ABILITY OF "OLD DOGS" to learn "new tricks" has
become increasingly important in our rapidly changing, technically
advanced society. Theorists and researchers generally agree that three major
factors have an effect on how much and how well adults learn: prior knowledge, motivation, and ability (Stolovitch & Keeps, 2004). OWLS like Sally
intrinsically understand the importance of active, daily involvement in the
learning process.

OWLS must be ready, willing, and able to participate in workplace
training and retraining activities—that is their responsibility as adult learners. On the other hand, WLP practitioners are responsible for providing the

opportunity, support, and accommodation that OWLS require to become fully functional workplace learners.

WLP practitioners who accept this responsibility need to become acquainted with OWLS as learners. To begin this task, we will take a step back in time and then follow the path that research on adult learning has set for us.

This chapter summarizes the research and theory on adult and later-life learning and then explores some workplace perceptions about OWLS as learners. The chapter ends with a performance support tool (PST) that will help WLP practitioners audit their organizations to identify how the workplace views OWLS as learners.

Adult Learning Theory and Research

An extensive body of research and writing on adult learning in formal and informal education and training settings began developing in the 1960s. This early body of work is summarized by writers such as Cross (1981), Knox (1981), Kidd (1973), and Peterson (1983). Adult learning theory and practice has evolved over the years, and although it is not always directly related to the later-life learner, it is still a relevant starting point for WLP practitioners who desire to learn more about OWLS as learners.

In its current state, adult learning is far too complex a phenomenon to explain with a single theory. "A much more vibrant model is what we have now—a prism of theories, ideas, and frameworks that allows us to see the same phenomenon from different angles" (Merriam, 2001, p. 96). We will take a brief look at two facets of Merriam's "prism"—foundational theories of adult learning and multidisciplinary research—and how these two facets describe the later-life learner.

Foundational Theories Offer Insights About OWLS as Learners

Foundational theories of adult learning include andragogy, self-directed learning, informal and incidental learning, and transformational learning. These theories began developing in the 1960s and are ongoing areas of research and practice. They suggest some general assumptions about adult learners that we can apply to OWLS.

Andragogy. A term introduced in the 1960s, *andragogy* refers to the art and science of helping adults learn. It is based on the assumption that the adult learner

- Is capable of being a self-directed learner
- Can draw on a wealth of experience to enhance learning
- Has learning needs directly related to personal changes in role or status
- Is problem-centered
- Is interested in immediate application
- Is motivated to learn by internal rather than external factors (Knowles, 1980, pp. 43–47)

The andragogical approach to designing workplace learning includes the following components:

- Establishment of a climate of respect, support, and encouragement
- Mutual diagnosis of the need for learning
- An organizational structure that involves the OWL in planning
- Clear learning or performance objectives, or both
- Systematic design, development, and implementation of learning and performance activities
- Clear and frequent evaluation and feedback

These components are particularly user-friendly for OWLS who are self-directed, experienced, motivated, problem-centered learners.

Self-Directed Learning (SDL). The concept of adults as self-directed learners is a part of—yet can stand apart from—andragogy and other adult learning theories. The basic concepts of self-directed learning are found in the work of

Houle (1961), Tough (1979), and Knowles (1975). The basic principle of self-directed learning is that as humans mature they develop the ability to proactively diagnose their learning needs and plan and implement their own learning. Brockett (1997) suggests there are two dimensions to self-direction: learners *can* control their own learning and *want* to or even *prefer* to control their own learning. Self-directed learning theory encourages WLP practitioners, especially trainers, to take advantage of self-directedness by using interactive, participative learning strategies.

Informal and Incidental Learning. Informal and incidental learning theory "has always been part of the landscape of adult learning"; however, because of the implications for training in modern organizations, there was an increase in research beginning in the 1990s (Merriam, 2001, p. 1). Informal and incidental learning theory is especially relevant to workplace learning because it focuses on the learner and "learning that grows out of everyday encounters while working and living in a given context" (Marsick & Watkins, 1990, p. 29).

Informal learning is "intentional but not highly structured"; incidental learning is a category of informal learning and "a by-product of some other activity, such as task accomplishment, interpersonal interaction, sensing the organizational culture, trial-and-error experimentation, or even formal learning" (Marsick & Watkins, 1990, p. 25). Examples from the workplace may include networking, coaching and mentoring, and self-directed performance improvement initiatives.

There are frequently elements of informal or incidental learning in on-the-job and just-in-time training. However, critics warn that although informal and incidental learning can enhance more formal training, it can also require formal training initiatives to undo what learners learned on their own.

Transformational Learning. Transformational learning theory began in the 1970s and is a major focus for research in adult learning today. Transformational learning calls to mind the process that caterpillars go through before they emerge as butterflies (Baumgartner, 2001). Given new information, past experience, and a period of critical reflection, the learner is empowered or self-directed to transform or change learning into performance (Brookfield, 1991; Mezirow and Associates, 2000; Freire, 1970). We will explore transformational learning in more detail in Part Three. For now it is time to move on and review some of the research behind the theories of adult learning.

Research Examines OWLS as Learners

Ron and Susan Zemke reviewed adult learning theory and research in the June 1981 *Training* magazine and again in the June 1995 issue. After examining more than three hundred new articles for the 1995 review, the Zemkes concluded: "As far as solid, reliable information goes, most of what the literature has to tell us today is what it told us then . . . but some important differences in nuance and understanding have occurred that add to our knowledge of the training craft" (Zemke & Zemke, 1995, p. 32).

Much of the new knowledge on the adult learner comes from multidisciplinary fields within and beyond education—educational anthropology, educational psychology, educational gerontology, industrial psychology, sociology, training, and women's studies, to name a few. For example, the research in the following discussion was conducted within a number of different disciplines and provides new insights on women and learning; the potential of OWLS; motivating adult learners; curriculum design for adults; participation of adults in education and training; and the role of experience in adult learning. WLP practitioners need to keep abreast of the research through journals, online searches, and conferences to uncover these new *nuances and understandings* and become more knowledgeable about OWLS as learners.

Women and Learning. Studies of women at all ages have found that relationships and interconnectedness play an important role in a woman's growth and development (Merriam & Caffarella, 1999). The research suggests that women of all ages benefit from collaborative learning and teaching techniques. From a female perspective, the instructor and learners should interactively plan and organize learning experiences, develop a mutually supportive learning climate, use cooperative communication techniques, and recognize the role of feelings in fostering learning relationships (Merriam, 2001).

Learning Potential of OWLS. Educational gerontology is the study of how and why older adults learn—an "interface of adult education and social gerontology" (Findsen, 2005, p. 15). There is substantial evidence from laboratory studies as well as programs like Elderhostel and Institutes for Learning in Retirement (IRLs) that OWLS can and do learn new skills and develop proficiency with previously learned skill sets. In addition, the increasing body of knowledge and practical insight about short- and long-term memory, multiple intelligences, generational differences, the multicultural workplace, and other factors affecting later-life learning assist organizations in establishing programs aimed at helping OWLS maintain their productivity (Binstock & George, 1996; Sherron & Lumsden, 1990). See Part Three.

Motivation and OWLS. Research indicates that adults seek out learning before, during, and after a life-changing event. Change opens a window of opportunity during which OWLS are more receptive to learning and are more apt to retain what they learn. For example, OWLS are often motivated to learn by changes in their current job or work status—job or process redesign, new technologies, mergers or acquisitions, rightsizing, retirement, and so forth.

Personal growth or gain also motivates adults to learn. It is possible to increase motivation in adults, and particularly in OWLS, by engaging their curiosity, cutting the risk factor, and focusing on the immediate utility of the new learning.

Curriculum Design for OWLS. Zemke & Zemke (1995) found that the adult learner's tendency to prefer "single-concept, single-theory courses that focus on applying the concept to relevant problems" increases as adult learners grow older (p. 33). They also reported that the following curricular elements are important to maximize the learning experience for adult learners of all ages: preassessment of the individual learner's skills and goals; advance organizers and other strategies for organizing and learning the content; and opportunities for practice, feedback, and recognition.

Curriculum design for OWLS should take into account that OWLS integrate new information with what they already know. Storytelling is one strategy that seems to make it easier for OWLS to integrate old and new information; however, if the new information contradicts what they know and value, it may take OWLS longer to integrate the new and the old knowledge (Zemke & Zemke, 1995).

Participation in Education and Training. Studies from the United States, the UK, and the Netherlands indicate that adults who have education beyond high school and are working, especially in professional or managerial occupations, are more likely to participate in education and training activities ["Briefing Sheet," 2005; Longworth, 2003).

Studies in Canada, the United States, and Europe also indicate that as OWLS move closer to retirement, they have fewer opportunities to participate in training, because upgrading their knowledge and skills is not considered to be a good return on investment ("Older worker adjustment programs," 1999).

Researchers generally agree that if you build learning with adults in mind, they will come—and they will bring with them a plethora of past learning and experience.

Role of Experience. Experience or prior knowledge "helps the learner acquire additional knowledge or skills more rapidly . . . the more you know about something, the easier it is to acquire additional knowledge and skills in that subject" (Stolovitch & Keeps, 2004, p. 2). OWLS who have more learning experience are better able to tackle memory and other test-taking tasks. This increases their self-confidence and lessens their anxiety level.

Prior education and other experiences also increase the chance that training material is familiar and meaningful to the learner. You and other WLP practitioners may need to adjust the amount and type of prelearning or supplementary learning activities to compensate for variations in experience or prior knowledge.

Research Clarifies Perceptions About OWLS as Learners

No matter what discipline they come from, or what area of research they probe, most of the researchers who study adult learning set out to prove or dispel specific perceptions about adults as learners. Assumptions about the adult learner in general may or may not be true of an individual OWL. As a WLP practitioner, you will need to use observation as well as research to validate that what you think is true about an OWL as a learner is really true—a reality or a myth.

Workplace Perceptions About OWLS as Learners

There are six major workplace perceptions about OWLS as learners:

- OWLS are self-directed learners.
- Young worker-learners *learn better* than OWLS.
- OWLS do not need training.
- Young worker-learners are more motivated to learn than OWLS.
- OWLS cannot learn new techniques or technologies.
- OWLS cost more to train.

We will discuss each perception and the research that is associated with the perception. These perceptions will also form the basis of the workplace perceptions audit survey (PST 4.1) at the end of this chapter.

OWLS Are Self-Directed Learners

Self-directedness has been associated with adult learning theory since the 1960s. It is no wonder, then, that writers in the field, WLP practitioners, and others assume that OWLS are self-directed learners.

Self-directed learners want to control the learning process. "They take the initiative with or without the help of others, in diagnosing their learning needs, formulating learning goals, identifying human and material resources for learning, choosing and implementing appropriate learning strategies, and evaluating learning outcomes" (Knowles, 1975, p. 18). Self-directed learners take responsibility for their own learning and prefer self-study, independent learning, or self-instruction.

Some critics of self-directed learning question whether self-directedness is a factor of age or an individual tendency that can be found in both adults and children—or not at all. These critics argue that even grade-school children can be self-directed.

Other critics feel that self-directed learners prefer to learn in isolation and do not function well in group training sessions. Knowles (1975), on the other hand, argues that self-directed learning usually takes place in association with teachers, tutors, mentors, resource people, or peers. In addition, he suggests that true self-directed learners realize there are situations in which they need to be *taught* and that "they enter into those taught-learning situations in a searching, probing frame of mind and exploit them as resources for learning without losing their self directedness" (p. 21).

Younger Worker-Learners Learn Better Than OWLS

"The powerful myth that adults lose their *ability* to learn as they age prevails, although for the most part it has not been substantiated in the literature" (Merriam & Caffarella, 1999, p. 168). Many researchers think that OWLS are neither better nor worse learners than younger learners; they are just *different* from younger learners: "At different ages the human being learns and knows in different ways" (Moody, 1985, p. 35). Studies conducted by the AARP found no evidence that learning ability declines before age seventy-five—the beginning age of the Old-Old OWLS (Kaeter, 1995).

There *is* evidence in the literature of age-related declines in learning *processes*. Since the 1950s, research indicates that cognitive development, recall, and problem solving may show some decline with aging; however, these findings are also influenced by variables such as educational level, training, health, and speed of response (Merriam & Caffarella, 1999). Schaie and Willis (2002) reported that as adult learners age, they score better on some measures of intelligence and worse on others, and the overall measure remains stable.

If there is an age-related decline, it may be mitigated by individual differences: "Despite the fact that much literature does support an apparent age decline in learning processes, individual differences in memory and intelligence serve to modify such declines and age differences may be lessened, and sometimes eliminated" (Hayslip & Kennelly, 1985, p. 78).

Age-related differences in learning can be explained by the interaction between cognitive and noncognitive factors (Hayslip & Kennelly, 1985). Cognitive factors are basic intellectual processes such as memory and intelligence; noncognitive factors are variables, such as motivation and health, that have an effect on the learner's ability to transfer learning into performance. We will discuss cognitive and noncognitive factors in Part Two.

OWLS Do Not Need Training

Many people still think that humans traditionally study, work, and retire. In Chapter One we mentioned that many organizations are aware of the aging workplace; however, they have not made plans to train or retrain OWLS. Stein and Rocco (2001) also report that when workers reach the age of forty many organizations begin to view them as less productive and begin to offer them fewer training opportunities.

Cross (1981) suggested that future generations would break the study-work-retire pattern and would follow a "blended life plan" of lifelong learning, working, resting when necessary, learning again, working again, and so forth. The blended life plan reinforces the concept that "[a]ll humans are learners, and workers learn every day" (Cross & O'Driscoll, 2005, p. 32). When researchers report that more older adults are staying in or returning to the workforce, it reinforces the concept of a blended life plan—a cycle of learning and working and resting that is truly a lifelong journey.

Young Worker-Learners Are More Motivated to Learn

Sometimes the perception that OWLS *cannot* learn gets all tangled up with the perception that OWLS *do not want to* learn new techniques or technologies. The research on motivation that we discussed earlier in this chapter indicates that adults of all ages are motivated to learn what is relevant and beneficial to them as individuals. OWLS are no exception.

Key findings from a UK learner satisfaction study in 2001–2002 also indicated that OWLS were more motivated than younger worker-learners who took the same accredited learning program. In fact, 89 percent of the fifty-five-plus age group said they "get a buzz" from learning ("Briefing Sheet," 2005).

OWLS Cannot Learn New Skills

The general consensus in the literature is that OWLS can learn new skills; however, it may take them longer. Kaeter (1995, p. 63) feels that OWLS take longer to learn because "things need to be unlearned first." Kaeter uses the example of unlearning how to use a typewriter or a word processor in order to learn to use a computer.

OWLS Cost More to Train

One related perception is that it costs more to train an OWL than it does to train a younger worker. However, Karl Gustafson, former vice president for human resources at Baptist Hospital of Coral Gables, Florida, insists that although the training strategies differ for older and younger workers, the costs and end results equal out: "The experienced older worker, when treated appropriately, has a lot to offer. They catch on readily in training and are able to work in the high-tech areas as effectively as younger workers" (as cited in Joyce, 2005). Baptist Hospital is known for hiring older workers and adjusting its training programs to meet the needs of OWLS.

Implications for Workplace Learning and Performance

Twenty years ago Hayslip and Kennelly (1985, p. 73) predicted that OWLS "will remain in the workforce and will be either continuing or beginning their education anew." Ten years later, researchers predicted that as even the Old-Old and Oldest OWLS become healthier and more active there will be an increase in the number who pursue education and training (Neikrug, Ronen, & Glanz, 1995).

In the Learning Age we will need a workforce with imagination and confidence, and the skills required will be diverse (Jarvis, 2001, p. 24). WLP practitioners who are responsible for learning and performance in an aging workplace need to understand the factors that affect OWLS as learners. They also need to recognize that "[t]he less adult learners possess of each of the ingredients of learning [prior knowledge, motivation, and ability], the more we trainers have to work to compensate for what they lack. Yes, that's our job—compensating for what our learners don't have, managing the learning context, and providing feedback and rewards for success" (Stolovitch & Keeps, 2004, p. 3).

Action Steps for WLP Practitioners

As a WLP practitioner you are strategically positioned to help your organization define meaningful learning for the OWLS they serve by focusing on the OWLS' needs, interests, expertise, and learning styles. Initiate the following actions to help yourself and your organization understand OWLS as learners and to help OWLS understand themselves and the business environment in which they learn and perform. Here are some steps you can take to help maximize the potential of OWLS as learners:

1. Learn more about workplace learner competencies and OWLS.

   Appendix 4.1, "Competencies for Older Workplace Learners," which appears at the end of this chapter, was written especially for this book by Dr. William Rothwell, Instructional Technology and Training Series editor and professor in charge of the workforce education and development program in the Department of Learning and Performance Systems at Pennsylvania State University. Dr. Rothwell was a member of the 1995–1996 ASTD Expert Panel on Human Performance Improvement that helped develop the ASTD Models for Human Performance Improvement. In his appendix he discusses workplace learner competencies and focuses on the competencies that are most important to older OWLS aged sixty-five-plus.

2. Learn more about OWLS as self-directed learners.

   The International Symposium on Self-Directed Learning (n.d.) is a continuing resource for information on past and present research on this topic. WLP practitioners can access the Symposium's Web site at http://sdlglobal.com.

3. Learn about the psychosocial development of OWLS.

   Part Two of this book—OWLS in Transition—contains more in-depth information about OWLS as workers and learners.

Its chapters will explain the normal cognitive and physiological development of OWLS, explore the learning styles and challenges that OWLS face daily in the workplace, and discuss the psychosocial development of OWLS in terms of ages, stages, and generations.

4. Help audit your organization's perceptions about OWLS as learners.

As a WLP practitioner with competencies in information gathering, analysis, and change initiation, and a fledgling expert on OWLS, you can use PST 4.1, How to Audit Workplace Perceptions About OWLS as Learners, to find out what your organization thinks about OWLS as learners. This is the final step in the organizational analysis process that began in Chapter One. The complete process looks like this:

a. Preliminary organizational analysis to determine the status of your organization in terms of the aging workplace and shifting demographics

b. Analysis of your organization's perceptions about OWLS as workers

c. Analysis of your organization's culture of retention regarding OWLS

d. Analysis of your organization's perceptions of OWLS as learners

In PST 4.1 you will collect data on the organization's existing education and training policies, processes, procedures, and practices that directly impact OWLS. Then you will analyze the data to determine whether OWLS as learners are valued and supported by your organization; make recommendations for change if needed, and communicate the findings and your recommendations to the decision makers in your organization. This is the substance from which OWL-friendly policies, processes, procedures, and practices are born.

PST 4.1. How to Audit Workplace Perceptions About OWLS as Learners.

1. Collect information about how your organization perceives OWLS as learners. Use the sample survey at the end of these instructions as a guide. Customize the survey to fit your organization if necessary. You may also use the sample survey as an interview guide and record the answers on the guide.

2. Quantify your findings using percentages, frequency counts, and so forth. Here are some suggestions for quantifying the data on this survey:

   a. Total the number of the respondents to this survey (N).

   b. Total the number of respondents by classification—executives, managers, and so forth (n).

   c. Total the number of respondents by classification and age group (20–29, 30–39, 40–64, and so forth).

   d. Calculate the percentage of the total number of respondents who selected each response to each item or perception.

   e. Calculate the percentage of the respondents within a classification—executives, managers, and so forth—who selected each response to each item or perception (see example below).

Sample:

6. OWLS can't learn new techniques or technologies.	Myth	Reality	Not Sure
Executives	20%	69%	11%
Managers	50%	45%	5%

   • Calculate the percentage of each classification who selected each response to each item or perception by age group (20–29, 30–39, 40–64, and so forth).

   • Calculate the percentage of the total number of respondents who selected each response by age group.

3. Analyze your findings. Use the following sample analysis questions as a guide:

   • What perceptions about OWLS as learners are selected as realities by 50 percent or more of the total number of respondents?

- What perceptions about OWLS as learners are selected as realities by 50 percent or more of the total number of respondents in each classification (executives, manager, and so forth)?

- What perceptions about OWLS as learners are listed as realities by 50 percent or more of *each* age group (20–29, 30–39, 40–64, and so forth) within *each* respondent classification?

- What perceptions of the individual respondent classifications were aligned with each other? (Example of alignment: More than 50 percent of all the respondents agreed that OWLS can learn new techniques or technologies. Example of misalignment: More than 50 percent of the managers, coworkers, customers, trainers, and OWLS and less than 50 percent of the executives and human resource staff felt that OWLS cannot learn new techniques or technologies.)

- What perceptions are aligned by age group? (Example: More than 50 percent of the respondents in the sixty-five-plus age groups feel that OWLS can learn new techniques or technologies; less than 50 percent of the respondents in the 20–29 age groups agree.)

- Other . . .

4. Draw conclusions or make deductions about the current situation based on the audit results. Here are some sample conclusions:

   - This organization *does/does not* have a positive perception of OWLS as learners.

   - This organization *does/does not* need to plan a strategy for developing a more positive perception of OWLS as learners.

   - The following classifications *are/are not* positive about OWLS as learners.

   - Our organization *is/is not* aligned in its perception of OWLS as workers *(specify areas of alignment or misalignment; for example, topics, classifications, age groups and so forth)*.

   - Other . . .

5. Make recommendations to encourage the organization to take action based on the results of the audit. The following are sample recommendations:

   - Suggest ways that the organization can learn more about its OWLS.

- Suggest ways that the organization can learn more about OWLS in general. For example, use employee newsletters, staff or committee meetings, intranet bulletin boards, and so forth to share information from this book with others in the organization.

- Suggest that it is time to start collecting and analyzing information about the current policies, procedures, and practices of the organization that affect OWLS as learners; for example, education, training, certification, and so forth.

6. Communicate the results of the survey to build awareness and, if action is required, to gain support for a change initiative that will improve opportunities for OWLS as learners. Send reports by email or fax; print the results and rec-ommendations in a newsletter or on the intranet, or discuss the results and recommendations at meetings, briefings, brown bag lunches, and so forth.

Sample Survey

Title: What Do You Think About Owls as Learners?

Purpose: The purpose of this survey is to find out what people in our organization really think about older worker-learners (OWLS). We plan to use the information from this survey to _____ *[What will the organization do with the survey results? How will the respondents benefit if they complete the survey?]*

This is an anonymous survey; however, to help us interpret the results we are asking you to provide us with the following information before you begin the next part of the survey:

Check (✓) *one* statement that best describes your work relationship with older worker-learners (OWLS) in the workplace:

- ☐ I am an executive with this organization.

- ☐ I work in Human Resources and I interview and hire OWLS, administer benefit and retirement plans, and so forth.

- ☐ I manage or supervise OWLS.

- ☐ I train OWLS.

- ☐ I work with OWLS.

- ☐ I am a customer of OWLS.

- ☐ Other . . . (please explain).

PST 4.1. How to Audit Workplace Perceptions About OWLS as Learners, *Continued.*

Check (✓) the age range that best describes you:

☐ Under age 20

☐ Age 20–29

☐ Age 30–39

☐ Age 40–54

☐ Age 55–64

☐ Age 65–74

☐ Age 75–84

☐ Age 85+

Thank you for your help. Please continue with the survey.

Instructions: The topics and statements in the table below were taken from the literature on older worker-learners (OWLS). Please read each statement and check (✓) the column to the right that best describes your *immediate* reaction to the statement.

If you want to add a statement or make a comment on the topic, please do so in the *Comment* box at the end of the survey.

	Myth	Reality	Not Sure
1. OWLS cost more to train than younger workers.			
2. OWLS cost the same to train as younger workers.			
3. The experience level of OWLS can offset any additional costs for adapting training to age-related limitations.			
4. OWLS can learn new techniques and technologies.			
5. OWLS prefer self-study or self-instruction.			

PST 4.1. How to Audit Workplace Perceptions About OWLS as Learners, *Continued.*

	Myth	Reality	Not Sure
6. OWLS do not function well in group training sessions.			
7. OWLS are self-directed learners.			
8. OWLS can't learn new techniques or technologies.			
9. The capacity to learn is not a function of age.			
10. Younger workers learn better than OWLS.			
11. People study, work, retire—in that order— so OWLS do not need education or training.			
12. Younger learners are more motivated than OWLS.			
13. OWLS take longer to learn new skills.			
Comment . . .			

Appendix 4.1. Competencies for Older Workplace Learners

WILLIAM J. ROTHWELL

What are workplace learning competencies? Why are workplace learning competencies important, and what competencies has research shown to be essential for individuals? What learning competencies are particularly important for older workers? This brief appendix addresses these questions.

What Are Workplace Learning Competencies?

Much research over the years has focused on the competencies essential for successful trainers in organizational settings (see, for instance, Bernthal, Colteryahn, Davis, Naughton, Rothwell, & Wellins, 2004; McLagan, 1989; Rothwell, Sanders, & Soper, 1999). Of course, a *competency* refers to a characteristic that is linked to successful or exemplary performance. A *learning competency* thus refers to a characteristic that is linked to successful or exemplary learning performance.

Why Are Workplace Learning Competencies Important, and Which Are Essential for Individuals?

Futurist Alvin Toffler (1994) once wrote that illiteracy in the twenty-first century will be linked more to the inability to learn than to the inability to read or write. And the key characteristic of *high potentials*—understood to mean those who are capable of higher-level responsibility—is greater-than-average ability to learn, according to management gurus Michael Lombardo and Robert Eichinger (2000). Hence, workplace learning competence is essential to successful productivity. And that is why it is so important.

Research conducted by Rothwell (2002) revealed that numerous individual workplace learning competencies affect learning ability in workplace settings. These include the following:

Reading skill

Writing skill

Computation skill

Listening skill

Questioning skill

Speaking skill

Cognitive skills

Individual skills

Resource skills

Interpersonal skill

Informational and technological skill

Systems thinking

Personal mastery

Mental modeling

Shared visioning

Team learning skill

Self-knowledge

Short-term memory skill

Long-term memory skill

Subject matter knowledge

Enjoyment of learning and work

Flexibility

Persistence and confidence

Sense of urgency

Giving respect to others

Work environment analytical skills

Sensory awareness

Open-mindedness

Humility

Analytical skill (synthesis)

Intuition

Information sourcing skill

Information gathering skill

Information organizing skill

Feedback solicitation skill

Willingness to experiment and gain experience

Internalization skill

Application of new knowledge skill

Ability to adapt knowledge to new situations or events

Critical examination of information skill

Learning how to learn skill

Self-directedness skill

Organizational leaders may use these competencies to assess individual learning competence and plan ways to improve individual abilities to learn in real-time workplace settings to address the practical problems that all workers encounter as they work. Knowledge is not static; rather, it is continually reformed by individuals through the learning process to address these real-time problems and challenges.

Of course, individual workplace learning competence is only part of a bigger picture. Organizational settings can encourage or discourage individuals' willingness to learn. That is associated with so-called *learning climate,* a way of operationalizing the notion of the learning organization.

Research by Rothwell (2002) revealed that workplace learning is encouraged to the extent that each of the following conditions is perceived to be met:

Sufficient financial resources exist to support workplace learning.

Realistic goals and expectations for learning have been established.

There is commitment by the organization to the learning process.

Sufficient trust exists in the organization.

Management shares a common understanding of vision and goals.

Sufficient time is provided to permit learning.

Good communication exists in the organization.

The organization fosters a means by which to collect and use feedback from customers.

Workplace learning is made a priority and is tied to performance expectations.

The leadership of the organization is perceived to support workplace learning.

Clear milestones have been established for the workplace learning process.

Managers, union leaders, and learners exhibit buy-in and commitment to learning.

Individuals are matched to learning experiences for which they have the appropriate education and background.

The learning effort is closely tied to business needs.

Work standards are consistently applied within the organization.

The organization possesses clear methods by which to examine and measure work performance.

Learners are open-minded and possess an attitude that favors learning.

Measurement and accountability have been established and linked to the workplace learning process.

The workplace learning process is guided by a plan.

A clear sense exists about "next steps" following the workplace learning process.

The organization's union, if the organization is unionized, supports the workplace learning process and effort.

External environmental factors support the workplace learning process.

Fear has been reduced within the organization so that individuals are not afraid to take risks and learn.

Learners feel empowered.

Learners feel they have incentives and rewards sufficient to encourage them to pursue workplace learning and see "what's in it for them."

Responsibilities for who should do what in the workplace learning process have been clarified.

Which Learning Competencies Are Particularly Important for Older Workers?

Although research remains to be done to pinpoint exactly which individual workplace learning competencies are essential for older workers—especially those who are over the traditional retirement age of sixty-five—it does not stretch the imagination to suggest that individual workplace learning competencies can be affected by the physical, mental, and experiential issues surrounding age. For the most part, research has shown that cognitive ability does not decline with age so long as individuals remain mentally active, and physical ability that influences eyesight, hearing, and other senses does not decline dramatically so long as individuals remain physically active. In short, it is possible to teach old dogs new tricks so long as the "dogs" remain active mentally and physically.

Of perhaps greater concern is the workplace learning environment that employers establish and maintain. The coworkers of older workers must remain sensitive to the feelings of older workers, lest the workplace learning climate become less encouraging to individuals. That is, and should remain, a key focus for concern.

All adults go through transitions as they develop over their lifespan. OWLS are no exception. They develop their cognitive skills and learn to deal with cognitive challenges, develop their personalities and their social skills in relation to the life they lead and the generation into which they were born, undergo physiological changes and learn to cope with and compensate for the normal aging process, enjoy good health and cope with poor health, and often pursue both structured and unstructured leisure activities.

Some transitions inspire and motivate OWLS; others have a negative impact on their learning or performance. All transitions make them what they and all of us really are—humans in search of wisdom, knowledge, self, function, and well-being.

This part contains the following chapters:

Five   OWLS in Search of Wisdom: Cognitive Development

Six   OWLS in Search of Knowledge: Learning Styles and Challenges

Seven   OWLS in Search of Self: Psychosocial Transitions

Eight   OWLS in Search of Function: Physiological Development

Nine   OWLS in Search of Well-Being: Health, Wellness, and Leisure

The chapters present useful research and theory from the following fields of study: adult development, education, learning, behavioral sciences, psychology, educational psychology, training, and gerontology. They also discuss how transitions impact workplace learning and performance and suggest action steps that WLP practitioners can take to maximize the potential of OWLS in transition.

5

OWLS in Search of Wisdom: Cognitive Development

Whether I'm working or not, I try to develop my mind. In fact, I consciously do this at least three times a week by reading something. I like mystery novels and I'm hooked on Harry Potter. I even buy those silly crossword puzzles and get my friends working with me. I also try to keep healthy and fit and open to new things. The rabbi says that when your mind goes, you lose everything. I have too much I still want to do. I don't want to lose my memory or my mind.

Ruthie, age seventy-four, semiretired social worker

R UTHIE INTUITIVELY RECOGNIZES that it is "most fruitful to interpret age differences in learning as a product of the interaction between cognitive and non-cognitive factors" (Hayslip & Kennelly, 1985, p. 75). She also understands that the best way to combat or compensate for age-related challenges to learning is to maintain or improve her cognitive abilities while maintaining or improving the noncognitive factors, such as health and fitness, that could contribute to age differences in learning.

In this first chapter of Part Two: OWLS in Transition, we will focus on five cognitive functions: memory, attention, executive control, visuospatial processing, and general intelligence. We will discuss how they develop as OWLS age. We will also discuss noncognitive factors that can impact learning.

At the end of the chapter we will summarize the implications for workplace learning and performance and suggest some action steps that WLP practitioners can take to turn information about cognitive development into practice. Carefully selected and crafted learning and performance practices can empower OWLS, engage their creativity, and expand and develop their cognitive ability.

Cognitive Development of OWLS

The following list summarizes major findings from research on the cognitive development of OWLS that could impact workplace learning and performance decisions:

- Normal cognitive development may affect cognitive *agility;* however, there are only mild signs that cognitive *ability* is affected in healthy OWLS.

- Slow cognitive processing speed may be linked to a decline in motor function.

- Cognitive and noncognitive factors interact during learning and performance. Some of the noncognitive factors—pain, depression, health, and so forth—*may* speed up or increase normal cognitive aging.

Cognitive and Noncognitive Factors

Cognitive factors that have an effect on learning include five major cognitive or intellectual functions: memory, attention, executive control, visuospatial processing, and general intelligence. Executive control helps the learner manage attention and selective perception; visuospatial processing refers to how learners visually perceive spatial relationships among objects. All five cognitive functions are crucial to how OWLS process sensory and nonsensory data during learning experiences, retain the knowledge and skills they need to maximize their workplace learning and performance, and retrieve stored knowledge and skills as needed.

Noncognitive variables also affect the learner's ability to process information and transfer learning into performance. Noncognitive factors that affect OWLS as learners may include motivation, education level, health and wellness, sensory status, functionality, and past experience.

Cognitive and noncognitive factors interact to either improve or hinder learning. For example, OWLS can remember new knowledge more rapidly if they can relate it to prior experience; experience improves their ability to tackle memory and other test-taking tasks (Stolovitch & Keeps, 2004). In addition to speeding up cognitive functions, prior experience may increase self-confidence and decrease anxiety.

Aging May Affect Cognitive Abilities

Cognitive abilities or skills vary from OWL to OWL. The normal aging process may affect the cognitive abilities of older adults, especially those in the sixty-plus age group (Callahan, Kiker, & Cross, 2003). To complicate matters, Lowenstein (2005) warns that trying to delineate "normal age-related cognitive decline" is "a work in progress."

Research on the effects of aging on cognitive functions tells us that although cognitive processing may slow down, in normal, healthy OWLS there are only mild signs of age-related change. Roth (2005, n.p.) suggests that WLP practitioners and others should use research findings to "dispel most employers' fears of diminished cognitive ability among their older workers."

New scientific research into the brain and reassessment of old research strongly indicates that age-related changes can make older brains slower to process information, less able to block distractions and irrelevant information during recall tasks, and less agile when it comes to switching from task to task. However, old brains can also replace lost neurons, and training can alter brain circuits: "old brains can be trained to act like young brains" (Begley, 2006).

Generally, there is only a "mild decline" in the cognitive processing ability of healthy and active OWLS between the ages of fifty-five and one hundred-plus; between ages sixty-five and seventy-four an OWL's cognitive abilities may not decline at all (Roth, 2005). Of course this is a generalized view, and, as in any age group, there are broad variations in cognitive functioning and ability.

Although certain cognitive abilities decline with age, others may even improve (Callahan, Kiker, & Cross, 2003). Table 5.1 compares the cognitive abilities that are preserved in healthy OWLS and the cognitive abilities that may show some decline as a function of aging.

Table 5.1. Cognitive Abilities Are Preserved or Decline with Age.

These cognitive abilities tend to be preserved in healthy older adults . . .	These cognitive abilities may decline as a function of aging . . .
Attention span	• Selective attention required to focus on and remember specific sensory input
Remote memory	• Immediate, short-term memory
Everyday communication skills	• Verbal fluency
	• Handling face-to-face, low-frequency stimuli
Understanding of thought sequences	• Complex logical analysis
Simple visual perception	• Complex cognitive or perceptual tasks requiring speed
Meaning, sound, and use of knowledge	• Complex mental image skills
	• Cognitive flexibility—shifting cognitive ways of attending to information, previewing it, remembering it, and thinking about it

Noncognitive Factors Can Affect Cognitive Abilities

Many of the cognitive deficits that we observe in OWLS may be "artifacts of the older learner's past status and experience in our society" (Hayslip & Kennelly, 1985, p. 87). Lowenstein (2005) and others suggest several biological, psychological, and psychosocial-experiential factors that may speed up or increase the effects of aging on cognitive abilities:

- Biological factors—pain, nutrition, medication, lifestyle, disease, and trauma

- Psychological factors—depression, paranoia, anxiety, attention or hyperactivity disorders, and stress

- Psychosocial or experiential factors—education, test-wiseness, motivation, examination environment, timed versus paced tasks, and mental ability

Many of the noncognitive factors are discussed in Part Two. All of these factors taken together could have an impact on how well the aging brain is able to use memory, attention, executive control, visuospatial function, and even general intelligence.

Changes in Cognitive Agility Affect Memory

Memory applies to "all aspects of our ability to learn, retain, and recall information" (Roth, 2005). OWLS and researchers can attest to the fact that "memory can be strikingly sharp even to age 100" (Plutowski, 2005). However, cognitive processing begins to slow in a person's late twenties. By the time OWLS are in their sixties they may take longer to perform cognitive tasks (Roth, 2005). This affects the amount of time it takes to process data for sensory, short-term, and long-term memory—and timing is a critical factor for some learning or performance tasks.

Perhaps the best way to understand this is to view memory not as a single entity or ability but as a complex cognitive process that is deeply affected by timing. Figure 5.1 illustrates the components and tasks of memory from an information-processing perspective. The discussion that follows will focus on the time factor.

Figure 5.1. Memory: An Information-Processing Perspective.

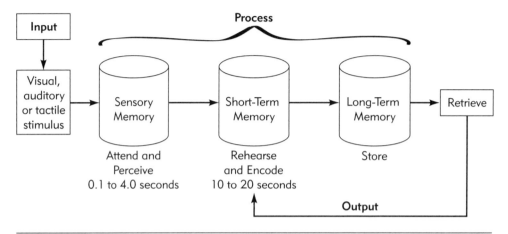

Sensory Memory. Sensory memory uses the five senses to select and process sensory information in the environment. Learners must attend to the sensory information as it enters the sensory memory, identify or decode the information, and send the information to short-term memory—and they have only one-tenth to one second to process a visual memory and two to four seconds to process an auditory memory. This is one of the reasons that the fast-paced MTV approach to training does not work well with OWLS who have lost some cognitive agility.

Short-Term Memory. Short-term memory has a duration of ten to twenty seconds. If the items are simply stored, short-term memory can hold approximately seven items; if the learner is trying to process the information, working memory can hold only two or three items (Sweller, van Merrienboer, & Paas, 1998).

Processing includes rehearsal, encoding, or both. Rehearsal is the process of repeating the input data over and over again without changing it; encoding is the process of connecting or associating the data with other data already stored in long-term memory. Both rehearsal and encoding are critical if a memory must be stored in and later retrieved from long-term memory. Again, OWLS may be at a disadvantage if their processing speed has decreased.

Long-Term Memory. In very simple terms, long-term memory is a lot like a giant file cabinet with multiple drawers, file folders, and files. It is almost limitless in capacity. Retrieval of information is either immediate or, more often, delayed, and it involves both recognizing and recalling the stored data. Research indicates that age has a bigger impact on delayed recall or retrieval than on delayed recognition. Even if OWLS can find the file, pulling it out of a tightly packed file drawer may take some time and effort. In addition, the type of memory that was stored—explicit or implicit—has an impact on recall and recognition and affects how WLP practitioners present the information.

Explicit Memory. Explicit memory is information that a person consciously learns and retains; for example, facts, rules, and definitions. Researchers have found that over the lifespan there are minimal changes to explicit memory in sensory and short-term memory and substantial changes to explicit memory in long-term memory after age fifty. The researchers also found that if healthy, active OWLS are given the time to learn new information "to the point where few errors are made," they remember the information as well as younger learners (Albert & Moss, 1997, p. 221).

Implicit Memory. Implicit memory refers to information that a person acquires without a conscious effort; for example, procedural knowledge, habits, motor skills, and perceptual skills (Papalia, Camp, & Feldman, 1996). Recall of procedural learning based on implicit memory may decline with age, depending in part on how easily and proficiently the skill or procedure was learned originally (Albert & Moss, 1997).

Attentional Capacity Affects Cognition

Attention is the ability to mentally focus on an object or task; attentional capacity is the totality of focusing abilities that are available to an individual. Attentional capacity includes both sustained and selective attention (Albert & Moss, 1997). WLP practitioners need to consciously plan how to help OWLS use both sustained and selective attention skills and keep their attention focused on what they need to remember.

Sustained Attention. OWLS must be able to control and sustain attention to short-term memory processing tasks in order to move data through working memory to long-term memory. They need to consciously work at it; attention must be effortful or concentrated, not passive. Sustained attention is usually well preserved over the lifespan; OWLS just need help blocking out distractions. OWLS need to stay focused and be actively involved in the tasks they are performing (Albert & Moss, 1997, p. 218). That's where selective attention comes in.

Selective Attention. Selective attention helps OWLS distinguish relevant from irrelevant information; block out interference, such as external environmental noise or internal mental distractions; and concentrate on relevant information. In a training situation, WLP practitioners can control external environmental "noise" such as loud voices or training rooms that are too hot or too cold. They can also use brain games and other strategies to train OWLS to block out internal distractions.

Decline in Executive Control Affects Cognition

Executive function is also known as executive control. It is an internal condition of learning—a complex set of cognitive abilities that enable OWLS to select and regulate the cognitive strategies they need to receive information, perceive it, remember it, think about it, act on it, and be confident that they have the ability to use it (Gagne, 1985). Research indicates significant age-related declines in executive function beginning with Mid-Old OWLS. Mid-Old OWLS with more education do not decline as soon; however, Old OWLS aged sixty-five and older show a significant decline in performance on tests that involve visually recognizing similarities among objects or completing a series of numbers or words (Albert & Moss, 1997)—two tasks that may come up in a training situation.

Visuospatial Functions Can Enable Cognition

Visuospatial functions are the skills used to visually perceive spatial relationships among objects. Most OWLS rely on the sense of sight to help them visualize objects and create internal mental images and pictures in both long-term and short-term memory.

OWLS who are strong in visual-spatial intelligence can develop flow-charts, read matrices, imagine options, and visualize solutions. They are the individuals who like to design, draw, build, create, and daydream. They "use the different functions of visual imagery to construct and/or acquire information" (Tracey, 2001, p. 3).

However, normal changes in the pupil and lens of the aging eye can play havoc with visuospatial functions (see Chapter Eight). WLP practitioners may need to adjust the size, color, and clarity of visual training elements, such as navigation charts or maps, complex spreadsheets, blueprints, or animated flow diagrams of an electrical system. They may also need to adjust the time they allow for OWLS to use the materials.

Intelligent OWLS

Another way of studying adult cognitive development is by looking at adult intelligence. General intelligence is an individual's inherited or genetic ability for acquiring new knowledge and skill. Intelligence varies from individual to individual and affects learning capacity and proficiency. Aging research emphasizes that flexibility and interindividual variability are inherent qualities of intelligent OWLS.

The Nature of Intelligence

Early literature looked at intelligence as a single trait, which included various verbal and reasoning abilities or aptitudes. The traditional view of intelligence includes the following:

1. Capacity to acquire knowledge

2. Ability to think and reason at an abstract level

3. Capability for solving "novel" problems (Eggen & Kauchak, 2001)

Another significant body of research distinguishes between fluid intelligence, which is determined by genetics and physiology, and crystallized intelligence, which is affected by cultural experience. Table 5.2 summarizes the difference between the two types of intelligence.

Table 5.2. A Comparison of Fluid and Crystallized Intelligence.

Fluid Intelligence	Crystallized Intelligence
Determined by genetics and physiology	Affected by culture and experience
Process of applying new information and mental abilities to novel situations without prior knowledge	Process of accumulating information based on experience
Tends to decline significantly between ages 25 and 75	Tends to increase with age and experience

Fluid Intelligence. Fluid intelligence is the ability to process new information and apply mental abilities to new situations without the benefit of prior knowledge (Perlmutter & Hall, 1985, p. 244). Researchers have found that there is significant decline in fluid intelligence–related abilities between the ages of twenty-five and seventy-five (Lowenstein, 2005). OWLS may be at a disadvantage when it comes to learning and performing new skills that are not directly in their repertoire of knowledge and skills.

Crystallized Intelligence. Crystallized intelligence "is the process of accumulation—which includes education and active information seeking, and is based on our experiences" (Jarvis, 2001, p. 55). Research suggests that crystallized intelligence increases with age and experience, so OWLS increase in intelligence as they age as long as decreases in physical or mental function do not interfere (Jarvis, 2001, p. 55). In fact, "up to ages 55 to 65, the improvement in crystallized intelligence is about equal to the decline in fluid intelligence" (Papalia, Camp, & Feldman, 1996, pp. 217–218).

Crystallized abilities include the development and use of vocabulary. This ability improves or remains consistent in later life and depends on the breadth of knowledge and experience acquired during a person's lifetime. Training developers may need to define and explain new vocabulary and help OWLS relate it to their past experience or knowledge.

Multiple Intelligences Are Mind-Expanding

Gardner pioneered the study of intelligence as a multidimensional concept. "The theory of multiple intelligences means that we can each acknowledge the other's specialisms without having to claim that one person or specialism is more intelligent than another is" (Jarvis, 2001, p. 56). Gardner's pioneering research, which resulted in the publication of *Frames of Mind* (1983), explains his perspective on how learners of all ages acquire knowledge and how the forms of intelligence work in synergy by interacting with and building from each other (Tracey, 2001).

Gardner (1983) originally identified seven intelligences: verbal-linguistic, logical-mathematical, visual-spatial, musical-rhythmic, bodily-kinesthetic, and personal, which includes interpersonal and intrapersonal intelligence. To make this multiple intelligence mosaic complete, he added an eighth intelligence, naturalist—an intelligence that "permits the recognition and categorization of natural objects" (Gardner, 1998, p. 20). Later in this chapter we will suggest how to capitalize on the multiple intelligences of OWLS. But first we will discuss some of the cognitive abilities that support cognitive processing; thinking, problem solving, and creativity.

Implications for Workplace Learning and Performance

This was a particularly challenging chapter to write because of the many components that are part of cognitive functioning. Therefore, rather than to treat all the workplace implications and the action steps as one unit—as we have in the previous chapters and in the following chapters—we decided to treat cognitive development, memory, attention, intelligence, and problem solving as separate issues with their own implications and action steps. We believe this will provide greater clarity of the discussion and give a more user-friendly practical approach.

Cognitive Development: Implications

Earlier in this chapter we discussed the cognitive development of OWLS and summarized major findings from research that could impact workplace learning and performance decisions. Cognitive development is like a kaleidoscope that is made up of many pieces or abilities with many reciprocal relationships. Most cognitive abilities tend to remain stable in healthy OWLS; however, pain, depression, health, and other noncognitive factors may make OWLS less cognitively agile and speed up normal cognitive aging.

Action Steps to Help OWLS Develop and Maintain Cognitive Ability

OWLS may need to overcome age-related factors that make it difficult to attend to information, perceive it, remember it, and think about it. You can use the following steps as guidelines for helping OWLS to develop and maintain their cognitive ability.

1. Help OWLS exercise their minds.

   Normal OWLS—those who are active, healthy, and not taking drugs or medication that interfere with cognitive functioning— can benefit from memory and other types of cognitive training (Lowenstein, 2005). Here are some suggestions:

   • Encourage OWLS to "exercise" their minds outside of the workplace to help to improve their information-processing skills in the workplace (*Aging Quiz,* 2004).

   • Integrate memory exercises into all training events. Memory exercises should range in level of complexity and should be both challenging and enjoyable. This is a chance to be creative; design or select memory exercises that are new and different, not the standard card game or brain teaser.

- Use a combination of physical exercise, good nutrition, and memory exercises (Jacoby, 2005). This will maximize the effectiveness of the mind exercises and all can be designed into real-time training situations and at least suggested in virtual training situations.

2. Adjust the timing of learning activities to compensate for decreases in cognitive agility.

- Avoid timed tests. Timed tests may not reflect the true ability of OWLS. Test givers may assume that older OWLS have "decreased cognitive functioning" or have "lost their mental competence"; however, "older adults don't lose mental competence; it simply takes them longer to process the necessary information" (Roth, 2005, n.p.).

- Avoid fast-paced presentations. OWLS did not grow up with MTV; "faster rates of presentation heighten anxiety, create over-arousal, undermine self confidence, and reinforce a tendency toward cautiousness—which leads to errors of omission—in older subjects" (Hayslip and Kennelly, 1985, pp. 79–80).

- Adjust timing when motor skills are required. Research links slow cognitive processing speed to a decline in motor function; some older OWLS may have less dexterity and coordination, move more slowly, and have a slower reaction time (Roth, 2005). Chapter Nine describes ways to accommodate them or to compensate for motor function problems.

3. Design well-facilitated, structured activities that will develop new cognitive skills and strengthen existing ones.

Supplement lectures or audio tracks and text with flowcharts, diagrams, and graphical forms. Well-designed graphics can benefit both OWLS who have strong visuospatial skills and OWLS who have visuospatial problems. When given supporting text or auditory input and sufficient time to respond to the visual stimulation, graphical representations can also help OWLS to process information and recall information over time.

Memory: Implications for Workplace Learning and Performance

The following research summary discusses age-related variables that WLP practitioners need to consider as they develop and maintain the memory skills of OWLS in their workplace:

- Recall of procedural learning may decline with age, depending in part on how easily and proficiently the skill or procedure was learned originally.

- Age has a bigger impact on delayed recall or retrieval than on delayed recognition.

- There are substantial changes in long-term memory of facts, rules, and definitions after age fifty.

- Changes in cognitive agility can affect how well OWLS rehearse and encode information before they store it in long-term memory.

- Memory cues during encoding and retrieval can help to lessen, but not eliminate, memory retrieval problems such as delayed recall in older adults.

Action Steps to Help OWLS Develop and Maintain Memory Skills

Memory strategies can help OWLS elaborate on information, process information at a deeper level, and ease the recall of information for later retrieval. The following suggestions will help you assist OWLS in developing and maintaining memory skills:

1. Use reinforcement strategies.

    Reinforcement is a technique used to increase or improve a desired behavioral outcome. As an instructional design technique, reinforcement is used to improve attention during memory processing or to change attitudes. Basically, reinforcement rewards *good* behavior and either does not reward or punishes *bad* behavior. Feedback is the key to successful reinforcement, and there are special guidelines for providing feedback to OWLS.

    - Focus an OWL's attention on a memory *task* rather than on the task *outcome* by providing the following type of reinforcement feedback: frequent and consistent reinforcement of *success* and infrequent and inconsistent reinforcement of *failure* (Hayslip & Kennelly, 1985).

    - Do *not* use continuous reinforcement. Continuous reinforcement may actually cause a feeling of helplessness in OWLS, which in turn increases anxiety and depression. Infrequent reinforcement does not mean you should eliminate feedback on failure; just provide feedback on success with more frequency and consistency.

    - Structure reinforcement. Balance the probability of success and failure by adjusting the difficulty level and sequence of training materials or tasks so OWLS move from easy to hard and back to easy tasks. Try to begin and end with an easy task.

2. Use rehearsal strategies.

    Rehearsal extends the time that the data stays in working or short-term memory and increases the chance for successful retrieval from long-term memory. Here are some rehearsal strategies:

    - Use drill and practice to help OWLS actively go over a perception before moving it into long-term memory.

- Encourage OWLS to repeat the data over and over again without changing it.

- Minimize interruptions during rehearsal. Sustained attention is a key component of short-term memory. If an interruption occurs, the information may be lost from short-term memory.

3. Use encoding strategies.

Encoding is the cognitive process that brings meaning to sensory data and connects or associates it with other data already stored in long-term memory. Organization, elaboration, and activity are three important components of the encoding process. Design education and training activities so that OWLS consciously and actively participate in the encoding process and sort through a variety of ways to make sensory perceptions meaningful. Encoding strategies include the following:

- Encourage OWLS to draw on their experience to help them organize new sensory input and make meaningful connections and associations between new and stored memories.

- Encourage OWLS to use experience to elaborate or expand on the existing groups of data that have already been stored and make room for the new input within the schema or patterns that already exist in their memory. This way the data can be stored in chunks, clusters, or groupings that make sense and are easier to retrieve (see step five).

- Limit the options. Too much experience can clutter the mind and confuse the response; having too many options is like opening an overflowing file cabinet. OWLS may get agitated and flustered, and consequently productivity tends to decrease. For example, ask yourself whether the OWLS need or want to remember the facts, rules, or definitions associated with a new procedure or it will be enough for them to remember how to perform the procedure.

4. Use memory cues or mnemonics.

   Memory cues such as mnemonics are visual or verbal mediational aids. They act as a medium that helps transfer information into a memory.

   • Use visual and auditory mnemonic devices, examples and nonexamples, and memory associations to help OWLS rehearse and later retrieve information from long-term memory (Albert & Moss, 1997).

   • Avoid cue overload. Using too many cues or using inappropriate cues will actually have the opposite effect.

5. Apply cognitive load theory.

   Cognitive load theory provides educators and trainers with three design strategies to help OWLS effectively perceive and process information in working memory and avoid cognitive overload. The three guidelines are chunking, automaticity, and dual processing.

   • Use *chunking* to transform information into smaller groupings that are more easily remembered; for example, remembering a credit-card number as 1234–5678–9012–3456 instead of 1234567890123456. Miller's chunking formula, $7 +/- 2$, suggests introducing from three to seven items of content per learning unit, depending on the difficulty and complexity of the content and the experience level and learning ability of the learners (Miller, 1956).

   • Repeat or drill knowledge or skills until they can be retrieved or performed automatically (automaticity); for example, memorizing the multiplication tables or typing on a computer keyboard.

   • Use both visual and auditory cues to process a specific memory (dual processing).

Attention: Implications for Learning and Performance

The following research findings have implications for improving the attentional capacity and function of OWLS:

- Significant age-related declines in executive function begin with Mid-Old OWLS and increase with age; Mid-Old OWLs with more education do not decline as soon.

- Old OWLS aged sixty-eight and older show a significant decline in performance on tests that involve the visual recognition of similarities or the completion of a series.

Action Steps to Help OWLS Control Attention

Attention is the energy that supports cognitive processing and helps OWLS make choices related to information selection and handling multiple sources of information. You can help OWLS control attention by using the following strategies:

1. Help OWLS reduce internal noise.

    Internal noise or interference may include health and wellness issues. WLP practitioners should

    - Encourage OWLS to seek appropriate treatment or apply other strategies for reducing or managing pain, depression, and so forth (Roth, 2005).

    - Use the Premack Principle or "Grandma's Rule" to help OWLS relieve training-related stress—another internal distraction that keeps OWLS from focusing on memory or other cognitive tasks. Always start and end an education or training session with a positive activity, and in between "sandwich" less-popular but necessary activities (Eggen & Kauchak, 2001).

2. Help OWLS reduce external noise.

External noise can include room temperature, lighting, sound level, number and timing of exercise or comfort breaks, and other ergonomic factors. Whenever possible, these factors need to be controlled to allow OWLS to attend to the learning activity. Here are some suggestions:

- Suggest that the learner find a quiet room or workstation to decrease distraction during virtual or individual learning activities.

- Allow OWLS to take breaks as needed during classroom training sessions.

- Adjust the training environment—lighting, temperature, time on task, activity level.

Intelligence: Implications for Learning and Performance

The research on intelligence tells us that fluid intelligence decreases with age and crystallized intelligence increases with age. For example:

- There is a significant decline in fluid intelligence–related abilities between the ages of twenty-five and seventy-five, which may put OWLS at a disadvantage when it comes to learning and performing new skills that are not directly in their repertoire of knowledge and skills.

- Up to ages fifty-five to sixty-five, the improvement in crystallized intelligence is about equal to the decline in fluid intelligence.

- OWLS increase in intelligence as they age, as long as decreases in physical or mental function do not interfere.

Research also offers the mind-expanding concept of multiple intelligences. Basically, this concept suggests that

- Each person processes eight intelligences to various degrees and can develop these intelligences to an adequate level of competency.

- There are many ways to be intelligent within each category.

Action Step to Encourage OWLS to Use Their Intelligence

Use PST 5.1 as a guide to design training that will encourage OWLS to use their multiple intelligences.

PST 5.1. How to Select Training Activities That Encourage the Use of Multiple Intelligences.

1. To encourage this intelligence . . .	. . . ask OWLS to
Verbal-Linguistic	• Read about . . . • Write about . . . • Talk about . . . • Listen to . . .
Logical-Mathematical	• Quantify . . . • Think critically about . . . • Conceptualize . . .
Visual-Spatial	• See . . . • Draw . . . • Visualize . . . • Color . . . • Create a mind-map about . . .
Musical-Rhythmic	• Sing about . . . • Rap about . . . • Listen to . . .
Bodily-Kinesthetic	• Build . . . • Role play about . . . • Get a gut feeling about . . .
Interpersonal	• Teach . . . • Collaborate on . . . • Interact with another about . . .
Intrapersonal	• Set personal goals related to . . . • Connect . . . with your personal life • Make choices with regard to . . .
Naturalist	• Identify . . . • Explore . . . • Categorize . . .

PST 5.1. How to Select Training Activities That Encourage the Use of Multiple Intelligences, *Continued.*

2. Help OWLS pay attention to their hidden intelligences—those that they shut out early in life because of negative experiences at home, at school, or at work. They may be the sources of new attitudes and new abilities that have been dormant for years.

3. As we look to the future, consider the possibility of new intelligences surfacing. We already know about emotional intelligence, but what about moral intelligence and spiritual intelligence? And dare we talk about social intelligence, the new science of success in the workplace (Albrecht, 2006)?

Thinking: Implications for Learning and Performance

The research on intelligence tells us that intelligence does not decrease with age. It also tells us that

- OWLS filter incoming information through a lifetime of experience and learning.

- OWLS tend to think more reflectively as they age.

- OWLS may be analytical, creative, or blended thinkers.

- OWLS who are analytical thinkers may prefer to research and reflect on their own.

- OWLS who are analytical thinkers may over-analyze the situation and delay action.

- OWLS who are creative thinkers may prefer group thinking activities.

Action Steps to Encourage OWLS to Think

You should encourage OWLS to think analytically, reflectively, and creatively. Here are some strategies:

1. Build a climate of trust and acceptance into all training and development activities to encourage thoughtful participation of all types: analytical, reflective, or creative.

2. Inspire OWLS to think creatively and support them when they do; use analogies, ask provocative questions, encourage them to think outside the box, help them identify new paradigms, and listen to them as they define problems and select solutions that work.

3. Encourage organizations to empower *all* workers to think creatively. Organizations can create positive work environments, provide workstations that block out external distractions, offer appropriate rest and food breaks to refresh the body and mind, encourage OWLS to think proactively, and reward OWLS and celebrate successes when they do.

Problem Solving: Implications for Learning and Performance

OWLS may be analytical, creative, or blended problem solvers:

- OWLS who use analytical problem-solving skills are convergent thinkers; they use a sequential and systematic problem-solving approach that focuses on one solution.

- OWLS who use creative problem-solving skills are divergent thinkers; they consider multiple novel solutions.

- OWLS who combine analytic and creative problem-solving skills increase the probability of a successful outcome.

All three types of problem solvers are needed to meet the needs of today's global organizations.

Successful problem solving is dependent on how the problem solver constructs the problem: "[W]hen faced with a problem the problem solver must reconcile what kind of problem it is, what its factors or components or parameters are, how they interact, and so on" (Jonassen, 2004, p. 81). OWLS have the cognitive ability to construct a problem and the experience to add history and depth to a problem. However, they may take longer to process the information and solve the problem.

Action Steps to Help OWLS Solve Problems

Problem solving is both an art and a skill. OWLS may need help to apply their unique experience and cognitive problem-solving skills to solve workplace learning and performance problems. To maximize the ability of OWLS to construct and solve problems, you can

- Provide the resources and information they need, or encourage analytical problem solving OWLS to do their own research

- Suggest a variety of problem-solving strategies such as case studies, simulations, peer instruction, story problems, and so forth, and train OWLS how to implement the strategies

- Ask probing and challenging questions to help OWLS fine tune their problem-solving abilities, focus on the problem, and capitalize on their generational cohort group uniqueness

- Provide relevant, timely, targeted feedback, basing your evaluation of their problem-solving performance on quality rather than quantity

Action Step: Learn More About Learning Styles and Challenges

Now we make a leap from cognition to workplace learning. All individuals have distinct and unique learning styles and challenges. WLP practitioners should observe and become familiar with the learning styles of OWLS in their workplace. Knowing this information will help WLP practitioners make OWLS more focused on quality, more productive in their learning and performance efforts, and more balanced in their output.

Chapter Six will discuss the variety of learning styles and challenges that could affect how OWLS perform in the workplace. We have only to look at our colleagues to realize that learning-challenged children do grow into learning-challenged adults.

ADDITIONAL RESOURCES

For more theoretical and practical information on adult cognitive development, memory, thinking, and problem solving, read the following:

Bransford, J., & Stein, B. S. (1993). *The IDEAL problem solver: A guide for improving thinking, learning, and creativity.* New York: Freeman.

Gredler, M. E. (2001). *Learning and instruction: Theory and practice* (4th ed.). Upper Saddle River, NJ: Prentice Hall.

Kirby, G. R., & Goodpaster, J. R. (2007). *Thinking* (4th ed.). Upper Saddle River, NJ: Pearson/Prentice Hall.

Merriam, S. B., & Caffarella, R. S. (1999). *Learning in adulthood: A comprehensive guide* (2nd ed., Chapters 7–9). San Francisco: Jossey-Bass.

Schank, R. C. (1999). *Dynamic memory revisited.* Cambridge, England: Cambridge University Press.

Smith, P. L., & Ragan, T. L. (2004). *Instructional design* (3rd ed.). San Francisco: Wiley.

See also selected articles from the professional journals *Memory and Cognition* and *Journal of Experimental Psychology: Learning, Memory, and Cognition.*

For more information about multiple intelligences, explore the following resources:

Armstrong, T. (1993). *7 kinds of smart: Identifying and developing your many intelligences.* New York: Penguin Books.

Armstrong, T. (1994). *Multiple intelligences in the classroom.* Alexandria, VA: Association for Supervision and Curriculum Development.

Thiagarajan, S., & Thiagarajan, R. (1996). *How to apply the theory of multiple intelligences to improve learning and training.* Workshops by Thiagi, Inc.: International Society for Performance Improvement Conference and Expo.

6

OWLS in Search of Knowledge: Learning Styles and Challenges

I have difficulty using the Yellow Pages and finding a word in the dictionary. Using an encyclopedia to help my grandchild do a school project is very challenging. I even have difficulty filing my tax preparation materials. I've always had problems with alphabetical order and spelling.

John J., age seventy, retired construction worker

SOME LEARNING CHALLENGES are just a matter of style. Each learner has a preferred mode or modality or "a consistent way of responding to and using stimuli in the context of learning" (Clark, 2000, n.p.) that the learner uses when trying to acquire new knowledge and skills—and that preference usually continues throughout the lifespan. As long as the learning environment supports the learning mode or method and the aging process does not interfere with the preferred sensory modality, learning styles are not a major challenge to learning and performance, whether the individual is an OWL or a younger worker-learner. In fact, OWLS and other learners can usually adapt to any learning style if necessary.

Other learning challenges have a more serious impact on an individual's ability to learn and perform. These challenges have produced an alphabet soup of acronyms: learning disabilities (LD), attention deficit disorder (ADD), attention deficit hyperactivity disorder (ADHD), or the 3-dys—dyslexia, dysgraphia, and dyscalculia. OWLS who are most affected by these learning challenges must continually compensate and cope, and the education, training, and work environments in which OWLS function must accommodate and support them. See the sidebar for further information on accommodation.

FROM PLAYGROUND TO WORKPLACE . . .

The terms *learning disability* (LD), *Attention Deficit Disorder* (ADD), *Attention Deficit Hyperactivity Disorder* (ADHD), and *dyslexia* were once used primarily to identify children and adolescents who need special educational accommodation in the K–12 system. Now the terms may travel with the individual throughout his or her lifespan. The Americans with Disabilities Act (ADA) and Section 504 of the Rehabilitation Act both require reasonable accommodation when an individual worker reveals his or her learning disability, whether the diagnosis took place in childhood or adulthood. The legislation acknowledges that LD, ADD, ADHD, or the 3-dys may require changes to the design, development, and implementation of education and training programs for affected OWLS.

This chapter will provide you and other WLP practitioners with an overview of the learning styles and learning challenges that may affect how the OWLS in your workplace learn and perform. The chapter will also discuss implications for workplace learning and performance and suggest action steps for you to take in your role as analyst, change leader, and intervention selector, designer, developer, implementer, and evaluator.

OWLS Have Style

Learning styles are a controversial issue. There is no single theory that explains the way people learn; rather, there are two major approaches or perspectives:

- Perceptual learning styles—the consistent, preferred way a learner uses the sensory modalities of sight, hearing, touch, and movement to perceive, observe, and acquire information

- Cognitive learning styles—the consistent, preferred way a learner uses memory, thinking skills, and problem solving to process information (see the discussion of Gregorc's Style Delineator on page 135)

Clark (2000) suggests there is also a third perspective—personality models—that focus on the consistent, preferred way a learner interacts with the learning environment to perceive, organize, and retain information. Using a fourth perspective, Dunn and Dunn (1972) combine environmental and perceptual modality preferences in their Learning Style Questionnaire. We will discuss all of these perspectives later in this chapter.

Not All OWLS Have the Same Style

OWLS as learners are not all cut from the same cloth; as a group they do not prefer one type of learning style over all the others. As a WLP practitioner, you may tend to design, develop, and deliver education and training the same way *you* prefer to learn. Therefore, you need to discover the various learning styles or preferences of your learners—and your own style as well. Only then can you attempt to accommodate as many learning styles as possible when you design or deliver education and training.

OWLS May Prefer to Look, Listen, Touch, or Do

The simplest way to begin gathering information on the learning styles of OWLS is to discover the sensory modality they prefer to use to acquire knowledge and skills. Often referred to as VAK (visual, auditory, kinesthetic) or

VAKT (visual, auditory, kinesthetic, tactile), the sensory modality approach to learning styles has been around since the 1920s. It has been used extensively in the K–12 system to help teachers design individualized learning programs and work with dyslexic children. Based on earlier work by Rose (1985), it is very popular with the global community of interest that has formed to support accelerated learning.

A VAK or VAKT inventory seeks the answer to one basic question: When you want to learn something, do you prefer to see it, hear about it, touch or feel it, or do it? Of course the question is usually asked in many different ways about many different kinds of learning to establish a sensory modality trend or preference—visual, auditory, tactile, or kinesthetic (Dunn & Dunn, 1972).

Survey Example. Since the mid-1980s we have surveyed the perceptual learning style preferences of adult learners in graduate classes, training programs, and professional workshops. We use a combination of a self-report survey and observation. During a recent analysis of a graduate class composed of twenty-five adult learners aged twenty-eight to seventy, the seventy-year-old student was the only auditory learner. Of the remaining students, whose ages ranged from twenty-eight to fifty, there were twenty-one visual learners and three visual-kinesthetic learners. This is the typical learning style profile that has been emerging since the authors began their survey activities. (See Figure 6.1.)

Old to Oldest OWLS and some Mid-Old OWLS show a tendency toward auditory learning. Many of these OWLS report that radio was really important to them as children and teenagers, or that their early learning took place in a teacher-centered classroom, and they liked it. Young OWLS are predominantly visual learners; they grew up with TV, computers, and, more recently, handheld digital devices.

A few lucky OWLS prefer a mixture of learning modalities. Learners who are very conversant with computers and handheld digital devices also show a preference for kinesthetic learning; in fact, OWLS of all ages show some tendency toward kinesthetic learning as a secondary preference.

Figure 6.1. Learning Style Preferences of Graduate Students.

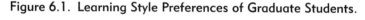
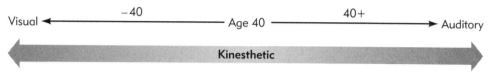

Age-Related Changes. Age-related changes in sensory capacity, psychomotor coordination, brain or physical function, health and wellness, and well-being may lessen or destroy an OWL's ability to use a preferred modality or compensate for a modality loss. Table 6.1 illustrates how six age-related changes can impact visual, auditory, tactile, or kinesthetic learning styles. If age-related changes impede their preferred modality, OWLS may become slower, less effective learners. In addition, both their self-esteem and their motivation to learn may suffer.

Table 6.1. Effect of Age-Related Changes on Preferred Learning Modality.

Age-related changes in the following . . .	. . . may have the following effect:
Sensory capacity	OWLS may need to switch to a weaker modality; for example, listen to a tape rather than read a book.
Psychomotor coordination	OWLS who are kinesthetic learners—prefer doing to seeing or listening or feeling and—may have difficulty with motor tasks.
Brain function	OWLS may have trouble processing sensory data to store in long-term memory.

(Continued)

Table 6.1. Effect of Age-Related Changes on Preferred Learning Modality, *Continued*.

Age-related changes in the following . . .	*. . . may have the following effect:*
Physical function	OWLS who prefer to learn by doing may have difficulty adjusting to another learning style when they lose strength or dexterity due to arthritis or related problems. Physical problems may also cause fatigue or pain, which interferes with all learning styles.
Health and wellness	OWLS who are healthy and robust enter into new learning with zest and determination. OWLS who do not have good health and do not feel well may lack the motivation and energy to cope with or compensate for learning modality problems.
Well-being	OWLS who experience high levels of frustration in workplace learning situations are especially susceptible to low self-esteem and a decrease in their motivation to acquire new knowledge and skills.

OWLS May Prefer Different Conditions or Stimuli

Dunn and Dunn included the Learning Style Questionnaire in their 1972 book on individualized learning in the K–12 education system. The questionnaire is extensive. It seeks to discover "the conditions under which a student is most likely to learn" and includes self-reported learner preferences for environmental, emotional, sociological, and physical "stimuli" (Dunn & Dunn, 1972, p. 93). The Dunns later developed the Productivity Environmental Preference Survey (PEPS) for use with adults.

Table 6.2 illustrates the four conditions that can encourage or stimulate learning and the major elements or components that are part of each condition. WLP practitioners may find it difficult to control many of these elements; however, OWLS are particularly affected by environmental and physical stimuli, and, whenever possible, the needs of the OWLS should be taken into consideration when selecting or preparing the learning area. Table 6.2 may be used as a checklist to evaluate and correct existing learning conditions or to plan for new learning experiences. (For more information on age-related physiological transitions that impact how OWLS learn and perform, see Chapter Eight.)

Table 6.2. Environmental Elements of Learning Style.

This type of learning stimuli . . .	*. . . contains these elements:*
1. Environmental stimuli	a. Level of sound
	b. Level of light
	c. Level of temperature
	d. Design of education or training area
2. Emotional stimuli	a. Motivation toward learning
	b. Level of personal persistence
	c. Level of personal responsibility
	d. Need for structured or nonstructured learning
3. Sociological stimuli	a. Individual or group learning preference
	b. Preferred role of authority figure
4. Physical stimuli	a. Perceptual preference (visual, auditory, tactile, kinesthetic)
	b. Need for food before or during learning activities
	c. Preferred time of day for learning
	d. Level of mobility required during learning activities
	e. Need for body and brain breaks

OWLS May Be Formal, Self-Directed, Eclectic—or Not

Merriam and Lumsden (1985, p. 68) summarized adult learning research from the late 1960s through the early 1980s and suggested that there are four categories of later-life learners based on the individual's learning experience preference:

- Formal-structured learners
- Self-directed learners
- Eclectic learners
- Nonlearners

Table 6.3 illustrates the learning experience preferences of OWLS who fall into each of the classifications. Formal-structured learners relate well to classroom style training and, if they are comfortable with technology, to nontraditional classroom-style experiences that utilize computers, satellite, or other distance learning technologies. They prefer interactive distance learning that provides opportunities to interact with the instructor and others in a class setting. Self-directed learners prefer self-study modules or hands-on experiences in which they can control what they learn, when they learn it, where they learn, how they learn, and why they learn.

Eclectic learners are a trainer's dream; they can adapt to either formal-structured or self-directed, independent learning experiences. Nonlearners are a trainer's nightmare: they see no value in learning, no matter how the learning experience is constructed, so trainers must focus on how to motivate these learners and encourage them to learn.

Table 6.3 is a useful planning guide for designing OWL-friendly training. WLP practitioners can turn it into a checklist to select or evaluate learning strategies that meet the needs of OWLS who fall into specific learning categories.

Table 6.3. Preferred Learning Experiences of OWLS.

OWLS who are . . .	. . . prefer these learning experiences:
Formal-structured learners	• Traditional, instructor-led classroom-style training • Interactive, broadcast distance training involving instructor and class cohorts
Self-directed learners	• Print, computer-based, or hands-on self-study • Independent learning activities
Eclectic learners	• Traditional or nontraditional instructor-led classroom training • Self-study or independent learning activities
Nonlearners	• No preference • Do not desire to enter into any type of learning experience

OWLS May Converge, Diverge, Assimilate, or Accommodate

The Kolb Learning Style Inventory is a simple descriptive test based on the theories of experiential learning. It describes the way the brain processes information—thinking, problem solving, remembering—and ties the individual learning modes to personality types—diverger, converger, assimilator, and accommodator (Kolb, 1984). Some researchers compare Kolb's Inventory to a "simpler version of the Myers Briggs Types Indicator (MBTI)" that is frequently used in business and industry to determine types or styles of personality (Clark, 2000).

Table 6.4 illustrates the different types of learning styles identified in the Kolb Inventory. The Inventory helps learners and instructors discover the degree to which the learners prefer abstractness (AC) or concreteness (CE);

active experimentation (AE) or reflection (RO). The inventory also helps OWLS identify their preferred learning style:

- *Convergers* combine abstract conceptualization (AC) and active experimentation (AE); their strength is the practical application of ideas.

- *Divergers* combine concrete experience (CE) with reflective observation (RO); their strength lies in their imaginative ability.

- *Assimilators* combine reflective observation (RO) with abstract conceptualization (AC); they can pull information together and create theoretical models.

- *Accommodators* combine active experimentation (AE) and concrete experience (CE); their strength is carrying out plans and experiments.

These learner classifications are especially helpful for setting up team learning assignments.

Table 6.4. Overview of Kolb's Learning Styles.

Style	Style Elements	Strength
Converger	• Think (abstract conceptualization) • Do (active experimentation)	Applying
Diverger	• Feel (concrete experience) • Watch (reflective observation)	Imagining
Assimilator	• Watch (reflective observation) • Think (abstract conceptualization)	Synthesizing
Accommodator	• Do (active experimentation) • Feel (concrete experience)	Executing

OWLS May Be Concrete or Abstract, Sequential or Random

According to Gregorc (1982), there are four basic perceptual learning styles: concrete sequential, abstract sequential, abstract random, and concrete random. OWLS and WLP practitioners can use the Gregorc Style Delineator to analyze their learning style preferences.

Gregorc based his four styles on brain hemisphere research. Although this type of research is no longer as popular or clear-cut as it once was (Santo, n.d.), it still provides us with insights into how learners prefer to learn. For example, learners who complete the Gregorc Style Delineator usually report that although they prefer one or two of these styles, they may use all of the styles at one time or another.

The four styles are not polar extremes, but lie on a continuum, so it is difficult to say where one ends and another begins. Table 6.5 lists Gregorc's four basic styles, some of the characteristics of each style, and a list of preferred instructional strategies for each style.

Table 6.5. Overview of Gregorc's Learning Styles.

Learning Style	Learner Characteristics	Learning Preferences
Concrete Sequential	• Hardworking • Conventional • Accurate • Stable • Dependable • Consistent • Factual • Organized	• Direct, hands-on activities • Tactile methods • Step-by-step instructions • Real-life examples • Workbooks with detailed instructions • Diagrams or flowcharts • Computer-assisted instruction • Documentation
Abstract Sequential	• Analytic • Verbal • Intellectual • Objective	• Highly verbal, logical, and analytical approach based on intellect • Solitude • Well-organized material

(Continued)

Table 6.5. Overview of Gregorc's Learning Styles, *Continued.*

Learning Style	Learner Characteristics	Learning Preferences
	• Knowledgeable • Thorough • Structured • Logical • Deliberate • Systematic	• Highly skeptical • Have trouble picking up subtle nonverbal cues • Do not like distractions • Accept change only after much deliberation • Written, verbal, and visual instruction • Lectures • Reading • Outlines • Conducting internet searches • Email • Listservs • Audiotapes • May enjoy searching the Internet for information as well as asynchronous communication
Abstract Random	• Sensitive • Compassionate • Perceptive • Imaginative • Idealistic • Sentimental • Spontaneous • Flexible	• Focus on relationships and their emotions • Visual methods of instruction, such as video clips, video-conferencing, TV • Group discussion, including chat rooms • Case studies • Guest speakers • Time for reflection • May be uncomfortable with distance education without a visible instructor and cohorts • Evaluating personal experiences

Table 6.5. Overview of Gregorc's Learning Styles, *Continued*.

Learning Style	Learner Characteristics	Learning Preferences
Concrete Random	• Quick • Intuitive • Curious • Realistic • Creative • Innovative • Instinctive • Adventurous • Impulsive	• Trial-and-error approach, with breakthroughs through intuitive insight • Stimulus-rich environment • Competition • Using their wits • Rarely accept anything on outside authority • Implementers of change • Do not like to read directions • Do not like structure • Independent study • Computer games and simulations • Multimedia • "Playing" with software

Research on Learning Styles Is Ongoing

Many other perspectives on learning styles have evolved over the years—far too many to cover in this short section. At the end of this chapter, under Action Steps, we have listed a number of resources you can access to gather further information about learning styles or to locate the learning style inventories that we discussed in this section.

Now we move on to a discussion of OWLS who have additional learning challenges.

Some OWLS Are Learning Challenged

From playground to workplace, the LD, ADD, ADHD, or dyslexic child grows up to become the LD, ADD, ADHD, or dyslexic adult. The LD OWL is quiet, the ADD OWL is a little "noisier," and the ADHD OWL shouts out to the world.

Some OWLS Have Learning Disabilities (LD)

Basically, LD is a quiet disorder and the signs are not always evident. LD OWLS may see or hear but not be able to process visual or auditory information, comprehend but not verbalize, read but not write, write but not read, or have multiple problems. Individual LD adults may or may not have trouble keeping a job or maintaining a satisfying social life. Their rate of employment, job status, and job satisfaction increases with any of the following factors: above-average intelligence, a middle- to upper-class economic background, and completion of college (Shapiro & Rich, 1999).

Definition. Official definitions for LD vary in focus and scope. Here are two definitions that are useful for employers and WLP practitioners who are involved with LD OWLS.

The first definition, from the Individuals with Disabilities Education Act (IDEA) defines a specific learning disability as "a disorder in one or more of the basic psychological processes involved in understanding or using language, spoken or written, which may manifest itself in imperfect ability to listen, think, speak, read, write, spell or do mathematical calculations." IDEA also classifies an LD individual as one who shows a significant discrepancy between ability and achievement despite "appropriate instructional experiences" (Shapiro & Rich, 1999, p. 16).

The second definition comes from the Rehabilitation Services Administration: "a learning disability is a lifelong condition due to central nervous system dysfunction [and may include] problems with attention, memory, coordination, social competence, and emotional maturity" (Shapiro & Rich, 1999, p. 19). This definition does not include the concept of a discrepancy between ability and accomplishment and does include social and emotional problems.

Intelligence. Learning disabled individuals do not lack intelligence; in fact, many are highly intelligent. However, LD individuals may show a significant difference between ability and accomplishment that may be traced to a specific problem in processing information or expressing thoughts and feelings.

Causes. Over the years there have been many approaches to explaining why some learners are "disabled" and some are not or why there are degrees of learning disabilities. The most common thinking is that learning disabilities are biological. Shapiro and Rich (1999) explain that the term *basic psychological process* used in the IDEA definition may be misleading because in this case it actually refers to cognitive processes such as perception, memory, thinking, speaking, and writing. The Rehabilitation Services Administration definition recognizes that learning disabilities are biological; they may be caused by structural or functional irregularities in the central nervous system, which includes the brain and spinal cord. Nerve cell connectors involved with perception, cognition, or motor skills may have a tendency to "misfire," interfering with the ability to perceive or process verbal and nonverbal information and express thoughts and feelings.

Duration and Scope. Learning disabilities do not "go away"; they are lifelong. In 1999 Shapiro and Rich reported that 3 to 10 percent of adults in the United States had learning disabilities and more than 50 percent of these LD adults were involved in adult literacy, basic education, and job training programs. LD is often called the "hidden disability"; adults learn to cope with and compensate for their learning problems.

Signs of Coping. Adults do learn to compensate and cope with processing or expression problems. Here is how five LD OWLS compensated during a classroom-style training session.

Brian has auditory processing problems, so he relied on the visuals, handouts, and other support materials to understand the content of the oral presentations. On the other hand, Diane relied on the oral presentations because she has problems processing visuals or print material.

Then there is Charlie, who reverses or omits letters and numbers when he writes, and Pete, who has totally illegible handwriting. Both of these

OWLS used a computer instead of a pen to produce prework or follow-up assignments and avoided writing their responses on whiteboards or flipcharts.

Celeste hates "interactive" training sessions because she finds it difficult to express herself in an orderly and clear manner. She compensated by going through the prework and writing out possible questions or comments. During the training session she relied more on show than tell—but mostly she sat quietly and said very little.

Some OWLS Have a Dys-function

Experts do not agree whether the 3-dys—dyslexia, dysgraphia, and dyscalculia—are types of learning disabilities or unique disabilities in their own right. What experts do agree on is that making sense of print materials, or putting pen to paper, or working with figures can be extremely challenging for some adult learners as well as children with these disabilities.

Definitions. There is no "unanimously accepted definition" for the 3-dys (Shapiro & Rich, 1999, p. 54), yet the terms are commonly used in education and training environments. The literal definitions are as follows:

- Dyslexia—difficulty understanding written language
- Dysgraphia—impairment of writing ability
- Dyscalculia—difficulty performing mathematical calculations

The difficulties may be severe to moderately severe and may be most severe when the individual is tired, depressed, or anxious.

Causes. Potential causes of the 3-dys include heredity and differences in the structure or function of the brain. For example, researchers report that they detect a difference in the electrical activity in the left hemisphere and in the frontal speech lobes of both hemispheres when they test the response of dyslexic children to sensory stimulus such as sights, sounds, or words (Shapiro & Rich, 1999).

Intelligence. The 3-dys do not correlate with low IQ or poor cognitive ability. However, adults who suffer from any of the 3-dys may appear less intelligent because they cannot fill out a handwritten form or follow printed directions or calculate the sales tax on an item.

Signs of Dyslexia. Some refer to dyslexia as "word blindness." When a dyslexic OWL reads a page of print, the letters, numbers, and words may actually appear to move around, reverse themselves, or even disappear. The OWL may complain: "I can't trust the printed page." Although this implies that dyslexia is a visual processing problem, experts now think that dyslexia may be a problem related to one or more of the following:

- Phonological or sound processing—difficulty recognizing, segmenting, blending, or producing the letter sounds that make up words

- Short-term memory—difficulty listening to a string of numbers or unrelated words and repeating them verbatim

- Long-term memory—difficulty retrieving words or names previously stored in long-term memory

- Temporal or time-related—difficulty processing rapidly changing visual or auditory sensory information

Signs of Dysgraphia. Dysgraphic OWLS reverse or leave out letters, numbers, and words when they write. Some may be able to spell a word orally, or on a computer, even without using spell check, but cannot write the word correctly.

Signs of Dyscalculia. Then there are dyscalculic OWLS. These OWLS may have problems with basic mathematical functions—addition, subtraction, and multiplication. They may also have trouble solving mathematical problems. These problems may cause or exacerbate "math anxiety."

Some OWLS Are ADD or ADHD

ADD or ADHD OWLS can't sit quietly, or, if they are quiet, they have a hard time paying attention. The incidence of Attention Deficit Disorder (ADD) or Attention Deficit Hyperactivity Disorder (ADHD) has progressed from being almost unknown in the 1980s to becoming "the most common behavioral disorder in American children, the subject of thousands of studies and no small degree of controversy" (Wallis, 1994, p. 43).

Definition. ADD and ADHD are neurobiological disabilities characterized by "exaggerated levels of any or all of the following: inattention, distractibility, impulsivity, and over or under activity" (Bond, 1994). ADD OWLS appear inattentive and distractible; ADHD OWLS are also hyper- or hypoactive and impulsive. More males than females are diagnosed with ADD or ADHD.

Cause. Some researchers speculate that ADD and ADHD may be genetic; others relate it to brain dysfunction. A growing body of research points to a biological basis (Wallis, 1994). The bottom line is that the cause is still not known.

Duration and Scope. Most researchers do agree that ADD and ADHD are lifelong: "You don't suddenly get ADD" (Wallis, 1994, p. 47). The National Institute of Mental Health (NIMH) estimates that 3 to 5 percent of children have ADHD and about 50 percent of these children carry the symptoms into the workplace (Read, 2005).

The diagnosis of ADD or ADHD in adults is complex, relying in part on the individual adult's recall of his or her childhood or on school records. However, what was once a disorder that was whispered about in school corridors is now becoming commonplace, if not culturally acceptable, and with much of the original social stigma gone, diagnosis has become more common.

Signs of ADD or ADHD. When the ADD or ADHD child ages, "the predominant symptoms tend to shift from external, visible ones (such as physical hyperactivity) to internal symptoms such as lack of organization and difficulty paying attention" (Byrnes & Watkins, 2005). Still, the key to recognizing ADD and ADHD is that both are characterized by extremes.

The characteristics of ADD and ADHD adults are usually more obvious and overt than those of LD adults. Even after years of acquiring the knowledge and skills to perform successfully, OWLS with ADD or ADHD may still find it extremely difficult to self-regulate what they produce and how they produce it. They may exhibit *exaggerated forms* of some or all of the behaviors listed in the sidebar.

ADD AND ADHD BEHAVIORS

☐ Inability to plan and organize work

☐ Inability to finish even a simple task

☐ Poor or nonexistent concept of time

☐ Problems with long- or short-term memory

☐ Vulnerability to distractions; inability to stay focused

☐ Impulsiveness

☐ Difficulty focusing

☐ Hot temper, tendency to overreact

☐ Overactivity or hyperactivity

☐ Excessive exuberance

☐ Underactivity or hypoactivity

☐ Difficulty following orders

☐ Inability to wait to take a turn

☐ Inability to "play by the rules"

☐ Forgetfulness

☐ Restlessness; inability to sit still

WLP practitioners can use the sidebar list as an observation guide or checklist to detect *possible* cases of ADD or ADHD in training groups. However, practitioners need to be aware of the danger of misdiagnosing OWLS or others as ADD/ADHD based on the characteristics listed in the sidebar without taking other factors into account. One heuristic or rule of thumb says that if the problems started in childhood, it is probably ADD or ADHD; if the problems surfaced in adulthood, it may be a manifestation of depression or anxiety. Another heuristic says that the keys to recognizing the symptoms of ADD/ADHD are exaggeration and consistency. An OWL who is occasionally forgetful or exuberant or disorganized or drifts off during a business meeting may just be having a very good or not-so-good day at work.

The Positive Side. Given the right job and a supportive learning and performance environment, OWLS with ADD or ADHD are conscientious, committed, creative worker-learners who bring energy, enthusiasm, and passion to their workplace. They are risk takers and aren't afraid to take quantum leaps outside the box when it comes to analysis and problem solving. Hyperactivity gives them boundless energy and drive, and their impulsivity can make them very decisive. They are spontaneous and extremely alert to changes in their environment.

ADD and ADHD adults are entrepreneurs and police detectives; they work in emergency rooms and on Wall Street (Wallis, 1994). In his 1997 book *Attention Deficit Disorder: A Different Perception* (1997), author Thom Hartmann refers to them as "hunters" rather than "farmers." Winston Churchill and Benjamin Franklin may be examples of highly successful ADD and ADHD OWLS.

Treatment. The most popular treatment for ADD and ADHD is stimulant-type drugs, which actually curb excessive activity. As ADD and ADHD children become adults and enter the workforce, and as more and more OWLS are diagnosed, drugs that combat hyperactivity and improve attention are "becoming more common in the workplace" (Read, 2005, n.p.).

Implications for Workplace Learning and Performance

Learning styles and learning disabilities are lifelong. They travel with the individual throughout his or her lifespan and may have a negative effect on the individual's self-esteem and motivation to learn and perform.

Adult development and life transitions impact how OWLS deal with learning challenges, and the impact of a learning challenge can differ at each stage of development (Shapiro & Rich, 1999). For example, OWLS may need to compensate for a learning style that is compromised by age-related physical changes or to cope with a learning challenge when attention and energy is taken up by the normal challenges of life.

At a very minimum, OWLS may find that age-related factors are decreasing their ability to be efficient, organized, and attentive learners. Enter the WLP practitioner with a toolbox of learning and performance interventions designed to accommodate learning-challenged OWLS.

Action Steps for WLP Practitioners

The following action steps will help you proactively wend your way through the maze of learning styles and challenges that affect the workplace learning and performance of your OWLS:

1. Learn more about learning styles and learning disabilities.

    In addition to the references that were cited in this chapter, you can find additional information at the following Web sites:

    Learning styles—general:

    http://www.usd.edu/~ssanto/styles.htm

    http://www.nwlink.com/~donclark/hrd/learning/styles.html

    Learning disabilities:

    http://ericec.org/faq/ld-adult.html

    Dyslexia:

    http://www.dyslexia-adults.com

    http://ericec.org/faq/dyslexia.html

    Dysgraphia:

    http://www.audiblox.com/dysgraphia_symptoms_causes.htm

    National Center for Learning Disabilities at http://www.ncld.org/index.php?option=content&task=view&id=468

    Dyscalculia:

    http://www.dyscalculiainfo.org/

ADD or ADHD:

National Resource Center on ADHD at www.help4adhd.org

2. Assess the learning styles of the OWLS in your workplace.

Assessment Tool	Resource
Gregorc's Style Delineator	Gregorc Associates, Inc., www.gregorc.com
VAK Learning Style Indicator	Free at www.businessballs.com/vaklearningstylestest.htm
VAK Learning Styles Self-Assessment Questionnaire	Free at www.businessballs.com/freematerialsinword/vaklearningstylesquestionnaireselftest.doc
Kolb's Learning Style Inventory	Hay Resources Direct, 800-729-8074 or www.hayresourcesdirect.haygroup.com/Learning_Self-Development/Assessments_surveys/Learning_Style_Inventory/Overview.asp
Productivity Environmental Preference Survey (PEPS), Dunn, Dunn, & Price (1993)	www.brevard.edu/fyc/resources/Learningstylesinstruments.htm#peps

3. Select or design, develop, and implement appropriate learning and performance interventions that support the learning styles of all OWLS.

   • Design learning and work spaces that block visual or auditory distractions.

   • Encourage the use of organizational aids—such as day planners and PDAs—to help OWLS organize their work. Use outlines, agendas, advance organizers, and the like to help OWLS organize their learning.

- Allow participants to use assistive technologies such as tape recorders, laptop computers, or calculators during meetings and training sessions if necessary.

- Offer blended learning programs or a variety of learning options so all styles—VAKT and cognitive—are covered. OWLS can get maximum benefit from their preferred style, and the other styles are useful for reinforcement.

- Provide assistive technology that makes computers and other devices more user-friendly for OWLS with specific visual or motor learning problems (see Chapter Eight for some examples).

- Teach "how to learn" side by side with "what to learn."

- Give OWLS time to think and process information.

4. Select or design, develop, and implement appropriate interventions for dyslexic OWLS.

   - Provide supplemental materials.

   - Use show and tell.

   - Include hands-on activities to support printed handouts.

   - Do not ask them to read out loud.

5. Select or design, develop, and implement appropriate interventions for dysgraphic OWLS.

   - Do not ask them to write on flip charts, whiteboards, or anything that other people will see.

   - Let them use a computer in training sessions to fill out surveys or share the results of class assignments. Smart-board technology means they can type a response into a computer and you can print or project the result.

   - Encourage your organization to use computerized forms for HRD, time reporting, status reports, surveys, and so forth.

6. Select or design, develop, and implement appropriate interventions for dyscalculic OWLS.

- Avoid assigning them jobs or tasks requiring math.

- Let them use calculators, adding machines, or full-function cash registers.

- Develop or help them develop performance support tools (PST) that precalculate cost-per-unit, sales tax, cycle time, and so forth.

7. Select or design, develop, and implement appropriate interventions for ADD or ADHD OWLS.

- Avoid assigning them repetitive, sedentary jobs or tasks.

- Avoid static lectures or presentations and information dumps.

- Provide them with opportunities for interactivity and hands-on learning.

- Let them walk around during training and take brain and body breaks.

- Give them time to prepare reports or assignments on a computer in advance of the meeting or training session.

8. Partner with the OWL and the employer to ensure that the type of intervention provides "reasonable accommodation" for the individual without creating "undue hardship" on the employer. Some guidelines are available in the Vocational Rehabilitation Act and the Americans with Disabilities Act (ADA), both of which protect learning disabled OWLS and other adult workers whose employers receive federal monies.

9. Learn more about OWLS in transition.

Chapter Seven continues with the transitions theme by discussing adult development and generational issues that may affect the learning and performance of OWLS. The chapter will discuss the ages and stages that make up the twenty-first century's unique multigenerational workplaces, implications for workplace learning, and action steps for WLP practitioners.

7

OWLS in Search of Self: Psychosocial Transitions

> I was sent here to replace a very popular store manager. At first, the employees really resented me. There was someone else in the store, an assistant manager who wanted my job, and they liked her too. I just made up my mind that I would be as friendly as I could be, find out about them and their families and all that kind of stuff, and give them a lot of positive feedback. The other day, one young checkout girl told me, "For an old manager, you're not so bad after all."
>
> *Barry, age fifty-three, store manager for a large retail chain*

BARRY IS just one of almost four generations of OWLS who, together with almost two generations of younger worker-learners, make up the new multigenerational workplace. Each generation is at a different stage of psychosocial development; each generation has its own values and priorities.

This chapter will focus on the psychosocial development of OWLS from a generational perspective and discuss some of the psychosocial issues that affect the relationships of OWLS and younger worker-learners. The chapter will end with the implications for workplace learning and performance and action steps that WLP practitioners can take to maximize learning and performance in the multigenerational workplace.

Adult Psychosocial Development

The study of adult psychosocial development is the study of how psychological and social changes influence how adults change and grow over their lifespan. Early studies and models of human development emphasized that humans change extensively from birth to adolescence, stabilize in early and middle adulthood, and decline in late adulthood. In the 1980s, researchers began to recognize that change is not limited to childhood and adolescence; it plays an important role throughout the entire lifespan, especially in late adulthood (Santrock, 1985). The 1976 book *Passages* by Gail Sheehy popularized the concept that stages of adult development continue throughout the life cycle and that "the stages of adult life are characterized not by physical growth but by steps in psychological and social growth" (Sheehy, 1995, p. 12).

Theory Base Comes from a Variety of Fields

Much of the theory base for adult psychosocial development comes from basic and applied research from the fields of psychology, sociology, and gerontology—research that has been steadily increasing since the 1950s.

Each field focuses on a different aspect of adult psychosocial development:

- Psychology studies changes in the human mind and emotions from birth to death

- Sociology studies the origin, development, and structure of human societies and how individuals or groups behave within a society

- Gerontology studies the aging process from maturity to old age and offers insights into how psychological and sociological variables affect aging

Although the research from these fields sheds some light on why OWLS are the way they are—that is, OWLness—and how they change over time, adult development theory does have its shortcomings: "in many areas of adult development we find little more than a variety of speculative theories . . ." (Schaie & Willis, 2002, p. 19).

One theme that does appear throughout the research is the concept of dividing adulthood into middle and late adulthood. Middle adulthood includes our Young and Mid-Old OWLS in the forty-to-sixty-four age group; late adulthood includes our Old, Old-Old, and Oldest OWLS aged sixty-five-plus. However, chronological age, like hair color, does not tell all.

Middle Adulthood Was Born in the Twentieth Century

The developmental concept of *middle adulthood* as a distinct phase between young adulthood and late adulthood is a twentieth-century phenomenon. The addition of middle adulthood to the adult lifespan came about because biological advances increased human health and longevity, and related social changes resulted in smaller families, empty nest syndrome, and retirements that last twenty years or more. Schaie and Willis (2002) tell us that the same factors—biological advances and social changes—make it increasingly difficult to define middle or late adulthood in terms of chronological age.

Some Young OWLS may be middle-aged at age thirty-five; others may still be raising a family after age forty—a developmental task traditionally assigned to young adulthood. Whether they are chronologically or developmentally in the middle adulthood stage of development, Young and Mid-Old OWLS are driven to perform one major developmental task: "regenerate or stagnate" (Erikson, 1963). OWLS in middle adulthood focus on creating and nurturing family and work-related "products." They are faced with issues of responsibility—to their families, their jobs, themselves. When OWLS fail to regenerate successfully, their feathers droop and they stagnate, suffering from low self-esteem and frustration.

Young and Mid-Old OWLS in the middle adulthood stage of development often play the traditional regenerative roles of parents to their children and caregivers to their own parents. Havighurst (1972) adds four tasks of "adjustment"—adjustment to middle age, to spouses, to growing and grownup children, and to aging parents. This is in addition to the tasks required for them to perform and advance in the workplace while still enjoying leisure activities and assuming societal responsibilities.

Late Adulthood Is Arriving Later

Research and observation tells us that OWLS reach late adulthood at various ages. Some OWLS are old at fifty; others "display the manners, attitudes, and even physical characteristics of people a decade or two younger" (Schaie & Willis, 2002, p. 51). OWLS today can and often do remain healthy, physically active, energetic, and creative well beyond age sixty-five.

Late adulthood as a developmental stage is further complicated by the fact that one stage does *not* fit all. Chapter Two discussed how OWLS aged sixty-five-plus can play out their lives in three different stages:

- Old OWLS (aged sixty-five to seventy-four)
- Old-Old OWLS (aged seventy-five to eighty-four)
- Oldest OWLS (aged eighty-five and older)

OWLS may also play different roles on each stage of late adulthood. For example, on the Old stage you will find OWLS who are mentally and physically more like OWLS in middle adulthood; these Old OWLS will probably play the role of a full- or part-time worker. Other Old OWLS may play the more traditional role of retiree; however, even in retirement there is diversity. Some "retired" OWLS seek full- or part-time work; others play golf or shuffleboard every day. Old OWLS will give diverse portrayals of retirement as active or inactive, outgoing or reclusive, obsolete or imaginative—depending on their mental and physical health and well-being. They demonstrate that ". . . there is a great deal of individual variation in adult personality development" (Santrock, 1985, p. 377).

Early psychologists like Erikson and others did not foresee the phenomena that we discussed in Chapter One—OWLS becoming younger and older and staying in the workforce. However, by the 1990s Fisher offered a model of late-life adult development that more closely reflects the graying of the workplace.

Erikson's Developmental Stages. Psychologist Erik Erikson (1963) believed that during the developmental stage of late adulthood adults focus on ordering their lives. They try to make sense of what has been, what is, and what will be; tie up loose ends; and even mourn what might have been. However, Fisher (1993) reports that once Erikson became an octogenarian himself, he "admitted to some surprise at the creative potential and generativity of older adults" and "suggested that increased life expectancy necessitates the reexamination of the stages of the entire life cycle" (p. 77).

Havighurst's Developmental Tasks. Sociologist Robert Havighurst (1972) looked at late adulthood from the perspective of "developmental tasks." He felt that late adulthood was the time when OWLS completed the process of "disengaging" from the workplace, one that had actually begun in middle adulthood:

- Adjusting to life events such as retirement, physical and mental health issues, and the death of spouses and peers

- Developing a new role in society

- Learning to interact "leisurely" with peers

- Planning new living arrangements

Sheehy (1995) reminds us that developmental tasks are not "defined by marker events" but by an "impulse toward change" (p. 12). Havighurst himself might have suggested taking a new look at the developmental tasks of late adulthood, given the major changes that are resulting in the aging of the workforce.

Fisher's Model. Fisher (1993) developed a five-period model of older adulthood based on "the major changes and transitions of older adulthood and the contexts in which they occur" (p. 88). Fisher's five periods are as follows:

1. Continuity with middle age—OWLS continue their middle-age lifestyle while they plan retirement and begin to substitute other activities for work

2. Early transition—involuntary and voluntary transitions events such as retirement, ill health, death of a spouse, or the need to relocate bring about the end of the middle-age lifestyle

3. Revised lifestyle—older adults adapt to the transition from middle age, begin a more stable lifestyle, and socialize with their age group

4. Later transition—older adults begin to lose health, mobility, and autonomy and to require assistance

5. Final period—older adults adapt to later transitions and develop a sense of mortality

Fisher's five periods portray a developmental process that is defined by context, not age: "For some, continuity with middle age extends well into the seventies; for others, the early transition occurs shortly after (or even before) retirement" (Fisher, 1993, p. 88).

Adult Development, Generations, and Today's Workplace

The research on adult development gave new meaning to the term *generation.* This new meaning was popularized by Gail Sheehy in *Passages* (1976) and *New Passages* (1995). Generations are cohorts or groups of people who were born in the same time period and whose development was influenced by the economic, social, and political realities of that time period (Smola & Sutton, 2002). The concept of generations provides a useful framework for studying how generation-related perceptions can influence behavior at work.

Today's workplace is made up of multiple generations of workers and the age range of the largest generational group is fifty and older. Speaking in terms of generations is a popular way to put adult development into perspective and clarify how the ages and stages of the adult life cycle affect learning and performance in the workplace.

What Is a Generation?

A generation encompasses, again, all the people who were born at approximately the same time. The literature on adult development does not provide us with standard birth years and age ranges for each group that forms a generation; even the name assigned to each generation is not always the same. In their book *Generations at Work* Zemke, Raines, and Filipczak (2000) concluded: "There are no hard stops or road signs indicating when one generation ends and another begins. . . . If we wouldn't utterly confuse everyone, we would overlap them (generations) by three or four years" (p. 3).

OWLS Are Represented in Four Generations

The multigenerational workplace contains five generations, spans birth dates from 1916 to 1998, and includes workers aged eighteen to ninety. Back in 1985, Merriam and Lumsden wrote, "older adults are a more diverse group than any other age group" (p. 56). Twenty years later, consultant Phil Goodman warned: "there's no simple 50+ generation in the United States. . . . There are three separate generations in that age group, all with individual mindsets" (as cited in Harris, 2005, p. 48). Actually, as OWLS get older and younger, they are represented in four of the five workplace generations: Senior, Silent, Baby Boomer, and Generation X.

Figure 7.1 describes the five generations that make up the 2006 workplace, including various names used to describe each of the generations, the range of their birth dates and ages, and typical characteristics attributed to each generation by themselves and others. The names and characteristics are derived from the literature, including Kaplan-Leiserson (2005), Woodwell (2004), Sheehy (1995), and, of course, Harris (2005), who would not let us forget the forgotten generation.

The characteristics attributed to each generation by themselves and others reflect the social, economic, and political factors that impacted the development of each generation. We recognize the danger of stereotyping and warn our readers that *all* characteristics may not apply to *all* individuals within a specific generational cohort—especially those who are at the beginning or the end of a generation.

Figure 7.1. The Multigenerational Workplace.

Senior

Also known as . . .
Veterans
Matures
GI Generation
Lost Generation
World War II Generation

Birth date range
1916–1935

Described variously as . . .
Conservative
Conscientious
Loyal
Work-centric—work over "life"
Savers
Real-time communicators
Narcissistic

Age range
Old,
Old-Old, and
Oldest OWLS
aged 71–90+

Silent

Also known as . . .
Forgotten Generation
Postwar Generation
Lonely Generation
Duck and Cover
   Generation

Birth date range
1936–1945

Age range
Old and
Mid-Old OWLS
aged 61–70

Described variously as . . .
Strong work ethic
Independent
Real-time communicators
Cautious
Unadventurous
Unimaginative
Withdrawn
Indifferent
Suffocated children of war
   and depression
Brooding
Indecisive
Socially conscious

Baby Boomer

Also known as . . .
Me Generation
Protest Generation
Youth Generation
Vietnam Generation

Birth date range
1946–1964

Age range
Mid-Old and Young
OWLS aged 42–60

Described variously as . . .
Individualists
Youthful
Unconventional
Seek respect
Work-centric—work over "life"
Seek flexible work options
Strong work ethic
Real-time communicators
Vocal
Self-absorbed

Gen X

Also known as . . .
Baby Bust Generation
Endangered Generation

Birth date range
1965–1976

Age range
Young Old OWLS
aged 40–41 and
younger workers
aged 30–39

Described variously as . . .
Entrepreneurial
Independent
Self-confident
Ambitious
Determined
Skeptical
Directionless
Spoiled
Entitled
Autonomous
Dual-centric—
   work-life balance
Mobile
Virtual

Give me a job that pays well and I'll do it...my way

I'm wired. Connect me, and I'll collaborate with you . . .

Gen Y

Also known as . . .
Net Generation
Digital Generation
Echo Boomers
Millennials
Second-Wave Boomers
Generation Next
Nexters
Cool Generation

Birth date range
1977–1988

Age range
Aged 18–29

Described variously as . . .
Digital decision makers
Self-absorbed
Entitled
Autonomous
Independent
Competitive
High tech
Spenders
Life-centric—life before work
Self-confident
Flexible
Virtual
Wired
Cool
Optimistic
Blunt
Savvy
Contradictory
Upbeat
Education-minded

Senior OWLS. Old, Old-Old, and Oldest OWLS aged seventy-one to ninety or beyond are the new OWLS in the workplace. The Senior generation of OWLS may work full-time or part-time; function as workers, consultants, or senior executives. Many are torn between the economic need to work, the desire to work, and traditional views of a leisurely retirement. Some have made work such a priority in their lives that they are not sure they will be able to function without it. As one eighty-year-old self-employed OWL put it: "When I can't work anymore, I will open the tent flap and walk out into the snow."

Senior OWLS are the stable ones in a work world of instability; the experienced ones whose experience may or may not be viewed as obsolete when fast-paced technological change encroaches on "business as usual."

Silent OWLS. This generation is composed of Old OWLS aged sixty-five to seventy and Mid-Old OWLS aged sixty-one to sixty-four. They are the traditional OWLS in the workplace. They are dependable, hard-working, and loyal to their organization. They seldom take chances, and caution characterizes their lives.

Boomer OWLS. Mid-Old OWLS aged fifty-five to sixty and Young OWLS aged forty-two to fifty-four are the Boomer OWLS. They are dependable and hard-working like Senior OWLS; they think nothing of working long hours. However, Boomer OWLS plan to work well beyond the traditional retirement age, despite the fact that they feel the Generation X and Y workers are starting to get "their" promotions. Many Boomer OWLS may be thinking of early retirement or alternatives to full-time employment. Boomer OWLS still put work over life. Boomer OWLS who are managers also worry that the X and Y generations do not take work seriously enough.

Gen X OWLS. Yes, there really are some Young OWLS aged forty to forty-one who technically fall into Generation X. They are truly on the cusp—borderline Boomers and Gen Xers who may tend to balance the work-life equation rather than reversing it totally like younger Gen Xers.

The major difference between Gen Xers and the Boomers is that Gen Xers tend to be entrepreneurial. They are independent and confident that they can attain, maintain, and upgrade the skills they need to compete in the marketplace. They tend to consider themselves "independent value adders" rather than "long term employees" (Woodwell, 2004).

Generation Y. These are the young kids in the workplace; the under-thirty-some-things who are the sons and daughters of the Boomers. In an online inter-view, Don Tapscott, author of *Growing Up Digital: The Rise of the Net Generation,* described them as "the authorities of the digital revolution" and John Patrick, former IBM vice president, Internet Technology, suggested: "They've grown up connected, they are connected, and when they come to a company they want to stay connected" (Stepanek, 2003, n.p.)

Harris (2005) and others look on this generation as the "me first" gener-ation; its members want to move fast, be fulfilled, and have it all. In an inter-view, Steven Darwin, former chief information officer of the Federal Bureau of Investigation (FBI), also referred to Gen Y as "the new engine" in business and industry; they will drive profound changes in the nature of work systems, management, compensation programs, and information technology (IT) (Stepanek, 2003, n.p.).

Variation on Gen Y. Marc Ellis, director of HR for Getronics, an Amsterdam-based, multinational communications technology company, describes a new generation of eighteen- to twenty-four-year-olds that is entering the work-place in Eastern Europe. This new generation is radically entrepreneurial, energetic, determined to absorb new information in the shortest possible time, and grateful for everything they get.

Ellis feels the new, unnamed generation is the "polar opposite of Boomers" (cited in Harris, 2005, p. 50), which could create multiple generational issues in the future.

Multigenerational Workplace Issues

John Izzo, a Vancouver-based consultant, feels that the two major issues that arise from generational differences in the workplace are (1) integrating dif-ferent workplace values and (2) retaining both OWLS and younger worker-learners (Harris, 2005). Cooperative and collaborative efforts along with synergistic approaches may be required to address these issues.

Different Values Call for Integration

Values are the accepted principles or standards of an individual or a group. Workplace values are reflected in how workers work and how managers perceive their work efforts. Both are affected by generation-based preferences, which in turn are based on the economic, environmental, and social context of the workers' or managers' growing-up years.

As consultant Phil Goodman from San Diego notes: "All five generations in the United States today have their own unique mindsets. . . . To expect any generation to behave the way its predecessor did is insanity" (as cited in Harris, 2005). The key is to facilitate the integration of the various principles or standards into an organization-wide set of values that all workers can accept. Table 7.1 compares some basic generation-specific values found in the workplace.

"The viewpoints and perceptions of different age groups can present significant barriers in a workforce where ages can span fifty years or more" (Lesser, Farrell, & Payne, 2004, p. 8). This is especially true when there are different values related to work, authority, and careers.

Values Related to Work. In a 2002 study by the *Families and Work Institute,* researchers looked at the differences among generations regarding family or work priorities and came to the conclusion that younger workers tend to be family- or dual-centric and older workers tend to be work-centric. Workers who are family or dual-centric have better mental health and better career advancement and are more satisfied with their jobs and personal life. Being work-centric can lead to burnout and resentment when more "casual" workers are promoted (Kaplan-Leiserson, 2005).

Although work has intrinsic value for older OWLS, "to many younger workers work is important only if it will help their personal growth or achievement" (Blank & Slipp, 1994, p. 118). Older workers feel work is work, not fun; younger workers want work to be fun.

OWLS are also interested in the conditions of work:

- Flexible working conditions that do not jeopardize their economic safety net—benefits and pensions

Table 7.1. Workplace Values by Generation.

	Senior	Silent	Boomer	Gen X	Gen Y
Work-Life Focus	• Work-centric	• Work-centric	• Work-centric	• Dual-centric • Family first	• Dual-centric • Family first
Gender	• Traditional	• Traditional	• Traditional	• Nontraditional	• Nontraditional
Career	• Get ahead at almost any cost • Long-term career plan	• Get ahead at almost any cost • Long-term career plan	• Get ahead at almost any cost • Long-term career plan	• Get ahead but stop to smell the roses • Mobility • Entitled • Ambitious	• Get ahead if it feels right • Updated, portable competencies • Stay mobile • Entitled
Work	• Independent • Conscientious • Stable	• Independent • Cautious • Stable	• Independent • Committed • Flexible	• Entrepreneurial • Autonomous	• Collaborative • Flexible • Do what it takes to get the job done
Authority	• Hierarchical • Bureaucratic	• Hierarchical	• Hierarchical	• Parallel	• Parallel • Shared • Virtual

- Ergonomically sound work environments that minimize repetitive-motion and related injuries because they are more susceptible to these types of injury

- Retraining to keep up with future new technologies

- The feeling that they are valued for the knowledge and skill they possess right now

Gen X and Y workers want work that is challenging and fun; career advancement; good pay; and a collaborative, flexible work environment in which their technological knowledge and skills are valued and they have a role in decision making. They want training so they can improve their knowledge and skills and become more competitive in their field.

Older workers also think that younger workers view them as drudges, workaholics, or "time nuts." They feel younger workers assume that older workers are weak or in poor health and cannot perform their jobs.

Values Related to Authority. In another study, Blank and Slipp (1994) reported that "younger workers feel entitled to know the 'whole picture' and to be part of the entire process from decision making to implementation" (p. 117). Older workers feel that younger workers are not comfortable supervising them.

Values Related to Careers. Younger workers do not want to wait for promotion; they prefer promotion tied to performance and want frequent feedback, training, and direction. They need to be respected for their knowledge and expertise and want credit for their work. They are cynical and not loyal; they feel the company is not loyal to them and they must be prepared to take their competencies somewhere else.

OWLS do not think in terms of career mobility but in terms of career longevity. They also need to be respected for their knowledge and skill, yet they often perceive that younger workers do not acknowledge their experience or appreciate their ability to see the big picture.

The Focus Is on Retaining OWLS

One of the great challenges of the twenty-first-century workplace is to retain multiple generations of workers and encourage them to collaborate for the good of the organization. To do this, the workplace must try to retain both younger workers and OWLS: OWLS for their historical perspective and experience, younger workers for their energy and technological know-how. Currently the global focus is on retaining OWLS.

"Over the last several years, the focus of the EU has changed from preventing age discrimination to mobilizing the aging workforce" (Lesser, Hausmann, & Feuerpeil, 2005, p. 2). Retention strategies in the EU include the UK's Code of Practice on Age Diversity, which aims at preventing age discrimination in "recruitment, selection, training and development, redundancy, and retirement," and New Deal 50+, which combines a grant for training older workers to reenter the workforce and a "working tax credit," which pays older workers a supplementary wage (Lesser, Hausmann, & Feuerpeil, 2005, p. 3).

In the United States, it is businesses that are initiating changes that help them hire and retain OWLS. For example, when CVS/pharmacy recognized that ". . . seniors are our workforce," the company instituted older worker training and promotion programs and "changed the nature of the jobs to accommodate older people" by offering flexible hours and working situations (Beigel, 2001). At the same time, congressional repeal of ergonomic requirements did not take into account the need to develop work environments that are not "discriminatory against older people" (Beigel, 2001).

Implications for Workplace Learning and Performance

Adult development theory provides us with a rationale for how adults behave in the workplace and why they behave that way; how they perceive the world in which they live and work and how they react to their perceptions. Armed with this information, WLP practitioners can determine how the various stages and generations of adulthood can "motivate and interact with learning" and

how best to "structure learning experiences" for OWLS (Merriam & Caffarella, 1999, p. 137).

Adult development theory also provides guidance for how to attract and
retain workers. Bill Chafetz of Deloitte Consulting suggests that companies
who want to be competitive in the recruitment-retention arena should focus
on "what matters most to employees: their personal development or growth,
their need to be deployed in engaging work, and their desire to be connected
to others in the organization" (as cited in Kaplan-Leiserson, 2005, p. 13).

"Facilitating the productive coexistence of a multigenerational workforce
is essential for the health and well being of the workers and the organization"
(Lesser, Farrell, & Payne, 2004, p. 8). The concept of generations helps us to
do this by putting the whole idea of psychosocial development into a historical context that fits both life and the workplace.

Action Steps for WLP Practitioners

As an analyst and a change agent, you should take an active role in facilitating
the psychosocial transitions of OWLS. Here are some suggestions:

1. Identify the generations that are working in your organization.

   Use existing HR data or information gathered during the organizational audit in Chapter One to answer the following demographic questions:

   • Which generations are represented?

   • How many worker-learners fall within each generation?

   • What percentage of worker-learners fall within each generation?

   • Are there specific areas or departments where worker-learners
     are predominantly one generation?

2. Identify the values that are held by the various generations in your
   organization.

   Use existing vision and mission statements and your knowledge
   of the general values held by various generations or survey OWLS
   and younger worker-learners to answer the following questions:

- What values are represented by generation in your organization?

- Do the values of the organization integrate the multigenerational values of the workers?

- If not, what can be done to integrate generational and organizational values?

3. Raise the OWL awareness level of your organization.

   Use the information in this chapter to help raise the OWL-awareness level of your organization regarding the two major issues related to adult development—integrating the values of multiple generations and retaining OWLS and younger worker-learners in the workforce. Spread the word through company newsletters, diversity training initiatives, staff meetings, brown-bag lunches, and so forth.

4. Facilitate organizational change.

   Use your knowledge of generational differences and your analysis skills to help your organization initiate organizational and technological changes that will maximize the potential of a multigenerational workplace. Predict how organizational and technological changes could affect the different generations in your workplace and make recommendations for actions to minimize potential problems and maximize learning and performance.

5. Determine the training needs of the various generations in your workplace.

   Use your needs analysis skills to answer the following questions:

   - What knowledge and skills are represented in each generation?

   - What new knowledge and skills will each generation need in the future?

6. Select the most appropriate type of training or nontraining interventions to maximize the learning and performance of your multigenerational workplace.

- Diversity training to sensitize employees to the similarities and differences among generations

- Engagement training to encourage all employees to take an active role in the organization

- Technology training to bring OWLS up to speed and keep younger workers up to date

- Blended learning and performance support strategies to meet the needs of a multigenerational group of worker-learners

- Nontraining interventions such as compensation and benefit policies to retain workers, flexible work options, communication strategies, and so forth

7. Address the multigenerational issues related to operating in a global marketplace.

"Generational distinctions exist throughout the world, but they're not the same" (Harris, 2005, n.p.). The OWLS in your organization may be affected by some of these distinctions, so you will need to help your organization focus on the following:

- What are the national, international, and regional generational distinctions in the specific global marketplace in which the organization functions or will function?

- How are OWLS affected by national, international, and regional differences?

- How can the organization design, develop, implement, and evaluate global learning events and performance interventions to overcome the differences and meet the needs of OWLS?

8. Learn more about OWLS as workers and learners.

Read Chapter Eight to find out about the normal and not-so-normal physiological changes that occur with aging. Find out what you can do to minimize the impact of these changes on workplace learning and performance.

8

OWLS in Search of Function: Physiological Development

I just realized this year that I'm old. My back hurts when I stand too long.

Maxine, age eighty-four, part-time hospital aide

AS OWLS GAIN in wisdom and experience, they simultaneously undergo physiological or functional "losses" due to the natural process of aging. Moody (1985) states " . . . both losses and gains are experienced as part of the present reality of old age, and at times the losses appear to be a condition of the gains" (p. 30). These gains and losses both affect the well-being of OWLS. "If an older person cannot read because of failing eyesight, cannot hear what is said in class because of hearing loss, or cannot copy notes or diagrams because he or she is arthritic, learning is going to be a frustrating, difficult experience" (Hayslip & Kennelly, 1985, p. 80).

Even Boomer OWLS, who are healthier, more fit, and live longer than preceding generations, cannot resist the ultimate losses associated with aging—losses that alter their physical appearance and affect their health and well-being: "Regardless of how long you live, time takes a toll on the organs and systems in your body. How and when this occurs (and how it affects your well being) is unique to you" (*Aging Quiz,* 2004, n.p.).

Physical Changes

So far, in the twenty-first century ours is still a youth culture, so appearance has a major effect on the well-being of OWLS. Age-related changes in skin, teeth, and body composition, and musculoskeletal changes that occur over time are very visible and are closely associated with how the rest of the work-place perceives OWLS and how OWLS perceive themselves. Directly and indirectly, these physical changes affect how OWLS learn and perform in the workplace. Changes in skin, teeth, and the musculoskeletal system may erode well-being and self-esteem or cause health problems; musculoskeletal changes may also affect attention and the ability to perform certain tasks.

Skin Changes Are a Visible Sign of Aging

Over the years the skin thins, becoming less elastic and more fragile, drier and more wrinkled. Smoking and exposure to the sun can speed up the wrinkling process. Brown age spots can occur, and skin tags are more common. Hair may turn gray and thin. Skin cancer becomes a health concern; OWLS "have a 40 percent to 50 percent chance of getting skin cancer at least once by the time (they) reach 65" (*Aging: What to Expect,* 2004).

Teeth May Cause Appearance and Health Problems

Even with good care, teeth may undergo some age-related changes that may create health and appearance problems and affect the well-being of OWLS:

- Teeth may darken slightly and break more easily.

- Dry mouth may decrease the amount of saliva needed to cleanse the mouth of bacteria, causing teeth and gums to become vulnerable to decay and infection. Dry mouth can also cause "bad breath" or make it difficult to speak, swallow, or taste.

- Many OWLS keep their natural teeth all of their lives; however, some OWLS may need dentures or dental implants, which may affect their speech and eating patterns.

- Receding gums are a natural result of aging, but may forecast oral problems such as gingivitis.

The Mayo Clinic also reports that oral cancer is more common among older adults (*Aging Quiz,* 2004).

Body Composition and Musculoskeletal Function May Change

The musculoskeletal system is composed of muscles and bones and connective components such as tendons, ligaments, and joints that support the frame. As the body ages, the composition of the body changes and affects the function of the musculoskeletal system.

Body Composition. Research suggests that "older people tend to weigh about 25 percent more than younger people and exhibit a decline in muscle and bone mass and a gain in fat mass relative to total body weight" (Bellantoni & Blackman, 1997, p. 415). Bones begin to shrink in size and density after age thirty-five (*Aging: What to Expect,* 2004). OWLS, especially postmenopausal female OWLS, may become shorter and more susceptible to osteoporosis and fractures.

As fat mass begins to naturally increase, the metabolism of OWLS generally slows so their bodies burn fewer calories. Calories once used to meet their daily energy needs are stored as fat and weight gain may occur. A more sedentary work and home life may exacerbate the weight gain.

Both decreased stature and weight gain may cause low self-esteem. Extreme overweight may affect an OWL's ability to perform job tasks and may also cause other health or musculoskeletal problems. Loss of bone density may affect stamina and strength. Highly physical jobs may put OWLS at risk for bone fractures.

Musculoskeletal Function. Both male and female OWLS will find that muscles, tendons, and joints naturally lose some strength and flexibility as they age. OWLS may suffer from varying degrees of arthritis. Some of their joints may stiffen, swell, become inflamed and painful, or not function properly. Some OWLS may even require replacements for joints affected by arthritis or wear and tear from sports or work activities.

Changes in bones, muscles, tendons, and joints may also cause chronic pain, a decrease in physical strength and flexibility, loss of range of motion, or a diminished sense of balance. These changes may affect an OWL's attention span during a learning or performance task or decrease the OWL's ability to perform physical tasks.

Age-Related Sensory Changes

Age-related changes in the five senses—vision, hearing, taste, smell, and touch—may have an even greater impact on the learning and performance of OWLS than the physical changes we just discussed. In fact, the U.S. Department of Health acknowledges: "It is not generally recognized that if an older adult is lacking comprehension, it may result from sensory rather than intellectual failure" (as cited in Ekstrom, 1997, p. 5).

Sensory changes begin to manifest themselves around the age of forty. McIntire (2005) reports that when Young and Mid-Old OWLS are compared to younger workers, the OWLS are more than two times more likely to have vision problems and five times more likely to have hearing problems. However, the Mayo Clinic Senior Center Web site offers this reassurance: sensory losses due to aging "might make some tasks more difficult. But an older worker can make up for these changes by offering wisdom and experience" (*Aging Quiz,* 2004, n.p.).

Aging Eye Affects Learning and Performance

It is generally accepted in the education and training fields that approximately 85 percent of all learning occurs through vision and that the percentage of the population with some defective vision increases dramatically as people age. Changes in vision actually begin during adolescence. Usually these changes do not interfere with learning and performance until around age forty, when focusing on close objects may become more difficult. Most of the problems are caused by age-related changes in the pupil and lens.

Changes in the Pupil. The size and flexibility of the pupils begin to decrease with age. The average pupil in the normal eye will admit only about one-half as much light at age fifty as at age twenty. As pupils become less flexible they also have difficulty adjusting to changes in lighting. This affects how OWLS react and adjust to glare from indoor or outdoor lighting, computer screens, and various presentation media. They may also need more direct light in training and work areas.

Changes in the Lens. The lens of the eye must change shape to focus on near or distant objects. As the eye ages, the lens compresses, becomes more dense at the center, and finally hardens. This causes the lens to become too stiff to change shape.

OWLS become more farsighted and need reading glasses, bifocals, or even trifocals to focus on near, mid-range, and far objects. As their lenses age they become opaque, and OWLS are bothered by glare from artificial or outdoor lighting and may develop cataracts. The lens also begins to yellow and screens out dark green, blue, and violet colors, while red, yellow, and orange appear more vivid; this makes it difficult for OWLS to distinguish colors.

Other Vision Problems. Other vision problems may occur because of drugs, disease, or environmental factors. Severe problems can require surgery or some other type of medical intervention. Table 8.1 describes the six most common vision problems that occur as people age: dry eyes, floaters, cataracts, glaucoma, retinal disorders, and presbyopia.

Table 8.1. Age-Associated Vision Problems.

Problem	Description
Dry eyes	• Aging eyes may be less able to produce tears and so may feel irritated and tire easily. • The condition may be accompanied by excessive tearing. • The condition is exacerbated if the heating and cooling system in a building produces dry air.

(Continued)

Table 8.1. **Age-Associated Vision Problems,** *Continued.*

Problem	Description
Floaters	• Tiny spots or specks float across the field of vision, especially in bright indoor or outdoor lighting. • Usually a normal part of aging. • Could be a sign of retinal detachment if the number or size of the spots changes or light flashes occur simultaneously.
Cataracts	• Cloudy areas form over part or all of the eye lens. • Light cannot easily pass through the lens. • Surgery can remove cataracts and improve vision.
Glaucoma	• The eye's drainage canals become blocked and put pressure on the optic nerve. • Vision decreases gradually until it is gone. • Older adults with diabetes are at higher risk.
Retinal disorders	• The retina is a thin lining on the back of the eye that takes in visual images and transfers them to the brain. • Retinal disorders include age-related macular degeneration, diabetic retinopathy, and retinal detachment. • Retinal disorders are the leading cause of blindness in the United States.
Presbyopia	• Age-related loss of the lenses' elasticity makes it difficult to focus on close objects and small print. • The condition begins after age forty and becomes progressively worse until around age sixty-five. • Eyes may tire easily, and OWLS may develop headaches and require reading glasses or contacts.

Effects of Vision Problems. Some of the effects of age-related vision problems include a decrease in the size of the visual field, less peripheral vision, changes in depth perception, and fewer nerve cells in the eye to absorb light. In addition, OWLS may lose contrast or color sensitivity.

Contrast and color sensitivity both affect readability and legibility. Readability refers to the ease of reading a page of text; legibility refers to the speed with which each letter or word can be recognized. Contrast sensitivity is the ability to detect slight changes in brightness between areas that have no sharp lines around them. The eye recognizes objects by their borders, so contrast sensitivity is essential for processing visual information, especially in dim light or under glaring lights. Loss of contrast sensitivity can be a major cause of visual difficulty, especially in dim light or under glaring lights (Ekstrom, 1997).

Contrast sensitivity remains relatively constant through middle age, but elderly people typically show a mild but definite loss in the ability to detect low-level contrast. Less light entering the eye and scattering of light in the older lens may explain much of this loss.

Color sensitivity reaches its optimum in the early twenties and then steadily declines, although the rate of decline varies from individual to individual. Color sensitivity makes it possible to differentiate between various hues or colors on the color spectrum. It can affect how an individual processes colored text or distinguishes text from a background color. Ekstrom (1997) reports that beginning around age seventy, Old OWLS show a definite loss of color sensitivity. The blue end of the color spectrum is most affected; there is less loss at the red end and almost no loss in red-green discrimination. Old to Oldest OWLS have problems discriminating among black, brown, navy blues, charcoal grays, and maroons and among light pastel hues.

Aging Ear Affects Learning and Performance

Hearing loss and reduced ability to hear high-pitched sounds may begin as early as age twenty and have a direct impact on learning and performance for Mid to Oldest OWLS. Age-related hearing loss usually begins around age sixty: "One in three people older than 60 and half of all people older than 85 have significant hearing loss" (*Aging: What to Expect,* 2004).

Hearing loss occurs because over the years sounds and noise damage the hair cells of the inner ears. In addition, the walls of the auditory canals thin, and the eardrums thicken. Changes in the inner ear or in the nerves attached to it, earwax buildup, and various diseases can also cause hearing loss.

The aging ear usually has trouble with soft and high-pitched sounds or frequencies. Some OWLS find it difficult to follow a conversation in a crowded room because they cannot block out interference from background sounds; they cannot differentiate between the main speaker and other conversations going on in the background.

PSYCHOSOCIAL EFFECTS OF THE AGING EAR

Hearing loss can have psychosocial effects that can have an indirect impact on learning and performance; for example, in a group setting OWLS may have trouble hearing voices that are pitched high or participants who speak softly. OWLS may also have more trouble blocking out background noises from machinery, paging speakers, or even piped-in background music. Younger workers may become annoyed if OWLS ask them to repeat or clarify information, or think that OWLS are "not paying attention," "don't care," or "are losing it."

Changes to Taste, Smell, Touch Affect Learning and Performance

The ability to receive sensory data from the environment affects work and life activities. Taste, smell, touch, or feel are often required to function both on and off the job.

Taste and Smell. Sensory organs of taste are predominantly on the tongue. Taste buds trigger impulses that relay taste messages to the brain. Smell influences taste. OWLS retain their sense of taste and smell with age, although they may experience minor decrements in sensitivity. Smell and taste influence food consumption, production, and enjoyment. Smell is crucial when OWLS need to be able to escape from areas made hazardous by gas fumes and other toxic vapors (Ferrini & Ferrini, 2000). Smell is vital in jobs requiring taste or smell tests.

Touch. As OWLS age they may have reduced blood flow and tactile feedback. Tactile acuity is less sensitive with age. For most OWLS this is not problematic; however, for those who are visually challenged, it interferes with the ability to read Braille. OWLS who work in areas that require tactile feedback—hot-cold, smooth-rough, and so forth—may find it difficult to function in their jobs.

Feeling the Heat. Aging is often accompanied by a decrease in the body's ability to regulate internal temperature when exposed to high external heat: "Older individuals respond to an imposed heat challenge with higher core temperatures and heart rates, lower sweating rates and a greater loss of body fluid compared to younger individuals" (Kenney, 1993, as cited in Roth, 2005, n.p.). A sudden increase in temperature can strain the heart and blood vessels and cause heat exhaustion, heart failure, or stroke: it "may well be a life-threatening problem for the aging employee who is working in continuously hot environments" (Roth, 2005).

Medication can also make it more difficult for OWLS to adjust to the heat. Diuretics for high blood pressure prevent the body from storing fluids and keep blood vessels near the surface of the skin from opening. Some tranquilizers and drugs used to treat diseases like Parkinson's interfere with perspiring. Chronic conditions such as circulatory problems, diabetes, a previous stroke, overweight, or a weak or damaged heart can also make it hard for OWLS to adjust to the heat.

Feeling the Cold. Roth (2005) reports that OWLS who work outdoors or in highly air-conditioned buildings may have problems adjusting to the cold. Whenever body temperature drops below normal (98.6 degrees Fahrenheit or 37 degrees Celsius), the blood vessels narrow and blood flow decreases to reduce heat loss from the skin's surface. Since the blood vessels of adults normally constrict with age, OWLS are at increased risk for hypothermia if they work in cold environments. OWLS who work outdoors for long periods of time in low temperatures—for example, postal, construction, commercial fishing, food warehousing, and agricultural workers—are especially susceptible. Low temperatures, high or cold winds, dampness, and cold water can even cause chilblains, frostbite, or hypothermia.

System Changes

The skin and the senses are not the only areas affected as the body ages. Other body systems also change with age, and the changes can affect the learning and performance of OWLS. Fortunately, many changes in the body systems are gradual and often go unnoticed until later in life. Some changes can, however, be problematic for OWLS and present challenges for the WLP practitioner. This section reviews the major body systems that affect OWLS in the workplace.

Cardiovascular System Changes Affect Learning and Performance

As we age, heart muscles have to work harder to pump the same amount of blood through the body and blood vessels become less flexible. Arteriosclerosis or hardening of the arteries may also occur. The natural loss of flexibility in the blood vessels, in combination with narrowing of the arteries, makes aging arteries stiffer, causing the heart to work even harder to pump blood through them. This can lead to high blood pressure or hypertension. Medication can help to control high blood pressure, but long, stressful hours on the job can negate the effect of the medication. Exercise breaks and reduction of stressful conditions can help to alleviate the problem.

OWLS who stand for long periods of time may suffer from circulation problems, including varicose veins and swelling of the legs, hands, and feet. Medication and surgery may offer some help; however, it may also be necessary to offer ergonomic workstations to ease circulation problems. For example, supermarket cashiers for one German supermarket chain sit in swivel chairs and the cash register and checkout counter are at chair level. They also take more frequent breaks than their American counterparts.

Older OWLS may have decreased cardiorespiratory function or lung capacity, which in turn decreases their ability to oxygenate red blood cells. When these OWLS are working in heavy labor jobs such as construction or manufacturing they may tire more easily and may need more frequent breaks.

Digestive System Changes Affect Learning and Performance

Many OWLS are not even aware that swallowing or other motions within the digestive system are slowing down, or that secretions required to digest food are decreasing. Other OWLS may eat more slowly; require smaller, more frequent meals; become less tolerant of certain foods; have problems digesting late night meals or snacks; or require more frequent restroom breaks. At times some may suffer from bloating, heartburn, reflux, or other discomforts that make it difficult to concentrate on their work. Work-related travel may become more difficult. In extreme cases organs begin to malfunction or become cancerous and may require surgery to repair or remove them.

Excretory System Changes Affect Learning and Performance

As OWLS age the kidneys become less efficient in removing waste from the bloodstream. Chronic conditions, such as diabetes or high blood pressure, and some medications may further damage the kidneys. The Mayo Clinic reports: "About 30 percent of people age 65 and older experience a loss of bladder control or urinary incontinence. Incontinence can be caused by a number of health problems, such as obesity, frequent constipation and chronic cough" (*Aging: What to Expect,* 2004).

Incontinence affects female OWLS, especially postmenopausal female OWLS, more often than male OWLS; however, male OWLS may suffer incontinence due to an enlarged prostate. Both female and male OWLS may need workstations that are within easy reach of restrooms, more work or training breaks, or adjustments for work-related travel.

Immune System Changes Affect Learning and Performance

The immune system includes the thymus gland, spleen, lymph nodes, bone marrow, and leucocytes. It protects the body from invading bacteria, viruses, fungi, and defective body cells. With age, the immune system functions decline, making OWLS susceptible to diseases. Loss of energy and general malaise accompany immune system deficits (Ferrini & Ferrini, 2000). OWLS may need more frequent rest periods or short food breaks to maintain optimum energy levels on the job.

Nervous System Changes Affect Learning and Performance

Some aging OWLS may find they have reduced nervous system responses, such as shaking in their hands, decreased ability to swing their arms, or increased rigidity. Age-related loss of neurons in the brain, coupled with an age-related decrease in dopamine, can increase the frequency of these and other neurological symptoms (Albert & Moss, 1997). It is accurate to say that "[t]he chief behavioral effect of most nervous system changes during adulthood may be a generalized slowing down of almost all functions and processes" (Troll, 1982, p. 23). This includes reading, writing, walking, talking, and other activities.

Respiratory System Changes Affect Learning and Performance

The physiology of the respiratory system tells us that breathing is a very complex mechanism. With age, there is a reduction in oxygen taken up from the environment by the blood (Whitbourne, 1985). There is also a reduction in vital capacity (movement of air in and out of lungs while inhaling and exhaling to capacity). The decrease in pulmonary efficiency has little effect on daily functions; however, OWLS who engage in heavy physical activity may need frequent rest periods because of tiring more easily and recovering less quickly (Ferrini & Ferrini, 2000).

The Aging Brain

This section discusses the general structural and functional changes that occur in the brain as OWLS age. Structural changes include brain atrophy; functional changes may affect memory and psychomotor activities.

Structural Changes Affect Learning and Performance

As the brain ages, cerebrospinal fluid increases, brain tissue decreases, and the brain begins to atrophy. Fortunately, although the white matter of the brain decreases, the gray matter does not; in one study the brain tissue of both thirty-year-old and seventy-year-old subjects contained 40 percent gray matter. Research indicates that human intelligence is determined by the volume and location of gray matter tissue in certain regions of the brain ("Human Intelligence," 2004).

The good news is that brain atrophy does not become significant until age seventy and beyond. Although there is a substantial age-related loss of neurons or cells in some areas of the brain that play a role in memory function, there is some evidence that the brain can regenerate neurons and training can help improve cognitive functions (Albert & Moss, 1997; Begley, 2006).

The other good news is that the brain itself compensates for losses from aging or injury: "compensatory mechanisms of growth and remodeling . . . may be part of the lifelong program to maintain and adapt brain function" (Cotman & Neeper, 1997, p. 292). For example, the brain increases or replaces lost connections between the cells, so OWLS can continue to function in those areas. Research also shows that mental and physical exercise can combat structural losses and have a positive effect on memory and general brain function (Cotman & Neeper, 1997).

Functional Changes Affect Learning and Performance

Some OWLS may lose some memory efficiency or find that psychomotor problems such as slower reflexes or problems with motor coordination are affecting their performance. Chapter Five explained what may happen to cognitive and perceptual memory functions as OWLS age. The sidebar lists some of the changes that may occur in psychomotor functions.

EFFECTS OF AGE-RELATED CHANGES
IN PSYCHOMOTOR FUNCTIONING

Employers, training professionals, and OWLS need to recognize that age-related changes in psychomotor functioning can affect the following:

- Motor coordination, speed, and dexterity
- Speed and reliability of reflexes
- Reaction speed
- Reflex time
- Ease and speed of movement or mobility
- Accuracy of motor performance
- Ability to grasp or hold objects
- Speed and accuracy of motor performance

Implications for Workplace Learning and Performance

The good news is that OWLS are indeed getting younger in both body and spirit, which may counteract many of the normal age-related physiological changes they go through as they age. When the Rehabilitation Institute of Chicago surveyed a thousand baby boomers, the respondents generally felt they would be "healthy and free from aches and pains well into their 70s and 80s"; 50 percent of the respondents said they "will not feel their age until after age 80" and 79 percent said they "will not limit their activities until after age 70" (*Denying, Defying Limits of Age,* 2004, p. 2).

Employers and WLP Practitioners Must Face the Challenge

Employers and WLP practitioners in the aging, multigenerational workplace need to recognize the new and improved OWL in the workplace. At the same time, employers and WLP practitioners must be ready, willing, and able to facilitate and support the normal physiological changes that may still occur as OWLS age. McIntire (2005) suggests that organizations should develop a "comprehensive strategy that includes training policies, technology procurement policies, accommodations, and ergonomics."

Accommodation is a major component of any strategy to decrease the negative effects of these losses and maximize the workplace learning and performance of OWLS. Accommodation helps OWLS continue to learn and perform despite changes in sensory capacity or physical functions, such as loss of vision, hearing, or physical dexterity.

Accessibility and Assistive Technologies Are the Key

Accessibility and assistive technologies are the key to accommodating OWLS in the workplace. Accessibility technology is computer technology that enables individuals to adjust a computer to meet their visual, hearing, dexterity, cognitive, and speech needs (Microsoft, 2003, as cited in McIntire, 2005). Assistive technology uses specially designed products to provide additional accessibility to individuals who have physical or cognitive difficulties, impairments, and disabilities.

Some accessibility and assistive technologies are built into computer operating systems; others are add-ons. For example, Windows XP has special built-in accessibility features for users with vision, hearing, or physical dexterity problems, and XP is also compatible with add-on assistive technology. The sidebar lists some specific examples of accessibility and assistive technologies that are useful in the workplace.

EXAMPLES OF ACCESSIBILITY AND ASSISTIVE WORKPLACE TECHNOLOGIES

- Reading glasses, contact lenses, and hearing aids are common examples of how technology can augment or enhance sensory capacity.
- Large-text settings in computer programs, magnification devices for computer screens, and glare shields for computer screens help OWLS compensate for vision problems.
- Larger keys for computer keyboards or telephone keypads and large trackballs allow OWLS to enter information or move a cursor without the need for fine motor skills.
- Voice-activated computers help OWLS compensate for decreases in visual capacity or physical function.
- Alternative input devices—such as specialized keyboards, trackballs, electronic pointing devices, screen magnifiers, touch screens, text-to-speech synthesizers, and so forth—assist the learning and performance of OWLS.

Action Steps for WLP Practitioners

As a WLP practitioner, you can help others in your organization to accommodate the physiological changes that OWLS go through as they age by implementing the following action steps:

1. Learn more about the physiological characteristics of the OWLS in your workplace.

   Use your analysis skills: Observe OWLS at work and in learning situations. Survey or interview OWLS, their coworkers, and their supervisors to get a feel for perceptions about the physiological condition of the OWLS in their department or area. For suggestions on what questions to ask, see the *Aging Quiz* (2004) and the organizational audits in Part One of this book.

2. Learn more about accessibility and assistive technologies and become a model of accommodation.

   • Go to the Mayo Clinic Web site www.mayoclinic.com to find ways to adapt the workplace to accommodate the different physiological needs of OWLS on the job.

   • Read "Workplace Design" (Medsker, 2006) to learn more about ergonomic issues related to WLP tools and settings.

   • Go to www.microsoft.com/enable to learn more about accessibility and assistive technologies.

   • Model accommodation in your training programs or when you design nontraining performance improvement interventions.

3. Accommodate the aging eye.

   Color and contrast sensitivity both affect readability and legibility, so manipulate the factors that determine readability and legibility, such as type arrangement, spacing, line length, type size, type style, ink color, and paper hue. Here are some suggestions based on research and practice:

- Use the typeface **Verdana**, instead of Times New Roman or **Arial**, because it is larger and does not have serifs or spurs on the letters, and the letters are more widely spaced. See Table 8.2 for examples.

- Use a minimum of 12-point type for printed text, 24- to 36-point for projected visuals.

- Do *not* use *italics* for headings or emphasis; *do* use **bold type.**

- Do *not* use ALL CAPS for headings or text.

- Use ragged right margins; do *not* justify right margins.

- Use white space to keep the text from looking crowded and to separate sections.

- Use fifty to seventy-five characters per line for 12-point type; five to seven words per line for projected visuals.

- Red and orange are good colors for aging eyes—but poor colors if your audience includes adults who are color-blind or color deficient.

- Increase readability and legibility for those who have some degree of color-blindness or deficiency by providing a brightness contrast of at least 30 percent between symbols and their backgrounds (Ekstrom, 1997).

- Make sure letters and their backgrounds are two to three values different from each other so they will be more easily read or seen by people with low vision (Hiatt, 1981).

Table 8.2. Typeface Differences.

Verdana	Times New Roman	Arial
Visuals	Visuals	Visuals

- Pay attention to the lighting levels for OWLS: "Appropriate lighting needs to be task-specific" (Roth, 2005). For OWLS this may mean more direct lighting at workstations or glare-free lighting in training rooms.

- Always be careful to match the compatibility of the delivery technology with the receiving technology; for example, it may be difficult for OWLS to learn from streaming video that distorts the picture, the sound, or both.

4. Accommodate the aging ear.

Here are some suggested action steps you can take when designing or delivering training or information for OWLS who have auditory challenges:

- Speak loudly and clearly. Use a microphone if necessary, but only if the sound system volume and tone are adjustable and you are familiar with how to use the system.

- Make sure participants can see the speaker's face and lips.

- Always use a "show and tell" blended approach to training presentations.

- Make sure the volume is adjustable if voice tracks are used for computer or video training programs.

- Minimize background noise for all types of training. In areas of high work noise, ear plugs and other noise-dampening devices are important accommodations, so you may need to design strategies that allow OWLS to use these devices during the training.

5. Keep OWLS cool.

- Air-conditioning, fans, broad-brimmed hats for outdoor work, and a dress code that allows loose, lightweight clothing can provide some protection from the heat.

- Cold water should be accessible and plentiful.

- Heavy meals can exacerbate the effects of extreme heat, so recommend that workplace cafeterias offer lighter, cold meals.

6. Keep OWLS warm.

   - Suggest that OWLS who may be exposed to the cold for long periods of time should wear warm clothing with at least three layers of insulation.

   - Suggest that OWLS take special care to protect their extremities with insulated hats, gloves, and socks. Heat is lost from feet, hands, face, and head—a bare head alone can account for up to 40 percent of lost body heat.

   - Suggest that OWLS who work or train in cold, damp conditions have a place to store and access dry clothing.

7. Accommodate the aging brain.

   You can design and deliver cognitive activities such as memory tasks and problem solving that will help OWLS exercise their brains and stay healthy. For specific action steps, see Chapter Six.

8. Encourage your organization to initiate nutrition and fitness programs for both OWLS and younger worker-learners.

   - Partner with a nutritionist and encourage your organization to offer nutritional options in company cafeterias. Nutrition studies demonstrate that eating the proper nutrients has a positive effect on body composition; helps to maximize immune, vascular, visual, and cognitive functions; and may delay or prevent chronic diseases (Blumberg, 1997).

   - Encourage your organization to set up on-site fitness centers or partner with an off-site facility and encourage OWLS to participate. Exercise can help OWLS maximize their cardiovascular health and function, increase muscle mass and function, increase metabolism, decrease or prevent hypertension and stress, and improve memory (Goldberg, Dengel, & Hagberg, 1997).

9. Learn more about OWLS and their search for well-being.

> OWLS who experience personal satisfaction, who are in control of their existence, who are responsible and accountable citizens, and who command and enjoy the respect of others, appreciate well-being and the role that health plays in defining it.

Chapter Nine will conclude the discussion of adult transitions with a description of how health and leisure issues over the lifespan affect the development of OWLS, impact workplace and learning, and provide action opportunities for WLP practitioners.

9

OWLS in Search of Well-Being: Health, Wellness, and Leisure

I didn't think I'd ever adjust to retirement but my sister insisted I go with her to our community college in town for their Institute for Learning in Retirement program. We hear all kinds of interesting things taught by people our age. We get free parking. We can use the college library and we're even served a light lunch. I'm learning about geology and rock formations, medical anthropology, and animal grooming. I think I'll get a cat for Christmas.

Frances, age seventy, retired cafeteria supervisor

FRANCES IS TYPICAL of many OWLS who have adequate financial resources for leisurely pursuits. She is happy with her life and her accomplishments and, above all, she enjoys good health, wellness, and well-being.

Health is both difficult to define and difficult to measure. The classic definition sees health as a state of complete physical, mental, and social well-being and not merely the absence of disease (Constitution of the World Health Organization [WHO], 1947). In effect, health is the totality of a person's existence:

the physical, psychological, emotional, social, spiritual, and environmental factors that determine quality of a person's life are interrelated (Edlin, Golanty, & McCormack Brown, 2002).

Wellness, on the other hand, is multifaceted. Individuals can achieve spiritual, social, emotional, intellectual, physical, and occupational wellness. For example, physical wellness deals with health promotion or lifestyle changes and personal well-being (Payne & Hahn, 2000). It is achieved and maintained through good nutrition, exercise, and so forth. We will discuss all six types of wellness later in this chapter. OWLS whose bodies are free from disease and acute or chronic pain; who are physically, intellectually, and emotionally active and engaged in life; and who have good mental attitudes most of the time, experience positive wellness.

Well-being is feeling good about life. It communicates a sense of personal satisfaction, control over one's life, self-sufficiency, and responsibility. Well-being is closely linked to personal happiness.

Health and wellness both focus on the well-being of the individual.

As individual OWLS advance through OWLhood, there are many challenges to their health, their wellness, and ultimately their well-being. Any or all of these challenges can affect the learning and performance of OWLS in the workplace. Learning and performance professionals need to be able to recognize whether the well-being of OWLS is being affected by health or wellness issues on the job and then be able to help implement policies, procedures, and programs to keep OWLS healthy and well.

This chapter looks at the health and wellness of OWLS and the effect of health and wellness on overall happiness, learning, and performance. It suggests typical leisurely pursuits that engage OWLS through a variety of learning options that keep the mind intellectually active and the body physically agile.

Health and OWLS

To be valued in today's workplace, OWLS need to be healthy and injury-free as well as wise. Employers ". . . want the brain power and the experience and knowledge that older workers provide, but not the lost work-time days, workers' compensation claims or any of the negatives associated with injuries/ illnesses" (Roth, 2005). OWLS, however, may be more susceptible to disease, injury, or illness and may require more time to recover.

Physical Health Affects Learning and Performance

In their study of the 1990s workplace, Crimmins, Reynolds, and Saito (1999) wrote that OWLS aged fifty-five to sixty self-reported that their health status had improved during the 1990s. Health has an effect on the ability to learn and perform; for example, cardiovascular disease may decrease the oxygen supply to the brain, which affects intelligence and cognitive functions such as memory as well as reaction time. Chronic health problems in general may cause anxiety and depression, which in turn affect physical and mental functioning as well as general well-being.

Serious health issues usually do not surface before OWLS reach middle age, and often OWLS do not have major health problems until late adulthood. Diabetes, heart disease, stroke, and lung disease become more possible as the body ages, even when OWLS have access to the latest in medical advances and lead a healthy and fit lifestyle (Vojta, 2003).

In addition, the longer OWLS live and work, the longer and harder they need to combat genetic, general environmental, and work-related factors that increase their potential for disease. OWLS need to be aware of the symptoms of disease and how to respond to the symptoms should they arise. Employers need to help OWLS by including health and fitness education, health monitoring, and health management programs as part of their benefits package.

Given the reality of the lost-time-is-lost-money workplace environment, organizations need to be able to ensure that OWLS continue to remain healthy and fit to work. Proactivity on the part of both employers and OWLS is the key to maximizing the workplace contribution of OWLS.

Mental Health Links to Physical Health

Disorders that may affect the mental health of OWLS include depression, anxiety disorder, schizophrenia, personality disorder, and dementia. There are also links between mental and physical health; for example, depression and anxiety have been strongly associated with "the incidence of coronary disease" and less strongly associated with asthma, arthritis, ulcers, and headaches (Tucker & Friedman, 1996, p. 310). When Gatz, Kasl-Godley, and Karel (1996) reviewed studies on the mental health of older adults, they concluded that older adults are less apt to suffer from depression and anxiety than middle-aged or younger adults.

Depression. There are two types of depression: clinical and subclinical. Clinical depression is a debilitating disease; it may require treatment including drugs, periods of hospitalization, and therapy. Subclinical depression is exhibited by feelings of sadness, discouragement, despair, and so forth; however, it is not incapacitating and does not impede social functioning. Research generally concludes that OWLS are not more depressed than younger adults (Costa & McCrae, 1996).

When older adults do suffer from depression, it is usually from early-onset, not late-onset depression; this means that they were depressed when they were younger and continue to fight depression throughout adulthood. Women are more apt to suffer from depression than men; however, the incidence is equal for men and women aged eighty and older. Boomers and other generations born after World War II are more apt to suffer from depression because of social factors such as urbanization, single-parent households, and so forth.

Anxiety. Anxiety can induce panic attacks and physical symptoms such as shortness of breath. Fewer older adults suffer from anxiety than any other age group; however, adults aged seventy-five and older are more apt to suffer from anxiety than from depression. It is unusual for anxiety disorders to start after age sixty-five. Anxiety is also associated with coronary disease.

Schizophrenia. This mental disorder usually starts between the late teens and early thirties; late-onset schizophrenia is rare. Onset after age sixty is sometimes called *paraphrenia* or delusional disorder and occurs more in women than in men. Biological changes play more of a role in paraphrenia than genetics.

Personality Disorders. Many researchers believe that personality forms early in life and does not change significantly as adults age: "The central fact in adult personality development, replicated in a host of longitudinal studies, is that personality shows little change after age 30 and until the advent of dementing disorders" (Costa & McCrae, 1996, p. 378). On the other hand, Magai and Nusbaum (1996) view personality as a "dynamic system" and suggest that emotions and emotional processes are agents of personality change: "Intense emotion provides the energetic force necessary to propel movement and change" (p. 416).

Magai and Nusbaum also categorize personality change as either sudden or gradual, elective or fortuitous. Sudden change may be triggered by extreme stress or a "mind-altering" experience. Gradual change is less dramatic or "profound" and can be triggered by "developmental or deliberate change" (p. 411). Elective change implies a conscious choice; fortuitous change is a happenstance—it happens by chance. For any change to grow and stabilize, there must be ongoing "cognitive-emotional work" as well as "interpersonal support" (p. 416).

Personality disorders such as hostility and neuroticism may begin early in life and continue through adulthood, affecting both the OWL's ability to cope and adapt and his or her perception of self and others. The causes may be genetics or severe trauma. Sometimes it is difficult to determine whether behaviors exhibited by OWLS—such as aggression, overreaction, impulsiveness, and so forth—are early- or late-onset personality disorders, warning signs of depression or dementia, or just plain frustration.

Emotionally Healthy OWLS Are Stable

"Emotions appear to constitute fractals in the stream of life experience" (Magai & Nusbaum, 1996, p. 418)—that is, breaks or cracks in the flow of emotional well-being. Fractals can trigger ramifications that change biological and psychological structures in unpredicted ways. Emotional health is closely interrelated with mental and physical health, biological and psychological development from childhood to adulthood, and personality. For example, Edlin, Golanty, and McCormack Brown (2002) describe emotionally healthy

OWLS as emotionally stable and mature. They are not under- or overemotional. Their emotional response to both positive and negative life events is constant and balanced. They are both inwardly and outwardly calm and even. OWLS who are emotionally healthy have positive self-images, feel positive about other people, and generally are able to meet life's demands.

OWLS who are emotionally mature generally function well under adverse conditions. They are able to adapt or modify their behaviors in the workplace as changes surround them; they are in control of their lives and they find satisfaction in helping other employees in the workplace and during training events.

Physical Disability Impacts Organizational Performance

Most OWLS experience good physical, mental, and emotional health. However, some OWLS may be more susceptible to disease, injury, or illness or may require more time to recover. OWLS may be unable to work because of disabilities caused by cardiovascular or respiratory problems, diabetes, or chronic pain from arthritis. In addition, "[t]he duration of disabilities increases with age, doubling from four or five workdays lost for workers ages 16 to 35 to 10 days for those 55 and older, according to the Bureau of Labor Statistics" (as cited in Vojta, 2003).

As OWLS become healthier and fitter, these statistics will begin to change. However, whether the disability is short-term, long-term, or permanent, time away from the workplace is always a loss for both the OWL and the organization.

When OWLS are absent from the job they deprive the organization of an important part of its knowledge and skill base and have an effect on the bottom line—both for the organization and for themselves.

Physical Injury Results in Lost Productivity

And then there are physical injuries. As people age, their physical capabilities—such as strength, stamina, and visual acuity—decline, making them more susceptible to injury and making certain physical tasks harder to perform (Vojta, 2003). The most common type of workplace injury is musculoskeletal. OWLS' decreased bone and muscle mass and weakened abdominal walls can make them more susceptible to spinal injuries. This susceptibility is increased when OWLS' jobs call for heavy lifting or holding a stationary or awkward position for long periods of time. Injuries lead to lost work days as well as increased costs from long- and short-term disability compensation plans. Accidents also pose a greater risk for OWLS; an OWL who slips and falls on a newly waxed office floor or who falls off a ladder in the supply room is more likely than a younger worker to suffer broken bones because the musculoskeletal system is weakened. In addition, the OWL may take longer to recuperate from a fall.

OWLS and Wellness

In the previous section we looked at the physical, mental, and emotional health of OWLS. Now let us turn to wellness factors that impact the lifestyles, work styles, and well-being of OWLS.

Wellness Has Six Types

The literature identifies six types of wellness:

1. Spiritual—Spiritual wellness is believing that some force unites human beings. OWLS who are able to examine personal values and beliefs and who have a clear understanding of right and wrong exhibit spiritual wellness.

2. Social—When OWLS interact successfully with their colleagues in the workplace environment or when they communicate with others because diversity and multiculturalism in the workplace are ingrained in their lives, they exhibit social wellness.

3. Emotional—Emotional wellness is the OWLS' ability to conquer stress. When OWLS take responsibility for their behavior in the workplace and when they exhibit a good sense of humor, they are emotionally healthy.

4. Intellectual—Intellectual wellness reflects new growth, new learning, new challenges. OWLS who see more than one side of an issue

and who exhibit adequate time management skills have intellectual wellness.

5. Physical—Physical wellness addresses daily tasks and positive life-style habits. OWLS who maintain a positive, health-promoting lifestyle and who invest in their physical health have physical wellness.

6. Occupational—Occupational wellness is the ability to complete a job to one's competence and satisfaction, thereby earning a just wage. OWLS who seek challenges at work and who know how to balance work with myriad other demands on life have occupational wellness (Anspaugh, Hamrick, & Rosato, 1994; Edlin, Golanty, & McCormack Brown, 2002).

Wellness Benefits OWLS and Organizations

OWLS who are concerned with increasing the quality of their lives and being the best they possibly can be experience a personal wellness lifestyle that produces a sense of well-being. It allows OWLS to act from an internal locus of control; increases physical, intellectual, and mental energy levels; increases job productivity; and improves awareness of self and relationships with others. "The biggest benefit of wellness is the attitude that helps each person to see life's possibilities and to work toward the ones that are most personally fulfilling" (Anspaugh, Hamrick, & Rosato, 1994, p. 5). This is the attitude that creates a feeling of well-being.

Well-Being Flows from Wellness

The well-being of OWLS is not so much a factor of age-related biological, psychological, and health changes as it is a factor of their attitude toward change, which affects how OWLS cope with these changes. For example, OWLS who are high-extraverts are more positive, whereas OWLS who are high-neurotic are less positive when they cope with change (Costa & McCrae, 1996). Costa and McCrae conclude that concurrent life circumstances such as "age, race, sex, income, education, and marital status combined accounted for only 6 percent of the variance in measures of well-being" (p. 375). It's all about attitude and coping strategies.

Signs That an OWL's Well-Being Is Not So Well

A number of signs may indicate that all is not well with a particular OWL. The OWL's energy level may begin to decrease, and he or she may tire more easily and have trouble sleeping. The OWL may also begin to exhibit signs of stress such as depression, anxiety, low self-esteem, personality changes, increased use of alcohol or prescription or recreational drugs, and an inability to focus on or complete tasks. The OWL may also become easily frustrated, overreacting to events at work, and jeopardizing work and personal relationships. Figure 9.1 illustrates how some OWLS feel when their well-being is not so well.

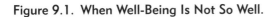

Figure 9.1. When Well-Being Is Not So Well.

Decreased Energy Level and Fatigue. The research of the 1970s and early 1980s does not support the effect of energy level and fatigue on intellectual functions. It may show that fatigue is interrelated with the difficulty of the content or learning task and practice; for example, practice may help the later-life learner combat the effects of fatigue and offset any increase in fatigue from extended practice.

Broken Sleep Patterns. How long OWLS need to sleep each day changes very little throughout adulthood. However, many researchers suggest that as OWLS age their circadian rhythm or internal clock advances. This means that some OWLS may wake up earlier and go to sleep earlier, so their "maximum work activities" also occur earlier (Mobbs, 1997, p. 246). On the other hand, there are the incurable night-OWLS who get up late, go to bed late, and avoid any work activities before noon.

Sleep Disturbances. The Mayo Clinic reports that OWLS need the same amount of sleep as they age: "Adults who need six hours of sleep nightly, will probably always need six hours—give or take 30 minutes. . . . Getting those same quality sleep hours is more difficult because they don't sleep as soundly" (*Aging Quiz,* 2004). OWLS may need to spend more time in bed to get the same amount of sleep. In addition, "by age 75, some people find that they're waking up several times each night" (*Aging Quiz,* 2004). Digestive or bladder problems are a major cause of sleep disturbance as the body ages.

Insomnia. Insomnia is the most common sleep problem for people of all ages, especially when it is difficult to stick to a regular schedule. For example, when workers change shifts every two to four weeks it is impossible to wake up and go to bed at the same time each day and establish a consistent sleep pattern. This may be more difficult for OWLS than for younger workers. Extensive business travel may also be more difficult for OWLS, especially when time zone changes are involved.

OWLS and Stress

Lack of well-being can lead to stress and may be exacerbated when aging is also a factor: "there has been much speculation concerning the relationship between 'stress,' which intuitively seems unpleasant . . . and aging, about which the same could be said" (Mobbs, 1997, p. 247). Aging can cause stress, and it can impair an OWL's ability to deal with stress. Identifying the cause of stress is important, but understanding how adults respond to stress may be even more important.

Common Causes of Stress in OWLS

OWLS are especially susceptible to stress related to the aging process itself, health, economic security, or job security.

Aging and Stress. OWLS may be threatened by the aging process when it alters their appearance and their ability to perform on the job. They may lose their self-esteem because they feel they are no longer the man or woman they used to be. They may become defensive in the presence of younger workers because they perceive that the younger workers do not value their wisdom and experience.

Health-Related Stress. Good health improves well-being; poor health can result in stress. Poor health may inhibit an OWL's ability to deal with the normal process of aging. It may also cause learning and performance problems.

Economic-Security–Related Stress. The quality of life for OWLS is generally looking up, according to AARP's 2004 report *A Close-Up Look at 50+ America.* However, several economic situations are stressing today's OWLS; for example, large plant closings. Then there is the stress that comes from a Social Security system in jeopardy. And finally, there is the pension plan situation. Approximately 50 percent of all workers have a pension plan; the others must rely on Social Security or their own savings (*A Close-Up Look,* 2004). For some OWLS, pension plans may be in jeopardy, as corporations are cautiously reviewing, carefully revising, and matter-of-factly dropping them. This is, indeed, a bitter pill to swallow for OWLS who have devoted their professional life and commitment to a company.

OWLS Respond to Stress in Different Ways

Responses to stress vary from individual to individual. In some OWLS stress may cause hypertension or high blood pressure and increase the risk of cardiovascular disease (Mobbs, 1997); in others it may trigger a positive surge of energy, determination, and attitude. Responses to stress are triggered by the individual's perception of sensory input as either positive or negative—a call to action or a threat.

Proaction. Some OWLS may seek help or try to alleviate the cause of their stress. While being proactive is a positive response, it may take time and energy away from the job. Proactive OWLS may have problems concentrating on work and relationships. They may overreact to workplace or personal situations and even undergo personality changes. Usually, however, their reaction is less extreme than that of OWLS who take *no* action to relieve stress.

No Action. Other OWLS may decide not to deal with stress. They become frustrated and depressed and "act out" on the job. They may begin to drink or take medication to "calm their nerves." Work performance and relationships may suffer as a result of their inability to deal openly with the causes of stress.

The Picture Is Not Entirely Gloomy

OWLS do experience physical and emotional transitions that are gradual. OWLS who are in control of their well-being adapt to these changes, and they view life's stresses as opportunities rather than challenges. They proactively work at being well and happy and stress-free, which often leads them to explore the pursuit of leisure.

OWLS and the Pursuit of Leisure

Leisure plays an integral role in the life cycle of OWLS and is crucial to their well-being. Leisure literature is conceptualized in a variety of ways. Aristotle saw leisure as a state of mind, somewhat spiritual and free from work or obligation. Others see leisure as discretionary time; that is, time remaining after subsistence and existence demands are met. Leisure is also a functional activity satisfying social, psychological, emotional, and physical needs. Finally, leisure is perceived as freedom. For OWLS, leisure supports autonomous decision making, social integration, and freeing of the mind to be and to do what is desired (Teaff, 1985). Learning is often a part of leisure.

Learning May Be a Leisurely Pursuit

Leisure wears many faces in the lives of busy and active OWLS. Many who work full or part time or who volunteer their services engage in learning activities that keep their minds and bodies vibrant and active. An advertisement for a training company reads "when you're through learning, you're through." There are many formal and informal opportunities for OWLS to learn and to keep their minds active outside of work.

In addition to work-related educational programs, universities and four-year colleges offer a variety of formal programs—and even some informal ones—for OWLS, ranging from courses specifically designed for older learners to a variety of continuing-education offerings for credit or for audit. Community colleges offer OWL avocational courses, and many specialize in financial management and estate planning programs (Lamdin & Fugate, 1997).

Public libraries, senior centers, YMCAs and YWCAs, and even companies and organizations offer less formal leisure learning programs for OWLS. For additional sources of leisure learning activities, see Action Step 8 at the end of this chapter.

Leisure Pursuits Impact Workplace Performance

The WLP practitioner should care about what OWLS do outside the workplace. Leisure activities, especially leisure learning, broaden their experience and perspectives. OWLS who actively pursue leisure activities can share new ideas and bring new insights into the workplace. They are healthier, more energetic, more fit, and have a sense of well-being. They may become more collaborative at work and infuse the workplace or training environment with their enthusiasm.

Implications for Workplace Learning and Performance

One day while out walking, the Buddha and some of his students encountered a line of ants in their path. One of the students said, "Master, why are the ants crossing the road?" The Buddha replied, "Because they want to be happy" (Edlin, Golanty, & McCormack Brown, 2002, p. 15).

Happy and healthy OWLS learn and perform at a higher level, resulting in greater productivity and fewer benefit expenditures. McIntire (2005) suggests that organizations should have a strategic plan to ensuring the health and well-being of all their employees—a comprehensive plan that includes health and wellness programs and safety training. Organizations should also encourage OWLS to pursue leisure learning and other activities that have the potential to keep OWLS energized and expand their knowledge and skills.

Action Steps for WLP Practitioners

As a WLP practitioner, you can assist OWLS in pursuing attitudes and behaviors that contribute to their quality of life. You can encourage them to maximize their personal potential in or out of the workplace. You can work with human resources (HR) to encourage and be supportive of OWLS who seek leisurely pursuits, especially those that have a learning dimension. You can also model health, wellness, and well-being yourself and encourage your organization to implement health and wellness programs for current and future OWLS. Here are some specific steps you can take:

1. Encourage your organization to establish an organization-wide health and wellness strategy.

    LuAnn Heinen, director of the Institute on the Cost and Health Effects of Obesity within the National Business Group on Health (a nonprofit organization devoted to physical and mental wellness issues), suggests: "If employers want an engaged and motivated workforce, they might want to consider implementing a health strategy for their organization. The benefits for companies that have employees who are in good physical condition include high productivity, lower health insurance costs, less absenteeism and an all-around better quality of life" (as cited in Summerfield, 2005).

    Heinen also urges companies to support healthy habits within their workforce or expect "health-related expenses to balloon, whether through productivity or benefits" (Summerfield, 2005, n.p.). Here are some ways that you and other WLP practitioners can help your organization plan for health and fitness:

- Get all levels of the organization involved in planning and communicating the plan.

- Encourage the organization to revise employee benefits plans as needed to support the health initiative. Partner with the Human Resources (HR) department to facilitate and communicate the plan.

- Suggest specific workplace programs such as health education, disease management, fitness, and nutrition.

2. Help your organization develop and implement health education programs.

Health education puts workers in the loop when it comes to making medical decisions about their health; however, older OWLS may tend to be less informed about their health care needs, health benefits, and treatment options than younger workers (Vojta, 2003). Employers who offer health education programs can turn OWLS into informed consumers and reduce medical costs. You can and should be involved in selecting, designing, developing, implementing, and evaluating these programs.

3. Help your organization develop and implement disease management programs.

Healthy OWLS are productive workers. Disease management is one of the fastest-growing cost-containment strategies offered by health plans in the United States. Disease management uses tools such as behavior modification, education, and intervention by trained nurses to empower OWLS and other workers to "manage and improve their health more effectively" (Vojta, 2003). You have an opportunity to be involved in both the behavior modification and education components of disease management for your organizations.

4. Help your organization develop and implement fitness and nutrition programs.

   Fitness and nutrition programs can improve or maintain workers' physical and mental functions. These programs are also useful for stress reduction and overall health and wellness. You can design programs or select outside vendors to design and deliver fitness and nutrition programs to OWLS and other employees. (See Action Step 8 in Chapter Eight for more suggestions about fitness and nutrition programs.)

5. Help your organization establish a plan for dealing with on-the-job stress.

   • Use your analysis skills to determine sources of stress, then help your organization preempt much of the work-related stress through education and change management efforts or special support programs for OWLS; for example, health education, disease management, and financial planning.

   • Research vendors and suggest programs such as meditation stress therapy. Some experts say that meditation can alleviate stress and even "enhance the qualities companies need in their human capital: sharpened intuition, steely concentration, and plummeting stress levels" (Conlin, 2004a).

   • Keep up to date on what other organizations are doing in the area of health and wellness and share best practices. For example, some organizations take planned breaks from handhelds such as cell phones and PDAs. These breaks can lead to less stress and improved performance: handhelds "boost errors and stress"; they "enable everyone to generate more and more work . . . and the flywheel moves faster and faster" (Conlin, 2004b).

6. Help your organization ensure a safe environment for OWLS.

   Wise OWLS are more cautious on the job and more aware of safety issues based on past experience; however, on-the-job safety programs may still face additional challenges now that more and more OWLS populate the workforce. Vojta (2003) suggests that employers should analyze the injury patterns and risk factors of OWLS and proactively use this information to redesign jobs or workplaces or change safety equipment requirements. As a WLP practitioner you can

   • Help your organization collect the data and analyze injury patterns and risk factors for OWLS.

   • Offer to help your organization strategize how to create an OWL-safe environment.

   • Provide training for managers or employees as needed to support the safety initiative.

   • Use your knowledge of OWLS to suggest accommodations that may help OWLS stay safe. For example, you might suggest the following accommodations (Bradford, 2005):

     ○ Give individual OWLS more time to get oriented to their surroundings.

     ○ Improve the lighting in work and transit areas.

     ○ Minimize the need for heavy lifting.

     ○ Design flooring that is solid and smooth.

     ○ Reduce noise levels.

7. Encourage OWLS to seek formal or informal learning opportunities outside of the workplace and encourage your organization to offer leisure learning activities to OWLS and other employees.

8. Collaborate with external education and training organizations to expand the learning opportunities for OWLS.

In addition to more formal sources of learning like colleges and universities, there are a number of organizations who provide leisure learning opportunities that can help keep OWLS healthy, wise, and well and make them more productive on the job. Here are just a few to share with your OWLS:

- Elderhostel, an international educational network for adults, challenges and excites OWLS to new opportunities and kaleidoscopic noncredit learning experiences.

- Institutes for Learning in Retirement (IRL) are organizations of retirement-age learners who are dedicated to meeting the educational needs of their members. Most of the course offerings are college level (Manheimer, Snodgrass, & Moskow-McKenzie, 1995).

- The Older Adult Services and Information System (OASIS), a consortium between business and not-for-profit organizations, offers a variety of educational, cultural, and health and wellness programs (Lamdin & Fugate, 1997).

9. Encourage OWLS in your organization to engage in volunteerism.

    Men and women who give generously of their time and effort reap the rewards of new insight, new learning, new adventure, and personal fulfillment. Through volunteering, OWLS "are making possible a new vision of the caring society" (Lamdin & Fugate, 1997, p. 157). This will reflect well on the organization that encourages and supports them.

10. Learn how you can transform OWLS into high-performance learners and workers.

    Go on to Part Three of this book to learn how you can transform OWLS into the learners and performers your organization needs to compete in the current and future marketplace.

The first two parts of this book provided the foundation—a knowledge and theory base upon which to build future workplace learning and performance interventions for OWLS. Next, in Part Three, you can learn how to apply what you have learned and adapt action learning, team learning, real-time learning, classroom learning, and virtual learning to maximize the learning and performance of the OWLS in your workplace.

Changing patterns in workforce demographics and changing views of OWLS as workers and learners require changes in how we transform OWLS through training. Part Three talks about transformations because we view learning as "the process of creating and transforming experience into knowledge, skills, attitudes, values, beliefs, emotions" (Jarvis, 2001, p. 34), and we recognize that "a permanently changing economy compels the education and training system to change" (European Union White Paper, 1995, p. 18).

This part contains the following chapters to help you design and deliver training that will transform both OWLS and organizations:

Ten	OWLS in Action: Sharing Experience and Motivation
Eleven	OWLS on Teams: Collaborating to Learn
Twelve	OWLS on the Job: Learning with the Workflow
Thirteen	Live OWLS: Learning in the Classroom
Fourteen	Virtual OWLS: Computerized, On the Web, At a Distance, Digitized
Fifteen	Collaborating with OWLS

Each chapter is a stand-alone reference for the WLP practitioner. It includes a general discussion of a learning delivery system—action learning, classroom, and so forth—plus suggestions on how to design and implement the delivery system to transform the learning and performance of OWLS.

10

OWLS in Action: Sharing Experience and Motivation

The new buzz word around here is action learning. Employees are empowered to take action on workplace problems while working in teams which emphasize insightful questioning and reflective listening. There is a commitment to learning and developing employees.

George, age fifty-nine,
university administrator and action learning coach

GEORGE SOUNDS really enthusiastic about action learning. He knows from experience that action learning helps organizations and individuals within organizations to develop and change. It is systematic and synergistic and can provide an ideal learning and development environment for OWLS. And perhaps the most important thing is that action learning accomplishes something—it does not end until action is taken, and that is something that OWLS—especially senior and silent OWLS—really appreciate.

About Action Learning

Action learning is a versatile, real-time strategy for finding and solving current problems, addressing organizational issues, and improving organizational performance while simultaneously building individual and team competencies (Rothwell, 1999). The goal of action learners is to solve real problems "while at the same time focusing on what they are learning and how they are learning it and how their learning can benefit each group member and the organization as a whole" (Marquardt, 1999, p. 4). It is both a process and a program:

- Action learners learn by doing; for example, they perform group and individual tasks such as research, reflection, problem solving, and decision making.

- Action learning is a program, not a one-time activity, whether the group meets on a regular basis to learn and develop their leadership skills or meets whenever a problem arises.

Action Learning Is Based on Experiential Learning

Experiential learning is "a process for drawing learning from experience" (Dick, 1997, n.p.). In a traditional example of experiential learning, the trainer or facilitator develops a case study and asks the learners to solve a problem, resolve an issue, initiate change, and so forth, based on the information in the case study and their own past and current experiences. An alternative way to set up an experiential learning activity is for the trainer or facilitator to provide a problem-solving process and ask the learners to provide the *case study* from their experience. In either case, the case study relates to the specific content of the training program or unit.

Dick (1997, n.p.) explains it this way: "You might say that experiential learning is the basis for the learning component of both action learning and action research." All three are cyclic, involve action and reflection on that action, and have learning as one of their goals. For example, action learning is a form of experiential learning that focuses on a real-time problem or situation instead of a case study, and is not related to specific training content.

Action Learning Requires Action

Many experts stress that not all active learning is action learning; for example, quality circles, task forces, outdoor learning programs, or business games are not true action learning unless they include both reflection and action (Van Tiem, Moseley, & Dessinger, 2001; Dixon, 1998). However, Thiagi does include action learning in his list of 25 "games people play" (Thiagarajian, as cited in Salopek & Kesting, 1999, pp. 32–33), and he indicates that games may be useful as action learning strategies.

Action Learning Is Broad in Scope

Action learning is appropriate for any business, industry, or service sector at any level in the organization. Rothwell (1999, p. 81) writes: "The scope of what action leaning teams can do is limited only by the imagination and creativity of team members and by the constraints imposed on the team as they begin addressing the problem or issue assigned to them." Marquardt (1999) calls action learning capable, flexible, and resilient, and believes it can adapt to and affect paradigm shifts "in truly creative and effective ways" (p. 18).

In general, "Action learning has the unique and inherent capability of being applied simultaneously to the five most important needs facing organizations today" (Marquardt, 1999, p. 5). These needs are problem solving, organizational learning, team building, leadership development, and professional growth and career development.

Action Learning Has Six Components

The five organizational needs just listed are embedded in the six basic components or elements of successful action learning—group, commitment, problem, process, resolution, and follow-up:

1. Group—a diverse group or team with a variety of viewpoints and perspectives; the members should have the knowledge, skills, and power to resolve the problem or issue and also be able to profit personally from the experience of resolving the problem or issue

2. Commitment—a continuing commitment to learning as well as action by the members of the action learning team and an equally strong commitment from top executives within the organization to be involved in and support action learning

3. Problem—a real, significant problem or issue that needs resolution

4. Process—basic steps of Focus–Clarify–Reflect–Resolve–Act

5. Resolution—a solution to the problem or issue that involves taking appropriate action

6. Follow-up—individual, team, and organizational feedback on both the solution to the problem or issue and the development of action team members

All six components must be in place to achieve a successful action learning experience and meet the needs of the individual participants and the organization.

One optional component is a facilitator—a trained internal or external person who guides and supports the members as they work through the process. Action learning groups may or may not use a facilitator. The decision may be influenced by whether the group prefers an analytical or creative approach to active learning.

Action Learning Is Analytical or Creative

There are two basic approaches to action learning: analytical and creative. The *analytical approach* is based on traditional problem-solving process models, which include identifying the problem, evaluating alternative solutions, planning the chosen solution, and implementing the plan. It is structured and formal even when organizations customize a problem-solving model for internal use or to meet quality-management or certification guidelines.

The creative approach forces the participants to think outside of the box to identify both the problem and the solution. For example, Rothwell (1999) suggests four creativity-enhancing techniques for action learning: brainstorming, magnification, minification, and random response:

- Brainstorming—the team generates possible causes and generates possible solutions; follow-up activities include reviewing and prioritizing the causes and solutions generated through brainstorming.

- Magnification—the team exaggerates the importance and cause before troubleshooting the cause.

- Minification—the team minimizes the importance of the problem and ridicules the causes before troubleshooting the problem.

- Random Response—two team subgroups go through several rounds in which one group states the problem or cause, the second group creates a completely unrelated word of phrase, and the original group tries to fit the random response to the problem.

PST 10.1 provides a "stepshot" or step-by-step view of each approach to help WLP practitioners select the most appropriate approach to resolve an issue or problem, given the organizational climate and the available resources. The next section of this chapter will discuss ways to ensure that no matter what approach the WLP practitioner selects, action learning becomes a useful learning delivery system for transforming OWLS.

PST 10.1. How to Select the Most Appropriate Action Learning Approach.

Purpose: To determine whether analytical or creative action learning is most appropriate for this action learning experience

Timing: Complete this form after you have been briefed on the purpose of the action learning experience and have generated a potential list of participants.

Instructions: The steps required to conduct an analytical and a creative action learning experience are listed in the table that follows. Review the steps and ask yourself the following questions:

1. Do we have the time-money-talent required for this action learning method?
2. Do we have the organizational support required for this action learning method?
3. Which method is best suited to the purpose of this action learning experience?
4. Are there steps in either method that we can change or delete to make the method more suitable without negatively affecting the outcome?
5. Other . . .

Analytical	Creative
1. Define the problem or issue.	1. Gather information.
2. Investigate the problem or issue.	2. Apply creativity-enhancing techniques.
3. Isolate causes of problem or variables affecting issue.	3. Reach new conclusions; creatively reframe problem or issue.
4. Propose solutions.	4. Propose solutions.
5. Experiment with solutions (prototypes, scenarios, simulations, and so forth).	5. Apply creativity-enhancing techniques.
6. Modify solutions as needed.	6. Reach new conclusions about the solution.
7. Try out solutions.	7. Experiment with reframed solutions.
8. Draw conclusions.	8. Modify the solutions.
9. Report to stakeholders.	9. Try out new solutions.
	10. Draw conclusions.
	11. Report to stakeholders.

About OWLS and Action Learning

The positive connection between action learning and OWLS is experience and motivation. OWLS can and do enhance the action learning process with their past experiences. They are motivated to participate in action learning because of its immediate, real-life relevance. Action learning in turn may trigger the OWLS' penchant for mentoring and coaching. All in all, OWLS and action learning can be a very good fit; however, OWLS may react to aspects of action learning in different ways, depending in part on the ages and stages at which they encounter it.

Some OWLS May Prefer Analytical Approaches

OWLS from Mid-Old to Oldest are often familiar with a structured approach to problem solving, so analytical action learning does not take them outside of their comfort range. On the other hand, these OWLS may or may not be comfortable with creative action learning techniques such as the ones suggested by Rothwell (1999) earlier in this chapter. Silent OWLS especially may be too cautious and unadventurous to think outside the box.

Certain Activities May Encourage OWLS to Act

OWLS generally have the experience to participate in action learning, and the motivation to get things done right. However, action learning "takes group members outside their areas of expertise and asks them to work on unfamiliar problems" (Van Tiem, Moseley, & Dessinger, 2001, p. 39). OWLS may fail to see the relevancy of the action learning activities or may find they are not able to respond as quickly as younger team members.

A trained facilitator—the optional component of action learning that we discussed earlier in this chapter—may be able to raise the comfort level of OWLS during action learning activities. In addition, some typical experiential learning activities may help OWLS tune in to their feelings; come to grips with their reactions to workplace issues, ideas, and practices; and maximize their workplace learning and performance. These commonly used activities include in-basket assignments, research, field trips, teaching, and task forces (Gomez-Mejia, Balkin, & Cardy, 2001; Silberman, 1998).

OWLS Can Handle In-Basket Issues. In-basket assignments include typical memos, messages, reports, and so on that might be found in a manager's in-basket. OWLS who are playing a role handle issues as they see fit. They are judged on their prioritizing ability, their creativeness, the quality of their decision making, and their responsiveness to action.

OWLS Can Research Issues. Assuming that time and data availability are not barriers, asking OWLS to conduct research and present their findings individually or in teams is a valuable form of workplace learning. OWLS not only learn from their colleagues but also gain valuable insight into the new language of work.

OWLS Can Conduct Field Trips. A third action learning project that engages OWLS is field trips to observe real-life settings relevant to the problem or issue that needs resolution. Observers develop a checklist of specific items they should look for in the setting and use the checklist as they interview and observe—an organizing strategy that many OWLS appreciate. The observers then share their questions, their insight, and their experiences with team members, and, in the case of OWL-observers, how the field trip aligned with their own experience both past and current.

OWLS Can Teach Others. Teaching projects allow OWLS to share their knowledge, experience, and sense of history with others. They can also share the heuristics or rules of thumb they have acquired over the years and apply them to current facts, skills, policies, procedures, and practices. This is a chance for OWLS to share their accomplishments, and it can minimize the potential for generational differences that affect clear thinking and active learning.

OWLS Can Work on Task Forces. Finally, task-force projects can give OWLS confidence in their ability to replicate workplace tasks. OWLS work with other team members to generate a plan or an outcome measure that addresses efficiency, effectiveness, impact, and value. If this type of activity is to be considered true action learning, OWLS must take an active part in the implementation as well as the planning.

Benefits of Action Learning

OWLS must be able to contribute to and benefit from the action learning teams. At the same time, OWLS need to feel motivated to join and participate in an effort that may take them out of their comfort zone. And finally, action learning must benefit the organization; it must be a value-added activity.

OWLS Benefit Action Learning Teams

Action learning team members must possess knowledge, skill, attitudes, or expertise that will help the team address the issue, frame and solve the problem, and formulate a goal or vision. OWLS are certainly an asset in the knowledge, skill, and expertise area. They can share both knowledge and know-how, and may have firsthand experience with the historical background of the problem or issue. They may also have experience in team roles such as leader, scribe, messenger, or timekeeper.

As for attitudes, OWLS tend to be independent and conscientious. They have a strong work ethic and want to do quality work that will benefit the organization.

Action Learning Benefits OWLS

Action learning team members should also be able to "benefit from the development experience likely to result from work on the team" (Rothwell, 1999, p. 46). Some of the benefits that could accrue from participation in the action learning experience include broad-based awareness of issues and concerns, new knowledge and skill related to the specific problem area and to the action learning process, extension of the participant's network within the organization, and the positive visibility that results from resolving the problem.

No matter how you approach it, action learning can benefit OWLS. In the context of action learning, OWLS can

- Develop confidence, trust, and a sense of being valued
- Share generational insights and differences
- Capitalize on new, invigorating learning

- Use their wealth of experience to solve workplace learning and performance issues

- Demonstrate their acumen as valuable employees

- Provide a steady, calming force within a team

- Teach, through example, ethical principles that should permeate workplace environments

- Communicate through word and action the fun and joy of growing older

There are three major benefits that motivate OWLS to participate in action learning team activities.

Increased Self-Esteem. Action learning can increase self-esteem in OWLS. When teammates and the organization acknowledge the knowledge, skill, experience, and wisdom that OWLS bring to the action learning process, this can make OWLS feel needed and valued.

Getting Things Done. Some OWLS are motivated to participate because action learning appeals to their desire to resolve issues or problems that keep them from "getting things done." These are usually the Senior or Silent OWLS who are work-centric and want to do it right.

New Competencies. OWLS may also gain new competencies from immersion in the action learning process itself or from gaining new perspectives and information related to the problem or issue. Taking a broad look at the term *competency* as a combination of knowledge, skill, attitude, motivation, and personality traits, participation in action learning activities can build a number of situational or contextual competencies (Rothwell, 1999). Situational competencies are direct outcomes of the experience of action learning; contextual competencies are by-products of action learning.

How highly OWLS value new competencies is sometimes determined by factors such as whether they want to be or need to be in the workforce, whether their specific job or work requires certification, and even to what degree they value work over life. Asking OWLS to make a commitment to increase their competencies through action learning may help OWLS focus on what they personally want to achieve as action learning team members. This may also motivate them to become more committed to the action learning process and outcomes.

PST 10.2 provides a form that OWLS can use to record the competencies they would like to acquire during a specific action learning experience. At the end of the action learning experience OWLS can revisit the form and determine which competencies were achieved and which may still require further effort.

PST 10.2. Action Learning Participant Action Plan.

Purpose: To establish, monitor, and evaluate the competencies you want to build during this action learning experience

Timing: Complete this form after you have been briefed on the purpose and process of the action learning experience you are about to begin.

Instructions: On your own, or working with a supervisor or team leader, proceed as follows:

1. Fill in your name.

2. Write a brief statement to identify the problem or issue your team will focus on during this action learning experience.

3. List the competencies you want to build as a result of the action learning experience. Here are some examples:

   - Knowledge—learn about the safety factors involved in a new manufacturing process.

   - Skill—learn how to use the new features on a piece of equipment.

   - Motivation—learn to motivate team members to achieve higher levels of performance.

   - Attitude—learn to understand and accept generational differences in the workplace.

   - Personality—learn how to manage Gen Y workers.

4. Review the list during or after the action learning experience and modify as needed.

5. Develop an action plan: What are you going to do with the list?

6. Plan for follow-up on the action you have planned.

7. Optional: discuss the outcomes with your supervisor, team leader, or team members.

PST 10.2. Action Learning Participant Action Plan, *Continued*.

Participant:

Problem or Issue Statement for this Action Learning Experience

As a result of my participation in this action learning activity, I will develop the following competencies:

Knowledge:

Skills:

Motivation:

Attitude:

Personality:

Action Learning Benefits Organizations

Action learning benefits organizations because it develops leaders and solves real business issues at the same time. A variety of companies have found action learning also helped them adapt to and accelerate change and promote continuous learning. Among the companies who use action learning are Accenture (formerly Anderson Consulting), Ameritech, AT&T, Boeing, Deutsche Bank, Dow, General Electric, General Motors, Novartis, and Whirlpool (Dilworth, 1998).

General Electric boasts of using action learning longer than any other company to solve problems and to develop skills in team building, change management, dispute resolution, coaching, and facilitation. General Electric action groups have been successful in improving morale by directly involving employees in decision making, using dialogue to increase staff trust, saluting management that embraces risk-taking philosophy, encouraging accountability at appropriate levels, and minimizing leadership control (Marquardt, 2004).

Selecting OWLS for Action Learning Teams

Careful selection of team members can also increase the versatility and raise the success factor of an action learning group. PST 10.3 suggests a general list of criteria for selecting action learning team members that applies to all potential team members, including OWLS. When selecting OWLS, the WLP practitioner should focus on how the team, the organization, and the OWLS could benefit from the inclusion of OWLS.

PST 10.3. Checklist for Selecting Action Learning Team Members.

Purpose: To determine whether a potential participant meets the criteria for participating in this action learning experience

Timing: Complete this form after you have been briefed on the purpose and process of the action learning experience and are generating a list of participants.

Instructions:

1. Fill in the name of the potential participant.

2. Check (✓) the boxes next to the criteria that best fit the participant.

3. Select the participants that will best match the action learning team purpose and process.

Potential Participant:

1. Possesses the know-how needed to analyze and solve the selected problem:

   ☐ a. Knowledge

   ☐ b. Skill

   ☐ c. Attitudes

   ☐ d. Expertise

   ☐ e. Other:

2. Could help the team to:

   ☐ a. Address the issue

   ☐ b. Frame the problem

   ☐ c. Solve the problem

   ☐ d. Formulate a goal or vision

   ☐ e. Other (for example, coaching or mentoring):

3. Could benefit from development in the area upon which the team will focus:

   ☐ a. Increased broad-based awareness

   ☐ b. Extended networking opportunity

   ☐ c. New knowledge, skill, expertise

   ☐ d. Greater visibility

   ☐ e. Other (specific to the problem focus or action learning process):

4. Comments:

Workplace Application: Welcoming OWLS to the Action Learning Team

All team members, even experienced action learners, need some type of orientation when they are selected for a new action learning team. Here is an example of how one multigenerational company conducts their action learning orientation.

Company A is an international utility company. Action learning is an integral part of the company's strategy for developing new and experienced leaders while solving problems related to their success in a global economy. Presently, many of their leaders are OWLS who may retire in the next five to twenty years. Most of their employees belong to Gen X and Gen Y and are highly skilled technicians or engineers. The action learning teams are made up of company leaders who are predominantly OWLS, engineers whose numbers are a combination of OWLS and Gen Xers, and skilled technicians who are from Gen X and Gen Y.

The first part of the orientation gives team members time to meet and mingle with each other. During this part of the orientation the team leader facilitates activities that help team members of all generations recognize the individual strengths each person brings to the action learning experience, and the competencies each participant hopes to develop as a result of the experience.

The action team leader also explains the specific purpose of the action learning experience and the strategies the team will use to achieve the purpose. Outcomes and deliverables are clearly defined. If some participants are not familiar with the problem solving or other strategies that the team will use, there are online Microsoft PowerPoint or video presentations available that describe why and how each strategy will be conducted. The orientation usually includes a chance to participate in at least one problem-solving activity. The online material blends video, auditory, and print materials that are designed to accommodate older eyes and ears. Accessibility and assistive technologies are available on all company computers if needed.

Company A has found that many OWLS are uneasy when they venture into new, uncharted territory. Sometimes a voyage of discovery is fun and interesting, but more often than not it is merely frustrating. OWLS may need continuing support and encouragement to make action learning a successful learning and performance experience. They need to focus and spend their energy on solving the problem or issue, not on the process for solving it. Company A pretrains OWLS and other team members to use the various techniques and tools they need to support the action learning activities for a particular action learning experience. The company has also established a follow-up system of coaches of all ages to monitor the progress of new OWLS-in-action and provide support and encouragement as needed. Once new OWLS become adept at action learning, they are often recruited to become coaches for other OWLS who are just beginning their action learning journey.

ADDITIONAL RESOURCES ON ACTION LEARNING

Read Chapter Eleven on team learning. The second workplace application— *Systematic, Experiential Design for Multigenerational Workflow Team Training in a Retail Environment*—is a combination of workflow team learning and action learning.

Also use the following as practical resources:

Rothwell, W. J. (1999). *The action learning guidebook: A real-time strategy for problem solving, training, design, and employee development.* San Francisco: Pfeiffer.

Rothwell's book contains background information on action learning and functional approaches to implementing action learning, plus examples and performance support tools (PST) to help learning and performance professionals design, facilitate, and manage action learning.

Marquardt, M. J. (2004, June). Harnessing the power of action learning. *Training and Development, 58*(6), 4, 26–32.

This article is an update on action learning and how to use it in today's workplace.

Silberman, M. (1998). *Active training: A handbook of techniques, designs, case examples, and tips* (2nd ed.). San Francisco: Pfeiffer.

This book provides helpful "how-to" information about various action learning activities including in-basket assignments, research, field trips, teaching, and task forces.

11

OWLS on Teams: Collaborating to Learn

Team learning contributes to the success of an organization. Collaboration is in and the individual problem solver, the Lone Ranger type, is out. A team functions well when each individual contributes. I believe each individual acts as a catalyst to other members.

Dennis, age sixty-eight, theater set designer

DENNIS IS an individualist and a natural collaborator, yet he belongs to the Silent generation of OWLS who tend to be independent, cautious types—individual problem solvers rather than team players. All through this book we have said that OWLS are not all alike. Planning learning experiences for OWLS means planning for almost four different generations and learners who could span sixty years of experience. Planning team learning is an even greater challenge because OWLS may or may not be comfortable with the highly collaborative nature of this increasingly popular learning strategy.

About Team Learning

Team learning is "the process of aligning and developing the capacity of a team to create the results its members truly desire" (Senge, 1990. p. 236); it is also a formal or informal learning strategy used to "organize and direct learning experiences" and provide "a context for the cross development of individuals and group learning" (Rothwell, 2002, p. 33). All team learning isn't the same: work team members in a bookstore gather in aisle three for fifteen minutes to learn about the latest children's book promotion; virtual collaborative in which geographically dispersed teams of engineers and scientists conduct experiments; managers participate in a literally off-the-wall, team-building cliff climb.

Teaming Up to Learn Is Not a New Concept

According to Cyril Houle, former professor emeritus at the University of Chicago, "all groups are learning groups in the sense that their members are constantly influenced by interaction with one another" even when learning is not a primary goal (Houle, 1996, p. 138). Teaming up to learn is a particularly relevant strategy for today's workplace. As more workplaces integrate work and learning in real time (see Chapter Twelve), "individuals will look to 'natural family groups'—such as their work groups or teams—as a natural grounding place and context for learning experiences" (Rothwell, 2002, p. 33).

Team Learning Is Collaborative

Collaborative learning is different from individual learning: "The individual learning environment engages the learner and provides a high degree of tailored interaction. Collaborative learning environments teach teamwork and group problem solving" (Goldin, Venneri, & Noor, n.p.). Team learning encourages and thrives on collaboration; the success of a learning team depends on the cooperation of its members. Team facilitators need to develop "cooperative confidence" among all the team members: "one uncooperative person can damage the motivation of even the most capable team" (Clark, 2006, p. 493).

Teams Learn at Work

In the context of the workplace, workers and other stakeholders join together formally or informally to share, discover, and grow the knowledge and skills they will need to improve learning and performance. Team learning may include old and new learning content, lessons learned and lessons to learn. In today's workplace, team learning may provide an almost seamless blend of work and learning.

Team learning groups may be set up informally by the members or formally by an organization or institution. In either case, team learning acknowledges that OWLS and other adult learners pursue learning for social reasons as well as for a love of knowledge or to achieve life or work-related goals (Houle, 1996; Tough, 1979).

Team learning activities are usually highly interactive; for example, games, role playing, team discussions, and simulations. The success of team learning is related to the quality of the interactions and relationships among the team members (Houle, 1996). This is why most team learning begins—or should begin—with team building activities—and that may mean "going out to play."

Teams Learn at Play

Organizations sometimes send teams off-site for a more "play-full" learning experience. Sometimes the off-site experience is a reward for high performance; more often the purpose is team building.

Team building is usually approached as a learning activity and a learning motivator. The purpose of team building is to uncover individual talents that group members may not know they possess; establish which team members will fill the various team roles—leader, scribe, timekeeper, messenger, and so forth—and help members learn how to implement their roles, learn camaraderie and trust, and bond with each other.

Team building learning activities may be as simple as individual coaching or mentoring before or during team sessions, or as complex as an off-site bungee jumping or crime scene investigation experience. They may be highly physical and active or cerebral and creative.

McDonnell (2005) reports that "corporate trainers are starting to focus more on creative and cerebral exercises than intense and physically demanding challenges" (p. C7). The new emphasis is on cooking contests, forming a band of percussion instruments, staging plays or improvisations, or even less physical outdoor activities such as sailing and crime scene investigating. These activities tend to focus on problem solving and critical thinking rather than coaching and leadership skills.

Teams Learn Virtually

The new, global organization may be too far-flung to allow team learners to occupy the same time and space, and new economic realities may preclude off-site learning experiences. In addition, many employees work part or flex time; some work at home; others are retired OWLS who work on an as-needed basis as consultants. Virtual learning teams may be the future of team learning. For example, NASA reports that "[t]echnology is being developed that will let scientific and engineering team members follow, and interact with, distant physical experiments, while running real-time simulations of their own" (Goldin, Venneri, & Noor, n.p.).

Building learning teams whose members are not physically present at one time and in one place is becoming a real challenge for the team-oriented workplace. Virtual teams of any type rely extensively on the use of technologies such as online email and file transfer; telephone, video, or online conferencing; instant messaging, chat room, and bulletin board technology; and so forth. Team members must be technically proficient as well as able and willing to learn without face-to-face interaction with other team members.

Team Learning Benefits Everyone

Peter Senge (1990, p. 239) felt that the potential of collaborative learning was "staggering": "we can be more insightful, more intelligent than we can possibly be individually. The IQ of the team can, potentially, be much greater than the IQ of the individual."

Team learning benefits both the team members and the organization. The internationally known performance and instructional technologist Thiagarajian (1999) points out the following instructional benefits of team learning:

- Facilitates holistic rather than linear learning
- Facilitates transfer of training
- Forces learner interaction
- Makes learning more interesting
- Provides specific feedback (p. 531)

Organizational learning also benefits from team learning. The spirit of cooperation and trust, as well as the knowledge and skill that is generated within learning teams, spread to other areas of the organization. As Senge (1990) tells us, "Team learning is vital because teams, not individuals, are the fundamental learning unit in modern organization" (p. 10) and "[i]ndividuals learn all the time and yet there is no organizational learning. But if teams learn, they become a microcosm for learning throughout the organization" (p. 236). And when it comes to virtual team learning, Goldin, Venneri, and Noor predict that "[t]he new learning environments will significantly increase creativity and knowledge, dissolve rigid cultural boundaries among teams, and create high-performance knowledge teams that enhance the global performance of diverse organizations" (n.p.).

About OWLS as Team Learners

OWLS will continue to be an integral part of the twenty-first-century workplace and an integral part of both formal and informal team learning activities. WLP practitioners need to recognize the potential weaknesses of OWLS as learning team members and adjust team learning activities to maximize the team learning and performance strengths of OWLS. Perhaps the best way to begin looking at OWLS as team learners is to use accepted team learner competencies as a filter.

OWLS May Need Team-Learner Competencies

Senge (1990), Rothwell (2002), Gagne and Medsker (1996), and others discuss special competencies that individuals should possess in order to be active and effective team learners. Some experts feel that there may be generational gaps when it comes to team-learner competencies. For example, Carolyn

Martin and Bruce Tulgan, nationally known authors and consultants on how to manage multigenerational workplaces, suggest that when it comes to team learning competencies, Gen Y workers tend to be collaborative, team-oriented, and good communicators. On the other hand, Boomer OWLS are more comfortable in top-down situations in which they are at the top, and Silent OWLS tend to avoid highly collaborative or interactive learning (Martin & Tulgan, 2001).

WLP practitioners, designers of team learning activities, and team learning facilitators need to be able to identify team learning competencies and help individual learners develop specific competencies as needed. PST 11.1 is a checklist of team learner competencies that WLP practitioners can use to assess the competencies of team learners, whether they are OWLS or younger workers.

PST 11.1. Checklist of Team Learner Competencies.

Purpose: To assess or evaluate the team learning competencies of OWLS or younger worker-learners

Instructions: You or the team leader can use the checklist to record observations of the learners during a team learning session; or, ask the team members to use the checklist as a self-assessment. Then, share the results with the team learners; help the team learners develop their areas of weakness, and plan team learning activities to maximize the strengths of all the team members.

Name: _____

☐ 1. Enjoys participating in workplace learning groups

☐ 2. Participates actively in workplace learning groups

☐ 3. Participates effectively in workplace learning groups

☐ 4. Is able to use team learning strategies to formulate, communicate, and test ideas generated by self and others:

    ☐ a. Brainstorming

    ☐ b. Dialogue

    ☐ c. Problem solving

    ☐ d. Other:

    ☐ e. Other:

☐ 5. Has a cooperative attitude when working with others; for example:

    ☐ a. Encourages other team members to participate

    ☐ b. Readily accepts tasks and assignments

    ☐ c. Adheres to the agenda and rules of the team

    ☐ d. Does not try to dominate the discussion

    ☐ e. Does not personally attack other team members

    ☐ f. Does not distract other team members

    ☐ g. Other:

Team Building Activities May Challenge OWLS

Extremely challenging and physically demanding team building activities may not be suitable or safe for some OWLS. Activities that require good reaction time, vision, strength, or dexterity may put OWLS at risk or stress them to the point of doing more harm than good. Training designers need to develop less physically demanding activities or allow for various levels of participation; for example, bungee jumper, coach, equipment manager, time or record keeper, and so forth.

The trend toward cerebral-creative activities for team building also allows OWLS to participate in team building activities more fully and on a more equal footing with younger team learners. However, even cerebral-creative activities such as disaster or survival simulations or cooking contests may need to be adapted to the physiological or cognitive challenges faced by some OWLS. OWLS may need more time, larger type size in printed material, auditory and visual prompts, a sous-chef to lift heavy pans or stir ingredients, and so forth. PST 11.2 is a guide to help WLP practitioners select new or evaluate existing team building activities for OWLS.

PST 11.2. How to Select or Evaluate Team Building Activities for OWLS.

Purpose: To select or evaluate team building activities that are OWL-friendly or to evaluate team building activities from an OWL-perspective, or both

Instructions: Check the items that are *true* for this team building activity. A truly OWL-friendly activity will have all or most of the items checked.

Team Building Activity: _____

Goals and Objectives:

☐ 1. Achieve a strategic business goal(s)

☐ 2. Provide OWLS with objectives that . . .

    ☐ a. Are clearly stated

    ☐ b. Are "up front" rather than "to be discovered as you go"

    ☐ c. Are relevant to their current work needs

    ☐ d. Are immediately applicable on the job

    ☐ e. Allow OWLS to add team-related personal objectives

Real Work Life Application

☐ 1. Team building activities clearly relate to the OWLS' situations in the workplace.

☐ 2. Team building activities will be useful for OWLS to use in future team activities.

Activity Design

☐ 1. Will *not* put OWLS at an age-related disadvantage in relation to other participants

☐ 2. Will *not* put OWLS "at risk" from physical or emotional stress

☐ 3. Will provide options for various levels of participation

☐ 4. Will let OWLS have some fun while they are learning

☐ 5. Will increase the OWLS' sense of being valued by the organization

☐ 6. Includes the following design elements to reinforce and support learning:

    ☐ a. OWL-friendly print, visual, and auditory learning support materials

    ☐ b. Coaching

    ☐ c. Feedback

    ☐ d. Debriefing session(s)

    ☐ e. Other . . .

Virtual Team Learning May Challenge OWLS

Virtual team learning is a growing phenomenon. Many OWLS appreciate the fact that virtual team learning allows them to work at home, maintain a flexible schedule in the workplace, or literally learn while doing. These OWLS will participate with enthusiasm and commitment.

However, some OWLS may not possess the knowledge and skill to use sophisticated virtual communication technologies. WLP practitioners will need to provide training, performance support tools, and coaching for OWLS who are not up-to-date on virtual learning technology. In addition, team learning designers should strike a balance between the technical bells and whistles that Generation Y learners love and expect and the more direct approach that appeals to many OWLS.

Some Old to Oldest OWLS may also prefer face-to-face contact with team members, and feel uncomfortable working and learning with people they never meet in person. Preparing OWLS in advance for the social realities of virtual learning can put OWLS at ease and also benefit the whole team. Team learning designers may do well to focus on the analogy that membership in a virtual learning team is like "interacting with the imaginary friends of childhood" (Thiagarajan, 1999, p. 527) and set aside time for team members to get acquainted at the beginning of each new team learning experience.

OWLS may also respond positively to the anonymity of virtual team learning. Thiagarajan (1999) suggests that the reality or perception of anonymity may be one of the benefits of virtual team learning: "You can fail with dignity in computer simulations or interpersonal confrontations . . . In chat rooms you can reveal your ignorance in total anonymity" (p. 525). Virtual team learning designers should make sure that anonymity is built into learning experiences.

(For more on the topic of virtual OWLS, see Chapter Fourteen of this book.)

Generational Difference May Impact Team Learning

There are differences between eighteen- to twenty-nine-year-old Gen Y worker-learners and OWLS aged forty and older in terms of both learning and communicating. Novicevic and Buckley (2001) found that "[t]his new generation of employees is filled with independent self-learners who are skillful and proactive communicators. They are different from the 40+ dependent learners who are more reflective and reactive learners and communicators" (p. 127).

Zemke, Raines, and Filipczak (2000, p. 53) tell us that all generations have participated on teams—the difference is the type and structure of the team:

- Many Senior OWLS participated in "huge" teams where there was a "strong central authority figure."
- Boomer OWLS participated in "community sized" teams with "shared leadership."
- Gen X OWLS participated in small virtual teams "with no defined leadership."
- Gen Y worker-learners will "form huge, civic minded teams" where "no one gets left behind."

Today's tendency toward small, virtual learning teams may necessitate a leap of faith for Senior or Boomer OWLS and be very appealing to Gen X and Gen Y worker-learners.

Gen Y Team Members Prefer Team Learning. Gen Y worker-learners constantly seek to update their skills and find team learning an efficient way to accomplish this: "Team-based learning allows them to be relational, connected, interdependent, and informal, while each person defines her/his role on the team" (Novicevic & Buckley, 2001, p. 127). OWLS may not be comfortable with team learning. They may feel "threatened" by the mental nimbleness and communication skills of younger team members. OWLS may feel that their experience is not valued and their tendency toward reflection makes them appear slow to grasp new concepts.

OWLS Bring History to Team Learning. The younger employees are grounded in the here and now and do not have the historical perspective to make informed decisions. OWLS—with their experience, tendency toward reflection, and loyalty to the organization—can help younger team learners see the big picture by adding historical or conceptual knowledge to the younger learners' current or experiential knowledge. OWLS can also balance the younger workers' "cool fantasy subculture" with their "plain reality subculture" (Novicevic & Buckley, 2001, pp. 127–128).

Implications for Workplace Learning and Performance
Team Learning Should be Accommodating

Workplace team learning should be universally accommodating—all workers should be able to participate. PST 11.3 lists some suggestions for designing, delivering, or evaluating team learning activities that are OWL-friendly.

PST 11.3. Suggestions for Designing, Delivering, and Evaluating OWL-Friendly Team Learning.

Purpose: To provide guidelines for designing, delivering, or evaluating OWL-friendly team learning

Instructions: Use this PST as a list of general suggestions for designing, developing, and delivering team learning that is OWL-friendly or as a set of criteria for evaluating existing team learning materials or activities.

☐ 1. Present instructions and other learning material in print *and* verbally to accommodate OWLS with vision or hearing difficulties.

☐ 2. Chunk content and adjust the length of activities to accommodate OWLS who cannot sit, stand, or stay in the area for long periods of time.

☐ 3. Avoid activities that require strength and physical dexterity, if possible.

☐ 4. When extreme physical activity is involved, provide an option for participants to function in leadership or support roles such as coach, scorekeeper, equipment manager, and so forth.

☐ 5. Adjust the environment if necessary—light, temperature, room setup, and so forth.

☐ 6. Avoid timed tasks, if possible.

☐ 7. Use verbal and printed advance organizers and other strategies to help OWLS focus and stay focused on current learning content and tasks.

☐ 8. Build mentoring, coaching, and feedback components into team learning activities.

☐ 9. Include opportunities for OWLS to share their knowledge, skill, and experience.

☐ 10. Value the contribution of OWLS and celebrate their successes.

☐ 11. Repeat or rephrase what OWLS say or help them "find the right words" if necessary.

☐ 12. Celebrate OWLness whenever possible.

Team Learning Should Be Structured

Even when team learning is accommodating, it may cause Senior OWLS and even Boomer OWLS some concern because of a "new sense of equality throughout the team" (Zemke, Raines, & Filipczak, 2000, p. 52). In addition, learning teams like other teams in today's workplace have a tendency to move away from strong, central leadership and embrace continual change. Senior and Boomer OWLS may adapt to these less structured learning teams; however, they will not put their hearts and souls into it: "Their adaptations are of behavior, not attitude or heart" (Zemke, Raines, & Filipczak, 2000, p. 54).

Workplace Application 1: Selecting Learning Content for a Multigenerational Retail Learning Teams

Recently, a national high-end department store chain changed hands. The new owners, who also owned five other department store chains, wanted to align the customer service policies and practices of all the chains and create a national, cross-chain customer service package. The new package would replace policies and practices that had been in existence since the early 1920s.

Once the customer service package was designed, the WLP practitioners needed to develop a training program for department managers, customer service representatives, sales representatives, and administrative staff. The purpose of the training program was to build awareness of and support for the new customer service package and train employees to implement the package with customers. One desired outcome was increased customer satisfaction; another desired outcome was cost savings due to changes in return policies, store brand warranties, and so forth.

The training designers decided to deliver the training through local cross-functional learning teams to save training costs and provide opportunities for interactive learning and an ongoing performance support system once the new policies and practices were implemented. The teams would reflect the multigenerational retail workplace in which the stores operated.

Each team could potentially be composed of worker-learners aged eighteen to seventy. This meant that the training designers were faced with developing team training strategies and content for multigenerational teams that could span four generations (Gen Y, Gen X, Boomers, and Silents) or fifty-two years or four age ranges—younger worker-learners and Young, Mid-Old, and Old OWLS.

The designers wanted the teams to be highly interactive; for example, they wanted the teams to role play situations in which customers would be less than delighted with the new service package, then brainstorm ways to overcome customer dissatisfaction. The designers also needed to know what content to include in the training.

One of the training designers went to a local professional association workshop on generational differences among learners. She shared what she learned at the workshop with the other two designers.

Armed with a better understanding of their training audience, the designers decided to develop a performance support tool to help them determine how to focus or "spin" the training content—new policies and procedures—to match the learning preferences of the multigenerational learning teams. PST 11.4 is the result.

PST 11.4. New Policies and Procedures Training: Let Generations-Based Learning Preferences Help Guide Content Selection.

Purpose: To help instructional designers and team learning facilitators select learning content for multigenerational teams when the topic is new policies and procedures

Instructions: Use the questions in the PST to help keep you focused on generational learning preferences—what OWLS and younger learners want to know—as you select "need to know" versus "nice to know" content for multigenerational learning teams.

When it comes to content, forty-plus OWLS may want to know . . .	When it comes to content, twenty-plus worker-learners may want to know . . .
What is the work process?	What are the work results?
What is the effect on employees?	What is the effect on the job?
Will it require new hires?	How many new hires will it require?
How much will it cost?	How much growth will it create?
Will it meet organizational or industry standards?	Will it satisfy the customer?
How is it different from the old system?	What do I need to know and do that's new?
What's in it for me and the organization?	What's in it for me?
Other:	Other:

Workplace Application 2: A Systematic, Experiential Design for Multigenerational Workflow Team Training in a Retail Environment

A chain of bookstores hires a truly multigenerational staff of sales associates and department managers. The majority of the staff are either Senior or Silent OWLS or Gen Y, with a few Boomer OWLS and occasional Gen Xers thrown into the mix.

The chain strongly believes in training all their employees. The main topics are customer service, marketing, new product training, and sales. There are no rewards or incentives tied to training results; however, employee turnover is low and morale is high. Their employees love books, enjoy learning about books, and want to learn new ways to build a customer base of fellow book lovers.

The general strategy is for work teams of five or six employees to "meet in aisle three" once or twice a week for a fifteen-minute training session before the doors open to customers. Each session is systematically designed by an outside vendor and reviewed, and approved by a team composed of an in-house senior instructional designer, a store manager, and a store employee.

The instructional designer follows a customized version of David Kolb's Team Learning Experience (KTLE) model. According to Kayes, Kayes, and Kolb (2004), experiential learning offers a way to "understand and manage how teams learn from their experiences" (n.p.). Experiential team learning can overcome some of the negative factors related to team learning: over-dependence on a dominant leader, a tendency to conform or "groupthink," and so forth. The major components of experiential team learning are conversation space, role leadership, and team development, and these components are reflected in the KTLE model.

Following the customized KTLE, the designer begins with orientation and clarification, then moves on to experience, reflection, generalization, and application. This is the design outline for each fifteen-minute "aisle three session":

1. The warmup (orientation)

   • Introduce the topic.

- Discuss the relevance and usefulness of what will be learned.

- Provide examples.

- Use icebreakers to acclimatize the participants.

2. The business session (clarification)

   - Establish learning objectives.

   - Present agenda.

   - Address housekeeping issues.

3. The happening (experience)

   - Introduce the topic.

   - Provide an "experience" for the learners that stimulates and involves the senses.

   - Include a learner-centered activity such as role-play, case study, hands-on activity, and so forth.

   - Call on common past experiences.

4. Think time (reflection)

   - Allow time to reflect on the experience individually.

   - Ask participants: What happened? What went on? How did you feel about that? Who else had a similar experience? Were there any surprises? What did you see?

   - Encourage participants to share thoughts and emotions through question and answer or group discussions.

5. The debriefing (generalization)

   - Ask the learners: Why was it significant? What conclusions can you draw? What does that mean to you? How does it fit together? What is operating here? Why is it important? What can we learn from the experience?

   - Encourage learners to draw conclusions, synthesize reflections, develop theories, look at patterns, provide "dos and don'ts" or "helps and hindrances."

- Insert brief mini-lectures to provide additional information if needed.

6. Doing it (application)

- Ask learners: How will you use this at work? What will you do differently next time?

- Encourage learners to use what was learned, practice, apply, and test theories.

- Ask learners to create an action plan, if appropriate.

7. Judging it (evaluation)

- Measure whether learning outcomes align with objectives.

- Verify the intended skills are developed, knowledge is gained, attitude is changed.

- Verify that the outcomes align with the business goals.

This Is an OWL-Friendly Design

The design is OWL-friendly. The training is systematically designed so it is orderly in content and flow. Learning objectives and intended outcomes are realistic, measurable, observable, and relate directly to learning objectives—and they are shared up-front with the participants.

Both the warm-up and business sessions focus on issues that are important to OWLS:

- Why am I here?

- Who are my peer learners?

- What is going to happen?

- What am I going to learn?

- How will I know that I have actually learned?

- What is coming up next?

During the "happening," past experience is called upon and valued. OWLS are given time to think during "thinking about it" and encouraged to share their thoughts with the others on the team. The use of action plans allows the OWLS to set and manage their individual learning and performance goals.

ADDITIONAL RESOURCE

For creative ways to activate and empower learning teams, read the following:

Thiagarajan, S. (1999). Team activities for learning and performance. In H. D. Stolovitch & E. J. Keeps (Eds.), *Handbook of human performance technology: Improving individual and organizational performance worldwide* (2nd ed., pp. 518–544). San Francisco: Pfeiffer.

12

OWLS on the Job: Learning with the Workflow

When I was a new employee on the afternoon shift, I got most of my training on the floor and during the work. I was confused and sometimes angry. It wasn't consistent and only gave me bits and pieces. I was young and it made me angry. I'm surprised I stayed so long. Now I hear they have a formal program . . . they're telling people what they need to know and do to perform successfully on the job. I often wonder if that's enough . . . do they give people help after the training?

Santiago, age sixty-two, manufacturing representative

H EY, SANTIAGO, welcome to workflow learning, where "learning fuses with real-time work . . . and the worker is plugged into the job" (Cross & O'Driscoll, 2005, pp. 31–32). Whether workers follow Harry around, learn just-in-time, or learn on-the-job, the concept is basically the same: workflow learning trains workers to know *what* they need to know and do *when* they need to know and do it and, if possible, *where* they need to do it—and above all, makes it easy to learn and do.

About Workflow Learning

Real-time delivery of learning and information is especially crucial for the manufacturing, service, and support sectors of business and industry. A salesperson may need product information to wrap up a sale; a repair team in the field may need troubleshooting guidelines "right now"; a geographically dispersed workforce may need to be updated on how to implement new policies, procedures, or standards in order to continue conducting the company's business.

The term *workflow learning* is an umbrella term for real-time learning. Workflow learning refers to the "fusion of learning and doing" (O'Driscoll & Cross, 2005, n.p.). It is synonymous with *performance centered design,* a concept that blends on-the-job training (OJT) and just-in-time training (JITT) with Gloria Gery's "concept of electronic performance support systems (EPSS)" (Cross & O'Driscoll, 2005, p. 32).

Workflow is "a sequence of activities that a person has to do to achieve defined desirable goals and results" (O'Driscoll & Cross, 2005, n.p.). Workflow learning uses workflow activities as a filter to screen out information that is not relevant for performance. Acknowledging the role of workflow as a filter keeps workflow learning right on—right content, right time, right place, right learners, and right device to make it all happen right now.

Just-in-Time Is a State of Mind

The concept of JITT leapt out of the manufacturing environment and into the workplace mainstream. JITT was originally a new concept for supplying parts to auto assembly and other plants just when they needed them, so the plants would not need to stockpile parts to keep up with production. In today's fast-paced, global workplace, many organizations face the same dilemma: they must "deliver critical information [and learning] to employees just-in-time, regardless of where they are, what time it is, and in what form the information is required" (Zarrabian, 2004).

JITT learning is real-time learning—the point where workplace learning and performance converge. JITT learning views OWLS and other workers as continuous learners who value an opportunity to immediately apply new knowledge and skills. It is best suited to situations in which workers need immediate practice to master new knowledge or skills and when it is possible to roll out a new procedure throughout an organization or in pockets of the organization.

On-the-Job Training (OJT) Is Formal or Informal

Traditionally, OJT is a strategy used to train new employees. Over time it has been melded with JITT and become part of a seamless, on-the-job learning continuum for workers. OJT can be either formal or informal. Both types of OJT are offered *when* the learner needs the training and *where* the employee will perform the job. OJT acknowledges that "instead of helping them where they are, too often we make them come to a class or interrupt their work to engage in content they find frustrating" (Cross & O'Driscoll, 2005, p. 32).

Formal OJT. Formal OJT is planned and may include a combination of classroom, "follow Harry around," practice, feedback, and testing. During the classroom component the new employee acquires the background knowledge required to perform the job—job description, job requirements, health and safety requirements, performance standards, and so forth. "Follow Harry around" is the show-and-tell part of the training. "Harry" is trained to walk the new employee through the job site and demonstrate what the new employee will need to do. Harry also monitors the new employee during the hands-on practice sessions, provides feedback, and may even test the new employee and certify whether he or she is ready to perform the job.

Informal OJT. Informal OJT has been around for years as an affordable and just-in-time way to train workers to perform new or different jobs. It is the practice of asking an experienced employee to teach a new employee the knowledge *and* skills required to perform a job. It usually begins and ends with Harry.

Harry provides the background, demonstration, guided practice, feedback, and testing. He may or may not be qualified as a trainer or coach, and the training may or may not be monitored by a supervisor (Van Tiem, Moseley, & Dessinger, 2001). Santiago may have been "confused and angry" because he had an informal OJT experience that was all show and tell and very little practice and feedback.

Workflow Learning Benefits the Organization and OWLS

Workflow learning can benefit both the organization and OWLS. It saves time and money and addresses the issues of immediacy and relevancy that appeal to OWLS as learners and performers.

Workflow Learning Can Benefit Organizations

At Colorado Springs Utilities, JITT and OJT are "centerpieces of the new customer service representative training program" (Solano, 2005, p. 40). By turning some content into job aids or tutorials that are available to trainees as needed, the company cut initial training time from fourteen weeks to eight weeks, with training usually delivered three times yearly. This translated to employees spending a total of ninety fewer days in the classroom—and away from their jobs—for both trainees and trainers.

Workflow Learning Can Benefit OWLS

"Real-time training emphasizes the average person's intrinsic interest in his or her work and the desire to be self-directed, to seek responsibility, and to develop the capacity to be creative with coworkers in solving work-related problems" (Ford, 1999, p. 26).

JITT Benefits. Most OWLS *like* the immediacy of JITT; they prefer to learn and apply new knowledge and skills right now rather than rely on memory to retain new knowledge and skills until they need to use them. They feel that they can build on their past experience to learn new processes or procedures and solve problems.

JITT provides a perfect opportunity to build on the work ethic and experience of OWLS while at the same time motivating them to learn and grow by offering immediate application and relevance. OWLS do *not* learn the new procedure for ordering office supplies six months before the procedure goes into effect; they *do* learn the new procedure and order supplies simultaneously.

OJT Benefits. In its earliest incarnation, OJT was informal or unstructured and was known as *apprentice training*. Many OWLS recognize the concept of apprenticeship; it is a familiar and accepted way to learn a job. However, formal OJT may have greater benefits for OWLS.

When OJT is consciously planned and effectively delivered, OWLS become productive faster, suffer less anxiety, and tend to stay on the job. During formal or structured OJT, learning challenges or problems with basic skills are more easily identified, and both the classroom trainers and Harry can make reasonable accommodations. There is also a consistent presentation of knowledge and skills and a commitment to safety and quality that OWLS appreciate (Rothwell & Kazanas, 1994).

About OWLS as Workflow Learners

Most OWLS like workflow learning because it is straightforward and immediately applicable. OWLS want to get the job done now, and they want to do it well. They also bring lessons learned into the mix. Workflow learning strategies that value the work ethic and experience of OWLS and can accommodate the OWLS' slower pace will succeed no matter what technology is used.

Some OWLS may *not* like the fast pace or sense of urgency that often accompanies workflow learning. Workflow learning stresses need-to-know rather than nice-to-know information; however, OWLS frequently want to know *why* or *why not* rather than what or how or when. They also may *not* be comfortable when technology is used, rather than humans, to deliver the training or when the training is delivered by someone who is younger, especially if that person does not respect the experience of OWLS.

OWLS Can Adapt to Most Workflow Strategies

OWLS are usually comfortable with the face-to face strategies used to implement workflow learning and less comfortable with strategies that involve technology.

Coaching and mentoring are common face-to-face components of both JITT and OJT. Classroom training is another face-to-face strategy used for

OJT or JITT workflow training. Classroom training usually covers the background knowledge that workers need to master performance. We will discuss OWLS and classroom training in Chapter Thirteen.

OWLS may be less comfortable with the use of performance support tools, a strategy common to both types of workflow learning. Performance support tools guide and sustain workplace learning and performance and may include electronic performance support systems (EPSS) or print-based performance support tools (PST), or job performance aids (JPA).

Single-source design strategy can also help to develop, deliver, and sustain JITT or OJT workflow learning and is usually transparent to the learners including OWLS. And while OWLS may not be savvy about highly technical simulations, carefully designed simulations can provide OWLS with opportunities for risk-free practice.

Coaching and Mentoring. Coaching and mentoring are important strategies for OJT and JITT. Many OWLS are familiar with the apprenticeship concept and naturally gravitate toward a coaching or mentoring role, although they may take less well to being coached or mentored by younger workers.

Coaching is frequently done by a manager, supervisor, or expert performer. It involves "one-on-one suggestions related to observable workplace situations and behavior" (Van Tiem, Moseley, & Dessinger, 2001, p. 348). Monica Higgins of the Harvard Business School suggests that mentoring goes beyond coaching because it contains additional elements of "career and psychosocial support, such as friendship and caring" (as cited in Coutu, 2000, p. 43). Coaching is more common when the workflow learning involves processes and procedures such as manufacturing or service; mentors are more frequently associated with leadership training.

OWLS respect coaches or mentors who are firm, fair, and ethical and obviously have the expertise to "do the job right." Organizations need to be selective in determining which supervisors, immediate managers, or experts coach or mentor during workflow learning. The individuals should know the job well and be able to perform the job tasks according to the highest possible standards; otherwise they will not be able to model the desired behavior.

OJT or JITT coaches or mentors must also be prudent and have a solid work ethic" (Mondy, Noe, & Premeaux, 2002).

OWLS frequently serve as coaches or mentors, but they may also find themselves in situations in which they need coaching or mentoring from younger employees, especially when OWLS must learn new technologies or entrepreneurial skills. This situation is often referred to as reverse coaching or mentoring. As a senior executive explained in a *Harvard Business Review* interview: "Like it or not, it's the younger generation that will have to mentor us rather than the other way around . . . I need these guys to connect. Otherwise, we won't be here in five years" (as cited in Coutu, 2000, p. 40). PST 12.1 offers some guidelines for planning successful reverse coaching or mentoring.

PST 12.1. Keys to Successful Reverse Coaching or Mentoring.

Purpose: To help workplace learning and performance professionals plan, select, or evaluate reverse mentoring or coaching interventions. *Reverse coaching* and *reverse mentoring* are terms used to describe situations in which the coach or mentor is younger than the person being coached or mentored.

Instructions: Use the following guidelines when you are planning a coaching or mentoring learning experience:

1. Use reverse mentoring and coaching prudently.

2. Make the program voluntary rather than mandatory.

3. Attempt to match the participants rather than randomly assign them.

4. Use the information in Chapter Seven and the Chapter References to help participants understand generational differences and bridge the gaps.

5. Clarify WIIFM (what's in it for me); OWLS will also need to know WIIFO (what's in it for the organization).

6. Stress that mentoring and coaching is a collaborative effort to build a better workplace; help participants find a common objective.

7. Stress that workers from all generations have knowledge and skill that are worth sharing.

8. Encourage mutual respect for what both OWLS and younger workers know and do.

9. Help OWLS and younger workers adapt their communication styles if necessary.

10. Help OWLS and younger workers build trust between each other.

11. Research and adapt the best practices of other companies; for example, General Electric (GE) and Procter & Gamble.

12. Approach the implementation of reverse mentoring or coaching as a change intervention; use change management techniques.

Print-Based Tools. Print-based job performance aids (JPA) or performance support tools (PST) were the precursors of electronic support systems (EPSS) and are often used to "direct, guide, and enlighten performance" (Rossett & Gautier-Downes, 1991, p. 4). Santiago, who introduced this chapter. would be happy to know that although print-based support tools may be used instead of training, they are also frequently used to support training.

According to Van Tiem, Moseley, and Dessinger (2001), "Inside every fat training course there is a thin job performance aid screaming to get out. . . . It provides just-in-time, on-the-job, and just-enough information to enable a worker to perform a task efficiently and successfully without special training or reliance on memory" (pp. 67–68).

A JPA or PST most frequently takes the form of a numbered list, checklist, flowchart, or decision matrix. Sometimes the formats are combined into a hybrid; for example, a numbered list of steps to complete a procedure may include a decision matrix whenever the next step involves an if-then decision (see Figure 12.1).

Figure 12.1. Example of a Hybrid Job Performance Aid (JPA).

How to Start XYZ Machine
 1. Press the ON button.
 2. Look at the light above the ON button.

3.	If the light is . . .	Do this . . .
	Red	Call the supervisor.
	Green	Go to step 4.
	Amber	Press the black HOLD button until the light turns green. • If the light turns green, go to step 4. • If the light does not turn green, call the supervisor.

 4. Set the timer to 0.
 5. Press the START button.

OWLS like the immediacy of a PST and JPA. OWLS also appreciate the fact that print-based performance support tools "enrich the environment" with information on how and sometimes why to do something, rather than "storing data or perspectives in someone's memory" (Rossett & Gautier-Downes, 1991, p. 15). They are immediately available on the shop floor, next to the computer, on the wall of a pizza-making station, or even in a shirt pocket. Print-based performance support tools should be stand-alone and self-explanatory; however, sometimes it is necessary to pretrain OWLS to use more complicated formats such as flowcharts, hybrids, or multicolumn matrices.

Electronic Performance Support Systems. Electronic performance support systems (EPSS) are performance support tools on steroids; they "provide integrated, on-demand access to information, advice, learning experiences, and tools to enable a high level of job performance with a minimum of training and support from other people" (Gery & Jezsik, 1999, p. 142). EPSS are the epitome of workflow learning; they are the "workware that unleashes human potential" (Cross & O'Driscoll, 2005, p. 32). EPSS are well received in the corporate world as viable alternatives to employee training and development (Chang, 2003).

In their simplest form, EPSS are "a virtual coach and an explicit task model" enabling OWLS and other workers to learn as they perform (Gery & Jezsik, 1999, p. 143). In more advanced forms, EPSS can provide the following benefits:

- Organize or structure jobs and job tasks
- Adapt to individual learning style
- Adapt to individual learning and performance level
- Complete frequently repeated tasks automatically
- Provide tools such as calculators and templates
- Include nice-to-know information, such as rules and relationships, to explain why a task is performed a certain way

- Allow performers to share information with others

- Adapt or withdraw performance cues to allow user to advance from novice to expert

A study by Nguyen, Klein, and Sullivan (2005) suggests that the use of any form—simple or advanced—of EPSS "to support task performance is better than having none at all" (p. 71).

WLP practitioners who are involved in designing JITT will find EPSS technology to be especially useful if learners have computer or web access on or near the job. They can design an intelligent system that allows learners to access the right information at the moment that they need it. And they can use the information in PST 12.2 as criteria for designing an EPSS that is OWL-friendly.

PST 12.2. Factors That Determine Whether an EPSS Is OWL-Friendly.

Purpose: To determine whether an EPSS will meet the workplace learning and performance needs of OWLS

Instructions: Check (✓) the items that are true. Items that are not true will need to be addressed and corrected before developing and implementing an EPSS in a multigenerational workplace.

☐ 1. Technology training of OWLS is adequate.

    ☐ 1.1 OWLS are trained in the technology required to use the EPSS (computer, handheld digital device, and so forth).

    ☐ 1.2 OWLS are *not* trained to use the required technology, but they are willing and able to learn what they need to know and do.

    ☐ 1.3 OWLS are *not* trained to use the required technology, but they will have the opportunity for adequate training prior to implementation of the EPSS.

☐ 2. EPSS design is OWL-friendly (see Chapters Five, Six, and Eight for a full discussion of the cognitive, learning, and physiological challenges that could affect the OWLS-EPSS interface).

    ☐ 2.1 Visual design elements (color, text design, screen size and brightness, and so forth)

    ☐ 2.2 Auditory design elements (clarity, use of high and low tones, use of auditory elements to support visual elements, and so forth)

    ☐ 2.3 Physical accessibility requirements (size of keys, portability, and so forth)

    ☐ 2.4 Cognitive processing requirements (memory, recall, timing, and so forth)

    ☐ 2.5 Hardware compatibility (OWLS have access to a computer compatible with the software used for the EPSS)

    ☐ 2.6 EPSS technology (semantic indexing of information, synchronization of information, decision rationale, and so forth based on a user model that included OWLS)

    ☐ 2.7 Other . . .

PST 12.2. Factors That Determine Whether an EPSS Is OWL-Friendly, *Continued.*

☐ 3. Environmental factors are OWL-friendly.

    ☐ 3.1 Adequate light level

    ☐ 3.2 No glare on the screen

    ☐ 3.3 Noise level not interfering with audio component of EPSS

    ☐ 3.4 Screen at eye level or adjustable

    ☐ 3.5 Seating available if necessary

☐ 4. OWLS are motivated to use EPSS technology.

    ☐ 4.1 OWLS recognize the value-added features of EPSS from previous experiences with EPSS.

    ☐ 4.2 OWLS recognize that what they will learn and be able to do as a result of using EPSS will have a critical impact on the success of the organization.

    ☐ 4.3 OWLS recognize that the EPSS will help them improve their job performance.

    ☐ 4.4 OWLS know that the organization will provide the resources to develop *and* maintain EPSS.

        ☐ 4.4.1 Organizational support

        ☐ 4.4.2 Know-how

        ☐ 4.4.3 People

        ☐ 4.4.4 Money

        ☐ 4.4.5 Time

    ☐ 4.5 OWLS know they will be able to provide input into the creation of the EPSS.

Single-Source Strategy. Single-source strategy saves time and money and "ensures that employees receive the training they need (about job skills, products or policies and procedures) when, where and how they need it" (Zarrabian, 2004). Learning content or objects are created and then reused in other courses, modules, or training programs. Designers may even adapt the content for use in a variety of media. OWLS and other learners are usually not aware that content is being reused, so a single-source strategy does not affect their learning, unless the original objects are poorly designed as learning sources or not well adapted to a different media. See the sidebar for one example of recycling learning objects.

MODULAR TRAINING FOR MULTIPLE USES

An international company purchased a new computerized system to handle all their accounting and finance processes. A majority of the system users were OWLS; the rest were Gen X and Y worker-learners. The training course on how to use the new system started off in life as a modular series of step-by-step instructions for using and navigating the system. Each module was process-specific and contained separate instructions for each task in the process. Instructors and participants at the home office used the modules for hands-on classroom training. Off-site employees received the modules by CD and used them with the help of an on-site trainer or as self-instructional modules or performance support tools (PST).

The modules were stored in the company's knowledge management system; each module or instruction could be updated, modules or instructions could be added or deleted, and users could access the modules or instructions as needed. Eventually the modules began a whole new life—they were reformatted as web-based training.

Simulations. Print and video simulations and simulation software provide a life-like, risk-free environment in which OWLS and others can learn and practice new skills. Simulation software is best known for training pilots in an environment that lets them learn without destroying expensive equipment or risking human lives. It is also useful for learning how to react in emergency situations or deal with interpersonal conflicts on the job. James Lundy, vice president of Gartner, a Stamford, Connecticut, research firm, "predicts that 70 percent of all off-the-shelf and custom e-learning content will include simulations of some type . . ." (in Boehle, 2005, p. 24). For information on how Gartner uses simulations during the hiring process, see the sidebar.

OWLS MAY HAVE THEIR FIRST SIMULATION EXPERIENCE UP FRONT

Gartner uses simulators for hiring purposes. The very best candidates are engaged with a multifaceted simulator on which they run an imaginary company for a specified time period. They experience a variety of jobs and play many roles, with tough problems to solve. They are evaluated on their workplace performance. Successful candidates form a bank of star performers who then are hired for Gartner's various branches. By not having to go outside for potential candidates, Gartner has saved hiring costs (Boehle, 2005).

From an organizational perspective, the use of simulations in hiring is cost-effective and provides valuable input to the candidate selection process. From an OWL's perspective, we do wonder whether candidates who are less familiar with or resistant to simulation technology are placed at a disadvantage.

Simulations are based on the learning principles of replication and repetition: "The best way to understand and internalize a task is by doing it over and over, as if in a live setting" (Zarrabian, 2004). Simulations take time and effort to develop, but once developed they are effective and efficient JITT tools. The beauty of simulation software from a just-in-time perspective is that "valuable information and training critical to successful job performance is never more than a click of a mouse away" (Zarrabian, 2004).

OWLS may take time and training to warm up to simulations. Many OWLS will need to learn and master the technology before they can use simulations effectively. Fast-paced simulations may frustrate them. Choice of colors, screen design, and visual and audio clarity are very important design factors for producing OWL-friendly simulations. Too much busyness can interfere with their visual, auditory, and cognitive processing.

Gen Y workers are a generation of computer game players. They like simulations because they can "learn and have fun" at the same time. Many were "born holding a joystick."

OWLS may feel that learning should not be fun! Older OWLS are really serious about their work and may be impatient with "game playing." In addition, they may not have the manual dexterity or eye-hand coordination required to run the simulation.

Workplace Application:
Designing a Multigenerational EPSS

DEG Company is getting ready to launch a new leasing option for customers who order one hundred or more units of specific products. Janine's team has been asked to help plan an intelligent JITT system that will give the dealership staff the right information at the right time and at the right level of detail so they can sell the new plan to their customers.

The company has used EPSS for other JITT training, so there is a group dedicated to developing EPSS training, and each dealership is required to provide its sales staff with PDAs or handheld computers that are compatible with company-developed EPSS materials. There is no formal program for training the sales staff to use the PDAs, but the same group that develops the company's EPSS also set up a call desk and online help for PDA users.

Janine's team is responsible for developing a user model or profile that will work with a multigenerational user base. The composition of the user base is illustrated in Figure 12.2.

Figure 12.2. Percentage of OWLS and Others Who Form the User Base for an EPSS System.

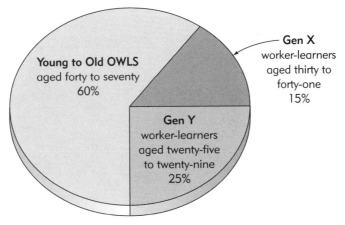

Janine's team decided to use PST 12.2, Factors That Determine Whether an EPSS Is OWL-Friendly, and Figure 7.1, The Multigenerational Workplace (see Chapter Seven), as guides for developing the user model. They developed PST 12.3, Preliminary Multigenerational Model of EPSS Users, to use as an interview guide and to record the overall results of data collection and analysis.

The team conducted online and telephone interviews with the potential user group. The team also used existing data from HR sources to develop the generational spread and other demographics. The example in PST 12.3 provides a preliminary model of the EPSS users. The user model has not been finalized; however, the EPSS designers are pleased with the results so far and have asked the team to document their process and develop an EPSS-based document that will guide future teams who need to develop user models.

PST 12.3. Preliminary Multigenerational Model of EPSS Users.

EPSS Project Title: _____

Date: _____

Model Developed by: _____

Generational Spread		
Percentage of Users	**Age**	**Generation**
15%	61–70	Silent
40%	42–60	Boomer
5%	40–41	Gen X

Technology Background

Percentage	Training Status
55%	Trained in PDA technology
35%	Not trained but willing to learn
10%	Not trained and do not want to be

Note: Generic PDA and EPSS training is available for all potential users.

Potential Design Issues

Design Element	Potential Issues
Visual	• Elements such as color and text font and size need to be adapted to aging eyes.
	• OWLS may have problems with screen size.
	• OWLS may have problems with picture clarity in bright light conditions.

PST 12.3. Preliminary Multigenerational Model of EPSS Users, *Continued*.

Design Element	Potential Issues
Auditory	• Auditory clarity could be an issue for OWLS. • OWLS and some younger users will have problems with high pitches. • Headphones may help block external noise.
Physical Accessibility	• OWLS may not be able to manipulate keys; key-strokes should be kept to a minimum. • Younger worker-learners will not have problems with the keys.
Information Processing	• Older users must be able to control the timing of the displays. • Younger users will want fast-paced, active displays. • The need for OWLS to recall information should be minimized.
EPSS Technology	• A majority of the users have had experience with PDA and EPSS technology. • Most of the remaining users are willing to use help desk and online help, but some suggest setting up coaching sessions. • Approximately 27 percent would like to participate in designing the EPSS.
Environmental Issues	• Environment will vary by individual. • OWLS will be affected if there is glare on the screen or environmental noise, so these factors should be considered when designing the EPSS.

User Motivation——Use of EPSS Technology

Generation	Motivation Level
Silent	Motivated to Not sure
Boomer	Very motivated to Not motivated
Gen X	Very motivated to Somewhat motivated
Gen Y	Very motivated to Motivated

Additional comments:

- Motivation was self-assessed on the following scale: Very motivated, Motivated, Somewhat motivated, Not motivated, Not sure.
- Approximately 59 percent of all users were Very motivated to Somewhat motivated to use the technology.

User Motivation——Content versus Technology

Generation	Motivation Level
Silent	Content
Boomer	EPSS technology and content
Gen X	EPSS technology
Gen Y	EPSS technology

Additional comments:

- Motivation was self-assessed on the following scale: Very motivated, Motivated, Somewhat motivated, Not motivated, Not sure.
- Boomer OWLS were split; some felt they did not need training to sell leases because they had prior experience with leasing; others wanted to learn about leasing but wanted classroom or other training rather than PDA training.

ADDITIONAL RESOURCES

Read the references associated with this chapter and also read Workplace Application 2: A Systematic, Experiential Design for Multigenerational Workflow Team Training in a Retail Environment in Chapter Eleven of this book.

In addition, the following books and articles will give you practical information and helpful workplace examples of workflow learning strategies. Don't be put off by the word *educational* in some of the titles or journal names; these resources speak directly to WLP practitioners, especially training managers and designers.

Aldrich, C. (2006). *Learning by doing: A comprehensive guide to simulations, computer games, and pedagogy in e-learning and other educational experiences.* San Francisco: Pfeiffer.

Appelman, R. L., & Wilson, J. H. (2006). Games and simulations for training: From group activities to virtual reality. In J. A. Pershing (Ed.), *Handbook of human performance technology: Principles, practices, potential* (3rd ed.). San Francisco: Pfeiffer.

Cross. J., & O'Driscoll, T. (2005, February). Workflow learning gets real. *Training, 42*(2), 30–35.

Elliott, P. (1999). Job aids. (1999). In H. D. Stolovitch & E. J. Keeps (Eds.), *Handbook of human performance technology: Improving individual and organizational performance worldwide* (2nd ed., pp. 606–625). San Francisco: Jossey-Bass.

Jacobs, R. L. (1999). Structured on-the-job training. In H. D. Stolovitch & E. J. Keeps (Eds.), *Handbook of human performance technology: Improving individual and organizational performance worldwide* (2nd ed., pp. 606–625). San Francisco: Jossey-Bass.

Rothwell, W. J., & Kazanas, H. C. (1994). *Improving on-the-job training: How to establish and operate a comprehensive OJT program.* San Francisco: Jossey-Bass.

For more information on *simulations,* read the following:

Thiagarajan, S. (1998, September-October). The myths and realities of simulations in performance technology. *Educational Technology, 38*(5), 35–41.

Villachia, S. W., Stone, D. L., & Endicott, J. (2006). Performance support systems. In J. A. Pershing (Ed.), *Handbook of human performance technology: Principles, practices, potential* (3rd ed.). San Francisco: Pfeiffer.

Zarrabian, M. (2004, December). The learning matrix—Just-in-time learning. *Chief Learning Officer Magazine.* Retrieved from http://www.clomedia.com/

13

Live OWLS: Learning in the Classroom

I sold my house and moved within walking distance of the college. I want to be able to pick up where my formal education left off. I want to register for an astronomy class. I like the formal class structure, the opportunities to share ideas with young minds, and the challenges associated with course work again. I haven't decided yet how I'll handle exams, but I'm going to do it for me.

Kaiser, age seventy-one, retired ophthalmologist

THE USE OF TECHNOLOGY to deliver workplace learning is rising steadily; however, live or real classroom learning is still the predominant training delivery method for more than 60 percent of the companies surveyed for ASTD's State of the Industry 2004 annual report (Sugrue & Kim, 2004). Sometimes classroom learning is stand-alone; sometimes it is part of a blended training strategy, which may also involve coaching and mentoring, computers, learning or performance support tools (PST, web-based resources, digital devices, and so forth. Classroom learning is always live and real, and that makes it comfortable for many OWLS.

About Live Classroom Learning

Yelon (1999) writes that any definition of live classroom learning should contain three distinguishing features: a live instructor, a group of students, and a location that is separate from the workplace. The first two features distinguish live classroom learning from individualized or self-instruction; the third feature distinguishes it from on-the-job training. Live classroom learning is a "legitimate, creative, and rewarding" workplace learning and performance intervention if it is well designed and suitable for solving a specific performance problem (Yelon, 1999, p. 486).

Live classroom learning is used for all types of learning: facts, concepts, principles and rules, procedures, interpersonal skills, and attitudes. Interactive live classroom learning is especially appropriate for learning concepts, principles, interpersonal skills, and attitudes.

Analysis is the key to determining whether live classroom instruction is the most appropriate delivery strategy for a particular type of learning. WLP practitioners need to analyze the learning or performance problem, the organization, the type of knowledge and skills required to solve the problem, and the available delivery strategies before deciding to select live classroom learning as the best performance improvement intervention. Analysis should also include three major issues: audience, practice, and cost.

Analyze the Audience

According to Malcolm Knowles (1980, p. 47), "adults feel accepted, respected, and supported in a classroom with other adults; there exists a spirit of mutuality between teachers and students as joint inquirers." In our aging, multigenerational workplace, the audience for any training initiative may include both OWLS and younger worker-learners.

OWLS tend to be real-time communicators and learners. Classroom learning provides face-to-face contact with the instructor, allows OWLS to network with other learners, and makes it easier for them to learn complex knowledge ("Skills for Tomorrow's Leaders," 2005). They are familiar with and comfortable in a classroom setting, although they may not like a highly interactive or informal classroom.

Younger worker-learners tend to prefer virtual learning. If they are in a classroom they want the delivery to be fast-paced, with a lot of interaction.

If there is a predominance of OWLS or younger worker-learners in your workplace, this will help you decide whether classroom learning is appropriate. If it is appropriate, you will need to decide what you are going to do to optimize the classroom environment for all the learners.

Analyze the Practice Factor

One of the key issues to consider when selecting classroom learning as an instructional intervention is practice. Some procedures require repeated rehearsal in order to master them; the classroom learning format does not always include sufficient time for practice. In addition, OWLS may or may not consider the classroom a safe environment for practicing new skills. "If practice in a classroom is possible, instructors can also probably administer other instructional activities (such as explanations, orientation, and motivation) in a classroom" (Yelon, 1999, p. 488).

Analyze the Training Aids

There are a variety of training aids that can be used to enhance classroom learning experiences. Familiarize yourself with them and how they can help or hinder OWLS from achieving maximum learning and performance. Some training aids are "old school"—like overhead projectors, movie projectors, video equipment, and flip charts—and will be familiar to OWLS. Some are "new school"—like PDAs, portable media players, and web cams—and OWLS may or may not be able to adjust to using them. Whatever you choose to enhance your instruction, be sure to

- Use the training aid that fits the learning event. In other words, after you carefully and thoughtfully prepare the instruction, decide on the training aid.

- Use the training aid that fits the learners, especially OWLS.

- Do not use the most current and expensive training aid when a simple overhead projector will suffice.

- Adapt your training materials to the physical and psychological changes in OWLS. Remember that aging is accompanied by many changes in receiving, processing, and responding to information; your choice of training aids needs to be adjusted accordingly.

- Ask your learners for feedback. Which training aid serves their immediate and long-range needs? You will find major differences here because of the different cohort groups that the class comprises.

- Maintain a personal Activity Log.

- After your instruction is completed, jot down what worked and what didn't and why. Get into the habit of self-evaluating your teaching efforts.

- Keep updated on new training aids that become available. Read about their practical application in various classroom settings. Take a risk and try something new. Then you will know whether or not the training aids work for you and your OWLS.

Analyze the Cost

Cost is another consideration. Live classroom learning may cost more than other interventions. Various types of computer or online-based learning have expensive up-front design and development costs; however, live classroom learning is the most expensive to implement when you consider hidden costs such as lost productivity, salaries, travel costs, site costs, trainer costs, and so forth.

How to Select Classroom Training

The *Intervention Selection Tool* (Van Tiem, Moseley, & Dessinger, 2001, pp. 317–336) is a PST that guides WLP practitioners through the instructional—and noninstructional—intervention analysis and selection process. As part of your audience analysis you will want to determine the age ranges and generations of your potential audience and find out how they feel about classroom training.

PST 13.1 offers a basic checklist to jump-start the process. The checklist may be adapted for use with other types of instructional interventions as well as live classroom learning.

PST 13.1. Is Live Classroom Learning the Answer?

Purpose: To help the WLP practitioner determine whether live classroom learning is the best instructional intervention

Instructions: Check (✓) all the factors that are true. In an ideal situation, you will check *all* the factors. If you are considering a blended approach, adapt the checklist to evaluate the use of other interventions such as computer-based training, e-learning, or PST and select the intervention(s) that fills in all the gaps.

Criteria	Success Factors
Is live classroom learning possible?	☐ Does the organizational culture support it?
	☐ Do current workplace realities—production needs, shift constraints, union requirements, and so forth—support it?
	☐ Does the organization have the appropriate resources—time, money, expertise—to design, develop, and implement it?
	☐ Does the organization have appropriate internal or external training facilities?
	☐ How do OWLS and other worker-learners feel about classroom training?
Is live classroom learning appropriate?	☐ Will it solve the performance problem?
	☐ Will OWLS and other worker-learners be able to learn what they need to know?
	☐ Will OWLS and other worker-learners be able to practice what they need to do?
Is live classroom learning the best solution?	☐ Is it the *best* way for OWLS and other worker-learners to learn what they need to know?
	☐ Is it the *best* way for OWLS and other worker-learners to learn what they need to do?
	☐ Is it the most cost-effective way for OWLS and other learners to acquire this specific knowledge and skills?

Criteria	Success Factors
Is live classroom learning a stand-alone solution?	☐ Would it be a *stand-alone* learning intervention?
	☐ Should it be part of a *blended* approach to learning?
	If you select blended approach, check (✓) the potential strategies you may want to add, then adapt this PST to analyze their suitability:
	☐ Action learning
	☐ Computer-based training
	☐ Distance learning
	☐ Electronic performance support systems (EPSS)
	☐ Just-in-time training (JITT)
	☐ Job performance aids (JPA) or performance support tools (PST)
	☐ On-the-job training (OJT)
	☐ Team learning
	☐ Other . . .

Classroom Connectivity

OWLS need to trust the instructor and the other learners before they feel comfortable enough to participate as interactive live learners. They also need to feel connected, both to the instructor and to their fellow classmates. Sometimes disconnects do occur.

A twenty-something worker-learner challenged the OWL sitting next to her in class, saying it was impossible for the generations to understand each other. In a voice loud enough for those around her to hear, the young woman said, "You grew up in a different world. We have TVs, jet planes, space travel, refrigeration, electrical cars and, . . ."

Taking advantage of the pause, the OWL responded, "You're right, young lady. We didn't have those things when we were young, so we invented them. What are you doing for the next generation?"

It is the responsibility of the instructor to develop connections or bonds with the learners and among the learners. Whitney (2005) makes the following suggestion to distance learning instructors: "You want to feel like you're having a conversation, not a one-way broadcast" (Whitney, 2005, n.p.). Live classroom instructors—and their learners—should also feel like they are part of a conversation or dialogue, not the recipients of one-way communication.

OWLS appreciate a "connected" classroom trainer. Use PST 13.2 to assess your "connectivity quotient" as a live classroom instructor or use it with your instructors as a self- or 360-degree-assessment tool and action plan. (Note: This PST is also applicable to online instructors.)

PST 13.2. Connectivity Quotient Self-Assessment for Live Classroom Instructors.

Purpose: To assess your connectivity quotient as a live classroom instructor

Instructions: Rate each of the connectivity items on the following scale. Then divide the total number of points by the number of items. If your connectivity quotients is 4 to 5, you are highly connective and make it easier for OWLS and others to interact and learn in a live classroom. If your connectivity quotient is 3 or lower, complete the basic action plan that follows, then reassess yourself after your next live classroom session.

Key: 1 = not sure, 2 = never, 3 = sometimes, 4 = most of the time, 5 = all the time.

	1	2	3	4	5
1. I think of the learners as my customers.					
2. I make an effort to know my learners.					
3. I let the learners know that I value their feedback.					
4. I think of the learners as collaborators in the learning process.					
5. I let the learners know we are collaborators.					
6. I focus on learning and learners rather than content and instructing.					
7. I feel comfortable engaging in "small talk" with the learners.					
8. I make frequent eye contact with all the learners.					
9. I can sense when learners need more clarification.					
10. I do not single out a learner who is having a difficult time.					
11. I do clarify or give additional help when needed.					
12. I feel comfortable letting the learners ask questions as we go.					

PST 13.2. Connectivity Quotient Self-Assessment for Live Classroom Instructors, *Continued*.

	1	2	3	4	5
13. I feel comfortable facilitating interaction among the learners.					
14. I use positive reinforcement techniques.					
15. I put my learners at ease.					
16. I turn negative classroom situations into positive learning experiences.					
17. I demonstrate a positive attitude toward the subject matter.					
18. I guide learners to reach answers themselves.					
19. I use learners as resources.					
20. I treat my learners in an unbiased way.					
21. Other . . .					

[a]You many want to add some items from Chapter Four to assess your perceptions about OWLS and younger learners.

Motivating OWLS in the Classroom

Stolovitch and Keeps (2004) tell us that motivation is a factor of value, confidence, and mood. OWLS will be more motivated to learn if they

- Feel valued in the live classroom

- Value the learning that is going on

- Feel confident, but not overconfident, that they *can* learn

- Feel open and optimistic about the learning experience

Most OWLS are motivated by learning that is purposeful and personal. They want to know why they need to learn and how it will benefit them and the organization. They want to add new knowledge and skill to what they already know and do, as long as new learning is value-added, not "out with the old and in with the new." When they are working in groups they need to feel they are in a safe environment in which they are accepted and valued.

Classroom Ergonomics Is a Motivator—Or *Not*

Live classroom settings are not always OWL-friendly. Some of the variables that may need to be adjusted to make OWLS feel more comfortable during classroom learning are temperature; lighting; seating; sound level; accessibility of restrooms, food, and beverages; and scheduled break times. Here's an example of a classroom schedule that is not OWL-friendly:

A Really, Truly Non-OWL-Friendly Classroom Schedule

7:00 A.M.	Class begins
9:30 A.M.	Break
9:45 A.M.	Class resumes
12:00 noon	Lunch
1:00 P.M.	Class resumes
3:15 P.M.	Break
3:30 P.M.	Class resumes
5:00 P.M.	Class ends

This schedule is an example of how organizations and even WLP practitioners can create non-OWL-friendly classroom learning. OWLS may need more frequent breaks and access to food or beverages. In this classroom schedule, participants could leave the classroom only during specified break times. In addition, the break times were too short, because the restrooms and the break room with food and beverage vending machines were located at the opposite end of the building, the cafeteria was two floors away, and food and beverages were not allowed inside the classrooms or in the hallways.

There were still more non-OWL-friendly problems with this particular classroom learning session. The lighting in the room was too bright to show PowerPoint slides, so the instructor turned off all the lights unless it was time for an activity. The instructor scheduled only one morning activity just before lunch and one afternoon activity just before the end of class, so the learners spent most of their time sitting in the dark with only the glow from the projector to light their way. The room was also very warm; however, there were no windows and the doors were closed because people were walking and talking in the hall. The result was a slumber party for OWLS—and for everyone else too!

Unfortunately, the situation just described is not unusual, especially when there is a tendency or policy to do "data dumps" rather than learning. It is not always possible to adjust temperature and lighting; however, a good instructional designer-instructor could have presented the content in smaller chunks, cut the number of visuals, added more activity, and allowed the learners to leave the room as needed.

Visuals Can Motivate OWLS—Or *Not*

Moody (2004) and others are adamantly opposed to what they call the "hidden curriculum" behind the use of slide presentations, especially in a classroom learning setting. Moody suggests that slide presentations encourage learners to "think in sound bites and bullet points" and reinforce what he calls the "sound bite cognitive style" (p. 14).

Even critics of slide presentations admit that they are a good way to show graphic and visual elements; however, critics also tend to agree that "how we communicate is sometimes more important than what we say . . ." (Moody, 2004, p. 14). This is especially true when it comes to helping OWLS learn—OWLS definitely do not think in MTV-like sound bites or slide presentation bullet points.

Focusing on the Learner Motivates OWLS

House (1996) makes the comparison between instruction that "crackles" and instruction that "fizzles." She tells us to plan instruction around learner outcomes, thoroughly prepare, set the stage initially, encourage learner interaction, and assess progress throughout. Learners will leave the classroom feeling good about their experience and themselves. What a gift to give to OWLS!

Workplace Application: OWLS and Others in a Graduate-Level Classroom

The first class of the semester began much like the previous semester's class, with roster review and introductions; syllabus review and the ubiquitous question "What do I have to do to pass this class?"; and an informal needs assessment to determine where students are in their current knowledge of the class content and what they hope to learn in the class. This graduate class in program evaluation seemed different, however.

There were nine adults in the class—eight females and one male. Of these, five were African American, three were Caucasian, and one was Chinese American. Two were doctoral applicants and seven were master's applicants. Their ages ran the gamut from twenty-four years to sixty-one years young. One student represented the Silent Generation, four were baby boomers, two were Generation Xers, of which one was an OWL, and two were Generation Y. The class of nine sported six OWLS and only three younger worker-learners. It was a multigenerational and truly diverse classroom—not the usual blend of mostly Gen Xers with a few Boomer OWLS and an occasional Gen Y or Silent OWL stirred into the mix.

All the students were working full-time and going to school on a part-time basis to earn their advanced degrees. All were in the early stages of their respective programs.. Their occupations were diverse: computer program developer, mental health volunteer, staff member from the Ministry of Education in Ghana, help desk administrator of a housing commission, elementary special education teacher, high school teacher, librarian, employee assistance provider, and the assistant director of education for a proprietary school.

The purpose of the course was to teach the students how to conduct a full-scope program evaluation. Class content focused essentially on the four components of full-scope evaluation (Dessinger & Moseley, 2006):

- Formative evaluation—used to improve processes

- Summative evaluation—used to determine the value of short-term results

- Confirmative evaluation—used to determine the value of long-term results

- Meta evaluation—used to evaluate the evaluation itself for quality improvement, validation, and lessons learned

The class content blended knowledge, skills, and attitudes. The students learned facts. They learned that the program evaluation standards set by the Joint Committee on Standards for Educational Evaluation are utility, feasibility, propriety, and accuracy (Joint Committee, 1994), and that confirmative evaluation uses return on investment (ROI) or cost benefit analysis (CBA) to measure the long-term efficiency of a training program. They learned the definition and scope of the terms *organizational impact* and *value.* They learned and practiced procedures, processes, and practices associated with conducting a solid program evaluation—focusing, designing, collecting, analyzing, and interpreting data, and managing and reporting results. They interactively learned attitudes and experiences dealing with evaluation trends, ethics, and politics; principles and rules associated with using quantitative and qualitative data-gathering instruments; and interpersonal skills involving stakeholders, clients, audiences, and sponsors in decision making and in communicating and reporting evaluation results.

Classroom discussions encouraged free and open dialogue in which students and teacher were joint inquirers, and face-to-face contact allowed students to network with each other and begin to respect the unique strengths and thoughtful ideas that each person brought to the live classroom environment. There was time for practicing skills and appropriate feedback; the instructor and peers were available for coaching as needed. Since the length of the class was only sixteen weeks, the students had to practice at work rather than in the classroom, and many would have liked more practice opportunities in the classroom as well. Discussions were both challenging and rewarding because the learners spanned so many generations and had different agendas. The Silent OWL was content just learning the material; the Boomer OWLS each had a different agenda; the Gen Xers wanted the degree so they could go out and make more money; the Gen Y folk were lost without their laptops.

The Gen X OWL's behavior was marked by skepticism. She questioned everything, and, sometimes, wouldn't let go even when she got the answer she wanted. On the plus side, she was resourceful and independent, and when group activities were assigned, she counted on her class partners and herself to get the work done.

The lone student representing the Silent Generation was guided by "conformity = success." She had a strong work ethic and enjoyed real-time instruction and communication. The baby boomers enjoyed life and their work both in and out of the classroom. They were youthful, vocal, and die-hard individualists. The Generation Xers chose to do it their way: they often designed their own protocols and templates that they discussed and shared with the entire group. They wanted to be expert evaluators who could become tomorrow's busy evaluation consultants because they felt that evaluation consulting pays well in the real world. They were certainly self-confident and very independent.

The Generation Y students wanted a more wired classroom experience; connect them and they would collaborate with the rest of the group. They were digital decision makers and seemed to be self-absorbed. These two students had to make the greatest adjustments, because the class was held in a temporary extension center that by day was a middle school, and there were few opportunities for interactive technologies—the instructor was limited to an overhead projector and email correspondence. They also had to adjust to being a minority in a multigenerational classroom in which OWLS outnumbered younger worker-learners by two to one.

Observation and the results of student evaluations at the end of the class indicated that the OWLS valued classroom learning, often prepared more than the instructor expected, and left the classroom feeling good about the learning experience and even better about their new skills in program evaluation. They liked the traditional classroom approach of tell-show-do. One student said: "Experience with this course is exceptional. It has impacted positively on my understanding and competence in focusing evaluation of programs and training. I have confidence to undertake evaluation projects in real life situations." And another student said: "The hands-on portions of classes were some of the best parts."

The professor overheard the Gen Y and the younger Gen X students talking about the fact that they would have liked more technology. These younger students preferred classes that used electronic whiteboards in the classroom and Blackboard online technology for communicating with the instructor and other students and sharing additional resources. One student said, "If the class was equipped with Blackboard, we could have posted several samples of completed program evaluations for guidance in completing the final course projects."

There was also a major difference between the learning styles of the OWLS and the Gen Y students. Most of the OWLS were willing and able—perhaps because of their past experience—to link new knowledge and application without explicit directions. The Gen Y learners had a "show me how right now and don't bother with why or what" attitude toward learning. They wanted to be told and shown exactly what to do and how to do it. During one of the classes, one younger student suggested that a visit from real-world evaluators or employers with an interest in program evaluation should be added to the course next time.

PST 13.2 was significantly helpful in both the initial planning for the class and the final evaluation and analysis after the course officially ended. It was also instrumental in helping the instructor reflect on some basic principles associated with effective and efficient classroom teaching strategies and learning applications for OWLS in the classroom.

Here are some lessons learned from this class:

- Always explain graphics, tables, diagrams, or photos—a picture is worth a thousand words to visual younger learners, but words are worth a thousand pictures to auditory older learners.

- Cite examples in your classroom training that involve real-life individuals, or create hypothetical individuals to talk for you.

- Use humor whenever it is appropriate, but do not offend your OWLS.

- Provide the stimulus material and listen to the discussion that unfolds. You will hear a cornucopia of ideas from your OWLS and will be able to capitalize on their experiences and give their self-esteem a boost.

- Finally, believe in yourself as a good classroom instructor and *the magic will happen.*

ADDITIONAL RESOURCES

For more details on how to adapt live classroom learning to meet the functional needs of OWLS, check out the discussion in Chapter Eight of this book. The tips for real-time trainers should be of particular interest and should help you communicate clearly with OWL audiences. These tips for how to design effective materials; how to write text for printed materials; and how to format and package printed materials.

You may also want to read the following:

Powers, B. (1992). *Instructor excellence: Mastering the delivery of training.* San Francisco: Jossey-Bass.

Rossett, A., & Sheldon, K. (2001). *Beyond the podium: Delivering training and performance to a digital world.* San Francisco: Pfeiffer.

Rothwell, W. J. (2005). *Beyond training and development* (2nd ed.). New York: AMACOM.

Rothwell, W. J. (2002). *The workplace learner: How to align training initiatives with individual learning competencies.* New York: AMACOM.

Silberman, M. (1998). *Active training: A handbook of techniques, designs, case examples, and tips.* San Francisco: Pfeiffer.

Stolovitch, H. D., & Keeps, E. K. (2002). *Telling ain't training.* Alexandria, VA: American Society for Training and Development.

Yelon, S. (1999). Live classroom instruction. In H. D. Stolovitch & E. J. Keeps (Eds.), *Handbook of human performance technology: Improving individual and organizational performance worldwide* (2nd ed., pp. 485–517). San Francisco: Pfeiffer.

14

Virtual OWLS: Computerized, On the Web, At a Distance, Digitized

Digital, mobile, virtual? I'm confused. I need one of those "technology for dummies" books. I didn't grow up with computers and I have always been in key positions where other people could do my techie stuff. I know I could learn the technology if I took time to learn it and practice it . . . Take a distance learning class? Never! You need good computer skills and great eye-hand coordination for that. I have neither . . . I have all I can do to keep up with my email and answer people back electronically.

Kyle, age sixty-four, department head

REAL-TIME OWLS are becoming virtual OWLS, whether they like it or not. Cross and O'Driscoll (2005) suggest that the future workplace will be "digital, mobile, virtual, and personal." Workers will have individualized, technology-driven interfaces with their job and their organization. Each interface will include "what's important, when you need it, on the device in your pocket, aware of your situation, cognizant of your background" (p. 34). Software designers will create this environment for each worker based on a user profile they have developed that tells them who the user is, where the user is located, what the user knows and can do, and what the user needs to know and do.

Workplace learning and performance is already going digital, mobile, virtual. It is up to WLP practitioners to make sure that workplace learning and performance is also personal. OWLS are real people with real learning and performance needs. They can and will interface successfully with training technology, if the training technology is designed to be OWL-friendly.

Computerized OWLS

Before the advent of e-learning there was computer-based training (CBT). At its simplest, learners could download training material from a floppy disc or a company server onto their hard drive. Now there are CDs or DVDs, or learners can go out into the web and download training programs or materials onto their personal or business computer.

OWL-Friendly CBT Is Designed

The first test of whether CBT is OWL-friendly is to look at where the CBT program falls on the design continuum illustrated in Figure 14.1.

Figure 14.1. The Design Continuum for CBT.

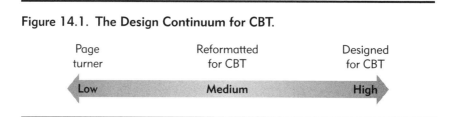

Just a Page Turner. At the low end of the continuum, CBT is just a page turner (not to be confused with the layperson's meaning—a gripping, suspenseful book), because CBT page turners come across as anything but exciting and positive. CBT page turners are print-based learning materials transferred to the computer *as is*. The screens are usually text-heavy and the user cannot work directly on activity or test pages, but must print the pages to complete the work. This type of format is not OWL-friendly.

Reformatted for CBT. When print-based learning material is reformatted for CBT, it is adjusted to take in screen shape and size and to take advantage of navigation, touch screens, branching, and other computer technologies. Learners can work directly on the screens to fill in the blanks, check responses, enter text responses, and so forth. Developers use special authoring software to reformat the learning material. If the authoring software allows the developers to use font styles and sizes, spacing, and other text design strategies that we discussed under the Action Steps in Chapter Eight, reformatted learning material can be OWL-friendly.

Designed for CBT. At the high end of the continuum is learning material designed specifically and originally for CBT. This level of CBT is limited only by the authoring software and the computer system parameters. Designers can "chunk" the content into small segments, keep the screens visually uncluttered, avoid colors that are not easily recognized by the aging eye, and provide frequent and immediate feedback—all factors that accommodate the physical and cognitive changes that OWLS undergo as they age.

Well-designed CBT training materials that can be downloaded on CDs or DVDs are especially user-friendly for OWLS. They can use the discs on their home or office computer, they have more control over their learning pace, and they do not need to use the Internet.

OWL-Friendly CBT Is Ergonomic

When it comes to designing OWL-friendly CBT, there are ergonomic considerations, some of which are listed in PST 14.1.

PST 14.1. Ergonomic Factors for OWL-Friendly CBT.

Purpose: To provide learning and performance professionals with a checklist of ergonomic factors that may influence how well CBT is accepted and used by OWLS

Instructions: Use this PST to design or evaluate the ergonomic side of OWL-friendly CBT. To evaluate Owl-friendly CBT, turn the list of guidelines into a numbered checklist.

- ☐ Computer screen
  - Size—larger screens can prevent eye strain
  - Adjustments—OWLS should be able to adjust the following on the screen as needed:
    - ○ Font size
    - ○ Glare
    - ○ Text density
    - ○ Text clarity
- ☐ Font size—text should be a minimum of 12-point; 14-point is preferred
- ☐ Font style—a simple sans serif, well-spaced style like Verdana is best for the aging eye
- ☐ Area lighting—OWLS may need nonglare area lighting
- ☐ Keyboard—OWLS may need ergonomic keyboards to compensate for arthritis or other problems; voice-activated computer software is available for OWLS who cannot use a keyboard at all
- ☐ Mouse—OWLS may need special training in how to navigate with a mouse or a JPA showing alternate keystrokes
- ☐ Toolbars—OWLS may need clear, consistent toolbars on every page as memory aids for navigating through the CBT
- ☐ Print option—OWLS may prefer to print worksheets and other learning support tools rather than viewing them on a computer screen

OWLS on the Web

E-learning is instruction that is carried out using a port to transfer training material through a company intranet or extranet. It is also called web-based learning, online learning, and internet-based learning. The e-learning market is booming and "could reach $21 billion by 2008 as mergers create larger firms with improved suites of products," says H. J. Nicholas in an *Information Week* article (as cited in *ASTD The Buzz,* 2005c, n.p.). More and more organizations use e-learning as an alternative to traditional training delivery strategies or as one component of a blended strategy that may also include classroom or on-the-job training.

In ASTD's *State of the Industry* annual report, Sugrue and Kim (2004) reported "[m]ore than half of technology based delivery was online in 2003 and 2004, and more than 75 percent of online learning was self-paced" (p. 5). The sidebar gives you an idea of where you will find e-learning in the global workplace.

HERE'S THE BUZZZZZZZZ ABOUT E-LEARNING

ASTD's weekly online newsletter *The Buzz* reports on global training and development initiatives. Here are just a few e-learning items that were buzzed to ASTD members from May to October 2005:

- The number of web-based learning lessons taken by workers at Caterpillar Inc. has jumped from thirty thousand in 2001 to two hundred thousand in 2004 (*ASTD The Buzz*, 2005a).

- To round out its Distributed Learning System, the U.S. Army has added an e-learning program that offers more than two thousand web-based courses to the entire Army workforce: active duty, reserve, ROTC, National Guard, and civilian. "Army e-learning has already been accessed by over 213,000 users, with 300 to 500 new users each week" according to "Army's e-learning," a *Federal Times* article by Davis (as cited in *ASTD The Buzz*, 2005b, n.p.).

- Brown and Galli note that e-learning has become "a training tool for a number of multinational corporations, such as Ford, Air Canada, Dow Chemical, and DuPont" (as cited in *ASTD The Buzz*, 2005a, n.p.).

E-Learning Benefits Organizations and OWLS

E-learning benefits both the organization and the participants. Even OWLS can find some benefits, especially if the e-learning is designed with them in mind and satisfies their need for content relevancy and timeliness.

Benefits to Organizations. Organizations save money and increase productivity when employees do not need to travel to remote sites and take chunks of time offsite for training. E-learning-related software also makes it easy for organizations to design, develop, and maintain the content of e-learning programs and to monitor who is being trained to do what and to what level of achievement. An additional benefit is the potential for sharing online training programs with other companies, industries, professional societies, or universities. Organizations or communities of practice can also partner with hardware and software companies to design, develop, and deliver e-learning (Rosenberg, 2001; Sloman, 2002).

Benefits to OWLS. OWLS also benefit from e-learning. They can learn at their own pace, without the extra time, out-of-pocket expenses, and disruption of personal life often associated with business travel. They can set up their own schedule for using e-learning material, because the material resides on an accessible company intranet or extranet or on the Internet. There is also a perception of anonymity, which makes it easier to take risks, especially during the early learning components.

How to Determine the Benefits of E-Learning

Aging and multigenerational organizations can determine the benefits of using e-learning programs by considering the outcomes and advantages and balancing them against the training needs of the organization and participating OWLS. PST 14.2 raises typical questions WLP practitioners might ask about specific e-learning program outcomes and advantages (Sales, 2002).

PST 14.2. Is E-Learning a Value-Added Activity?

Purpose: To help WLP practitioners determine whether e-learning is a value-added activity for their organization

Instructions: Use the following questions as a guide to interview or survey other WLP practitioners, supervisors, managers, executives, and so forth. Don't forget to ask OWLS, too.

Use the results to build a business case for or against using e-learning in an aging or multigenerational workplace.

	Yes	No	Not Sure

1. Has this organization used e-learning in the past?
   a. If yes, why?
   b. If no, why not?			

2. Have OWLS achieved the desired outcomes after they participated in e-learning?			
3. Are the OWLS in your organization motivated to learn from e-learning?			

4. Do you think e-learning benefits this organization?
   a. If yes, what are the benefits?
   b. If no, what are the disadvantages?			

5. Does e-learning help the organization recruit and retain OWLS?			
6. Should the organization adapt e-learning programs to individual learner needs, especially the needs of OWLS?			
7. Does the organization have the internal resources to design and develop, implement, and evaluate customized e-learning for OWLS?			
8. Does the organization have the resources to select customized e-learning from outside vendors?			
9. Will the organization's culture accept outside vendors?			
10. Will the e-learners be invited to collaborate on the design process for e-learning?			

OWL-Friendly E-Learning

The design and ergonomic factors we discussed in the CBT section also apply to e-learning. OWLS who are successful e-learners are comfortable with computer and internet technology and are motivated to learn. They are viewed by learning and performance professionals as "collaborators" rather than "users"; they are encouraged to help plan e-learning programs and are supported by an online tutorial or easily accessible help desk. For online instruction to be truly successful, content, instructor, peers, and requirements must be ingrained into the lives of online participants (Rossett, 2005).

OWLS, like any other e-learners, are "but a mouse click away from abandoning even the most well-planned instructional site" (Michalski, 2001, p. 199). As a prerequisite to planning successful e-learning, WLP practitioners need to understand what motivates their e-learners and what OWLS and other e-learners expect to accomplish as a result of their online experience.

OWLS at a Distance

Whenever the learner and the instructor are separated by time, space, or both, we have distance learning (DL). Distance learning is defined in many ways, but basically it is "formal instruction in which a majority of the teaching [or training] function occurs while educator [or trainer] and learner are at a distance from one another" (Verduin & Clark, 1991, p. 13).

Asynchronous Is Individualized

Asynchronous DL is accessed by individual learners or learning groups at a time and place most convenient to them. A variety of instructional media may be used to bridge the separation between learner and instructor: video, audio, text, and graphics may be delivered by fax or phone; snail mail or email; intranet, extranet, or Internet; CDs or DVDs; or even satellites. Correspondence courses were probably the earliest examples of asynchronous distance learning, dating back to ancient civilizations in which tutors and pupils corresponded with each other over a "rudimentary postal system" (Verduin & Clark, 1991, p. 15).

Synchronous Creates a Virtual Classroom

Synchronous DL occurs simultaneously for all the students, even though they all do not occupy the same space. Synchronous distance learning is a virtual classroom: the students are not physically present yet there is "a real-time exchange of video, audio, text, and graphic information" (Van Tiem, Moseley, & Dessinger, 2001, p. 55). Interactivity may be built in through the use of telecommunication technology; learners and instructor may see each other on a TV or laptop screen.

THE SKY'S THE LIMIT
Ford Motor Company uses its satellite-based FORDSTAR Network to beam both data and digital video to train Ford dealers around the world. The system is a true workflow learning tool: "In addition to distance learning, all data movement between Ford and its dealers occurs over the satellite" (Dessinger & Conley, 2001, p. 178).

OWL-Friendly Distance Learning

Human interface, timing, and technology are the major barriers to acceptance of distance learning by OWLS. OWLS in general seem less comfortable with asynchronous distance learning than they are with synchronous distance learning. They really like the personal touch.

OWLS Prefer to Interface with People

Older OWLS are not as comfortable with the concept of asynchronous distance learning; they usually prefer occupying the same space with the instructor and the other students. At least in synchronous distance learning there is an instructor or a group of learners on the screen or in the chat room. For example, in satellite-based distance learning the learners may be scattered at various learning centers, but the instructor is on screen and everyone can communicate with the instructor through telephone, fax, or keypad technology. There may also be an audio track for both the instructor and the learners.

OWLS May Need More Time

Timing is a real factor in designing synchronous distance learning, especially when the distance learning event is broadcast via satellite. Air time costs money, so the learning event must begin and end within strict time parameters. OWLS may need longer to process some content or to respond using keypad technology. In asynchronous distance learning the OWLS are constrained only by other demands on their time.

Technology Is a Major Barrier

OWLS may or may not feel comfortable with the technology they need to master to become interactive participants in both asynchronous and synchronous distance learning. They may fight the technology because they prefer real-time interaction or because they have physiological problems such as aging eyes or decreased manual dexterity. Even when timing is not a factor, the learner is expected to view the material on a computer screen and use a computer keyboard.

Breaking the Barriers

There are a number of ways to break down the barriers that interfere with learning from a distance. Personalizing the instruction and providing individual support may be the least cost-effective barrier breakers; however, they are the most effective. You will find some less costly suggestions in PST 14.3.

Trained Instructors Can Add a Personal Touch

The instructors must be well trained as both facilitators and instructors. Although the learning content is carefully scripted and timed for maximum instructional impact, instructors need to realize that "being online doesn't mean you don't have to connect, interact and perhaps even bond with your learners" (Whitney, 2005, n.p.).

Whitney (2005) also suggests that online instructors should "make more of an effort to connect by engaging in small talk, considering employee satisfaction and establishing trust with consistent, thoughtful and purposeful communication" (n.p.). PST 13.2 features the Connectivity Quotient Self-Assessment for Live Classroom Instructors. This PST is also useful for online instructors.

On-Site Facilitator Personalizes Distance Learning

When a group of learners meets at a synchronous or even an asynchronous distance learning site, a site facilitator may be assigned to verify the room setup, check attendance, coach users, and handle technical problems or questions from learners. This may help put OWLS at ease. It will also provide feedback regarding how OWLS react to the distance learning experience (Dessinger, Brown, Reesman, & Elliott, 1998).

Additional Barrier Breakers

PST 14.3 lists some strategies for maximizing the asynchronous or synchronous DL experience for OWLS. The tips are based on information gathered during a four-state distance learning series. The series had both asynchronous and synchronous components. A WLP practitioner observed OWLS during both distance learning experiences and asked them to share their reactions.

PST 14.3. Tips for Designing OWL-Friendly Distance Learning.

Purpose: To provide a list of tips to help WLP practitioners select or design and develop, deliver, and evaluate OWL-friendly distance learning

Note: If you use this PST to select or evaluate distance learning, format it as a numbered checklist.

OWLS Learning at a Distance:

- OWLS can handle less direction than younger learners.

- Conducting a learning styles inventory with OWLS, including an environmental inventory, helps pinpoint learning strengths and weaknesses and the environmental conditions under which OWLS do their best work (see Chapter Seven).

Asynchronous Distance Learning:

- This is individualized learning or self-study, so you should design stand-alone materials that are complete, accurate, and unambiguous; this helps the OWL block out interference.

- Remember, OWLS can handle less direction than younger learners.

- Add follow-up options to support the learners: mentoring or coaching components; phone, computer bulletin boards, or email support; online tutorials; and so forth.

- Develop visual and audio materials that are OWL-friendly—remember what you learned about the aging eye and ear in Chapter Eight.

- Let the learners know what you are going to teach them; teach them, then summarize what you taught them; use visual, audio, or print advance organizers and follow-up summaries.

- Chunk the material into short units or modules so the learner can control the pace of the learning whenever possible.

- Provide print support for audio or visual material.

- Follow the appropriate guidelines for OWL-friendly CBT and e-learning, provided earlier in this chapter, and the guidelines for OWL-friendly EPSS in Chapter Twelve.

PST 14.3. Tips for Designing OWL-Friendly Distance Learning, *Continued.*

Synchronous Distance Learning:

- Teach the technology. Don't assume the learners know how to fax or phone their responses or use the automatic response keypad devices.

- Don't surprise the learners—give them time to think. Let your audience know that responses are voluntary, or tell them ahead of time that you will call on them to respond to a specific topic or issue.

- Give immediate, frequent, and timely feedback.

- Provide follow-up opportunities via phone, email, computer bulletin boards, and so forth.

- Encourage groups of learners to participate together.

- Establish guidelines for the physical setup of the room in which the session will take place—lighting, noise, heating and cooling control, and so forth.

- Provide an on-site facilitator to make sure the technology is working and the room is set up appropriately; make sure the facilitator is able to communicate with the broadcast site to troubleshoot technical or other difficulties if necessary.

Digitized OWLS

Even as we write, there is new technology afoot to make learning faster, easier, and transportable. Digital audio or MP3 files are easily transportable and can deliver learning on a number of different devices, including computers, portable media players, or cell phones. Companies like Nokia are integrating MP3 technology into more and more of their cell phones. It's getting to the point where learning can literally "take place anywhere, at any time" ("MP3 and iPods," 2005, n.p.).

Recently, a well-known TV daytime soap opera began telling viewers not to worry if they miss an episode—all they need to do is check out the daily Podcast. If an OWL misses a meeting or training session, there may soon be a Podcast to help him or her stay in touch. See the sidebar on how Capital One is using iPods.

TRAINING GOES DIGITAL

Capital One is using Apple iPods for new-hire training. Capital One views the iPod as "a tool to enjoy learning via mobile audio . . . and enhance the learning experience"; the trainees appreciate the fact that they do not have to go to class but can listen to the material on their iPods while they are at home or on the road ("MP3s and iPods," 2005, n.p.). Organizations like Capital One can also subscribe to training programs that are available on commercial or university audio learning channels.

OWL-Friendly Digital Learning

In Chapter Six we discussed the fact that older OWLS tend to be auditory learners. From this perspective, digitized audio mobile devices may be a perfect solution to bridging the technology gap for OWLS and may even give them an advantage over younger, more visually oriented worker-learners.

The problem with devices like iPods, MP3s, and cell phones is the very thing that makes them easy to transport—the size. Older fingers may have problems pressing buttons and keying in text; older eyes may have problems with the visual displays. Glare from the sun or other lighting sources may also work against older eyes if the digital device also has a screen display. OWLS may be less motivated to use digital devices unless the hardware becomes more accommodating to aging eyes and fingers.

Workplace Application: Assessing Readiness for Distance Learning

A computer parts manufacturing company with manufacturing, distribution, and sales operations in the United States, Germany, and Taiwan is planning to transform its classroom-based training programs into asynchronous online distance learning. The training programs are currently scheduled for new employees or existing employees only on an annual basis.

The business case for the efficiency of distance learning has already been made. Distance learning would make the courses available on demand; for example, when new employees are hired they would be able to go through company orientation immediately instead of waiting for the scheduled monthly class. In addition, although up-front development costs are high, they are not as high as the current costs for travel, trainers, trainees, and lost productivity.

The final piece of the business case is to provide data on the potential effectiveness of distance learning. The WLP practitioner assigned to the project suggested that as one of the steps in assessing potential effectiveness, the planning group needs to establish the readiness and expectations of the potential learners.

The planning group decided to conduct an online survey of all employees through the company intranet. The purpose of the survey is to determine whether the potential learners are ready for distance learning, provide the support some will need to get ready, and help align user expectations with the new distance learning programs. The planning group intends to use existing training for those learners who need to develop specific hardware or software skills. The readiness program will also include trained on-site distance learning coaches.

The results will be anonymous; however, the survey will ask respondents to include their age range: eighteen to twenty-nine, thirty to thirty-nine, forty to fifty-four, fifty-five to sixty-four, or sixty-five to seventy-four. The age ranges reflect those of the current employees and will help the planning group determine whether there are OWL or other learner-related issues that must be addressed to ensure the effectiveness of distance learning.

Here are some of the questions generated for the survey:

My experience with online distance learning and computers:	Yes	No	Not Sure
1. I have participated in distance learning education or training programs that did not have an instructor; all the work was done on the computer.	☐	☐	☐
2. I have regular access to a work computer.	☐	☐	☐
3. I have regular access to a home computer.	☐	☐	☐
4. I can use the Internet to find information.	☐	☐	☐
5. I can use the Internet to send email.	☐	☐	☐
6. I have participated in chat rooms on the Internet.	☐	☐	☐
7. I can write, send, receive, and save email.	☐	☐	☐
8. I can download and upload attachments to email.	☐	☐	☐
9. I have participated in discussion boards on the Internet.			
10. I can set up and work with a spreadsheet in the _____ (name) _____ program.	☐	☐	☐
11. I can set up and work with a database in the _____ (name) _____ program.	☐	☐	☐
12. I can develop documents in the _____ (name) _____ word processing program.	☐	☐	☐

**My experience with online distance
learning and computers:**

		Yes	No	Not Sure

13. I can use the _____ (name) _____ presentation program. ☐ ☐ ☐

14. I know how to use the number keypad on the computer. ☐ ☐ ☐

15. I know how to find information on the company intranet. ☐ ☐ ☐

16. I can troubleshoot minor technical problems when they arise and seek assistance when necessary without becoming frustrated. ☐ ☐ ☐

My expectations about online distance learning:

Yes   No   Not Sure

17. I can take as much or as little time as I need to complete the training program components. ☐ ☐ ☐

18. All the class activities, assignments, tests, and so forth must be done on the computer. ☐ ☐ ☐

19. There may be prework that I need to complete before I can begin the program. ☐ ☐ ☐

20. I must have a password to log onto the program. ☐ ☐ ☐

21. I can work on the program at work or at home. ☐ ☐ ☐

22. I have the time management skills to set aside time to work on the training program. ☐ ☐ ☐

23. I have the self-discipline to continue working on the training program until I complete it, even if it is difficult. ☐ ☐ ☐

24. The primary means of communication with the instructor and my classmates will be discussion boards, email, and chat rooms. ☐ ☐ ☐

	Yes	No	Not Sure
My expectations about online distance learning:			
25. I will be able to contact my instructor by phone if I have problems with the training.	☐	☐	☐
26. I will be able to talk to other trainees by phone during the training.	☐	☐	☐
27. I can call someone for technical support if I need it.	☐	☐	☐
28. I will have online help to solve technical problems.	☐	☐	☐
29. I will have a printed manual to help me solve technical problems related to the training program.	☐	☐	☐
30. It is easy for me to read and understand instructions, course content, and instructor feedback in printed form.	☐	☐	☐
31. It is easy for me to read and understand instructions, course content, and instructor feedback on a computer screen.	☐	☐	☐
32. I will have a printed supplement with course content and instructions.	☐	☐	☐

If you have a home computer, answer questions 33–39. If you do *not* have access to a home computer, you are finished with the survey and you can go to the directions for returning the survey to _____.

	Yes	No	Not Sure
My home computer system includes the following (fill in the names of your software programs):			
33. Dependable internet service	☐	☐	☐
34. Regular access to a word processing program (_____)	☐	☐	☐
35. Regular access to a spreadsheet program (_____)	☐	☐	☐

My home computer system includes the following (fill in the names of your software programs):	Yes	No	Not Sure
36. Regular access to a presentation program (_____)	☐	☐	☐
37. Regular access to a database program (_____)	☐	☐	☐
38. Dependable virus protection (_____)	☐	☐	☐
39. Dependable technical support	☐	☐	☐

Given the cost of live classroom training in a global organization, the cost-effectiveness side of the business case for distance learning was easy to establish. The planning group is confident that the last, but not least, component of the business case for distance learning—alignment with learner expectations and learner needs—is about to fall into place. The planning group is hoping to finalize the survey, distribute it online, collect and analyze the data, and report the results along with their recommendations so they will be ready to present their case well in advance of planning for the next fiscal year.

ADDITIONAL RESOURCES

For additional information on how to design or adapt computer or web-based learning for OWLS with special needs, go to www.ibm.com/research or www.microsoft.com/enable.

For more information on virtual learning technologies, read the following:

Marquardt, M. J., & Kearsley, G. (1999). *Technology based learning: Maximizing human performance and corporate success.* Boca Raton, FL: St. Lucie Press/ASTD.

Mayer, R. E., & Clark, Ruth C. (2002). *E-learning and the science of instruction: Proven guidelines for consumers and designers of multimedia learning.* San Francisco: Pfeiffer.

Ochoa-Alcanta, J. M., Borders, C. M., & Bichelmeyer, B. A. (2006). Distance training. In J. A. Pershing (Ed.), *Handbook of human performance technology: Principles, practices, potential* (3rd ed.). San Francisco: Pfeiffer/ISPI.

Piskurich, G. M. (Ed.). (2003). *Preparing learners for e-learning.* San Francisco: Pfeiffer.

15

Collaborating with OWLS

When I first used the computer I was fearful that every time I touched the wrong key, I hurt the machine and wouldn't know how to fix it. I'm beyond that now. . . . I spend more time emailing messages at work than I do talking on the phone. I have a Palm Pilot that I use for organizing myself and keeping up with our team meetings and training sessions. I recently read that there's a fancy new iPod on the horizon that will play videos and music. I look forward to purchasing one. . . . I was reluctant to embrace technology, and I'm still hesitant. But in all honesty, technology has revolutionized my job . . . and me.

Philip, age sixty-four, library administrative assistant

THE LATEST BUZZ is that the world is flat, and it will continue to flatten—according to author and columnist Thomas Friedman (2005), once "the wall [Berlin] came down and Windows went up" it was only a matter of time (p. 48). Friedman explains that while giants like Microsoft, Netscape, and Google worked on the connection process, new workflow software development enabled collaboration processes like open sourcing, outsourcing, offshoring, supply-chaining, insourcing, and in-forming. Then there are the "steroids"—new and improved digital, mobile, personal, and virtual technologies that "amplify and further empower all the other forms of collaboration" (p. 170).

While all these world-flattening factors were emerging and converging, the worldwide workplace was aging—and business and industry was being warned that workplace learning and performance needed to change to accom-modate the increasing number of OWLS. Back in 1985, the 1978 Age Dis-crimination in Employment Amendments eliminated mandatory retirement before age seventy, "encouraged the development of retraining programs for older workers," and "created major training responsibilities for business and industry" (Lumsden, 1985, p. 20). Ten years later the European Union white paper *Teaching and Learning* (1995) urged that changing demographics and "a permanently changing economy compel the education and training system to change" (p. 18). As the world continued to flatten, Woodwell (2004) warned business leaders around the world that for the next two or more decades OWLS would drive changes in workplace learning and performance.

OWLS will need training and retraining, certification and recertification to keep up with technology as they remain in or reenter the workplace. OWL leaders will need new leadership skills to cope with the flattened worldwide workplace and new coaching and mentoring skills to help organizations train new leaders for the future. They will also need consulting and other skills to help them reenter the workplace as consultants or begin a whole new career. Then there are the training needs related to well-being—which could include everything from health and fitness to financial planning.

OWLS will also change the face of workplace learning and performance as organizations seek to accommodate individual age-related cognitive and func-tional changes. As Mary Sue Rogers, global leader, IBM Business Consulting Services Human Capital Management group, sees it: "The scale of this age-driven change will alter the way work and knowledge are managed within companies moving forward" (as cited in Whitney, 2005, n.p.). The sidebar gives a brief overview of how IBM is collaborating with business to make it happen.

IBM HELPS BUSINESSES
ANALYZE AND RETAIN OWLS

In October, 2005, IBM's Human Capital Management group introduced a new consulting service to help companies figure out how to retain, motivate, and utilize OWLS. IBM will work with companies to analyze OWLS as learners and performers, develop or adapt knowledge management systems and business processes to OWLS, manage the knowledge and skillsets that OWLS bring to the workforce, enhance the productivity of OWLS, and use OWLS to train new leaders to fill the gap when OWLS retire.

This chapter encourages the reader to think outside the box and take advantage of OWLS in the workplace. This chapter builds a business case for collaborating with OWLS to analyze, design, develop, implement, and evaluate training and development. These steps parallel the Human Performance Technology (HPT) Model that many WLP practitioners use as a strategy and guide for identifying and solving workplace problems, realizing performance improvement opportunities, or looking at challenges related to employees in the workplace. The model is reproduced in Figure 15.1.

Owl-Driven Training

Changing workplace demographics will force training professionals to face a number of issues related to the aging workforce. "Corporate based learning is growing and in many organizations it encompasses all three categories of human resource development—employee training, employee education, and employee development" (Richey, 1992, p. 17). Training program areas for the future may well include interpersonal skills, leadership skills, and consulting skills to deal with a multigenerational workplace. In addition to these three program areas, OWL-driven training will focus on job-related training and retraining, certification or recertification, technology interface, communication, coaching and mentoring, health and wellness, and so forth.

Figure 15.1. The Human Performance Technology Model.

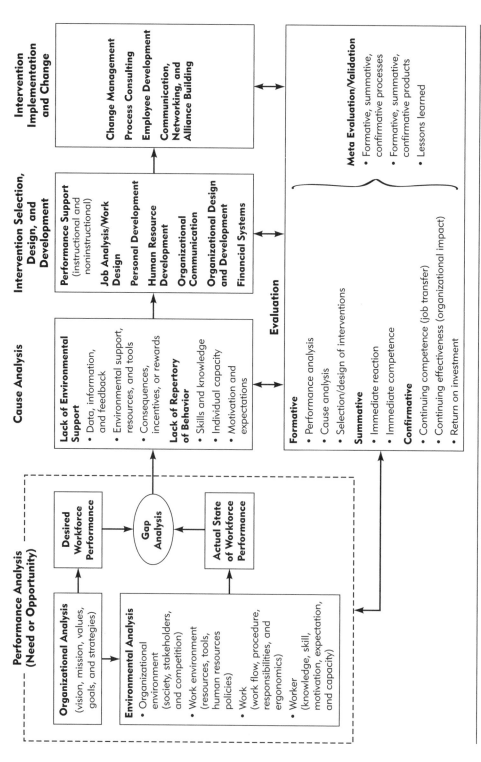

Source: VanTiem, D.M., Moseley, J.L. and Dessinger, J.C. (2004). *Fundamentals of Performance Technology: A Guide to Improving People, Process, and Performance* (2nd ed.). Silver Springs, MD: International Society for Performance Improvement (ISPI). Reproduced with permission.

Training or Retraining Is Inevitable

If organizations really want to retain OWLS in the workplace or rehire OWLS once they retire, they need to recognize that the opportunity to grow, learn, and develop should be the inalienable right of all workers, not only the new and the young. Organizations today cannot afford to let OWLS lose their skills or become obsolete; for one thing, it may be too hard to replace them.

OWLS will always need training or retraining in new business processes, new technologies, and new ways of thinking. They will need training to connect and collaborate as the economic playing field continues to flatten; for example, they may need to learn how to use the latest personal digital device or how to work in horizontal instead of vertical teams—teams that may span both time and space. They may also need retraining to handle telecommuting or other home-based working arrangements. In fact, as OWLS take on new and nontraditional roles, there will be many opportunities to train others in the organization as the entire organization learns how to collaborate with OWLS as consultants or telecommuters or part-time team members.

Certification or Recertification Will Require Training

Often training or retraining is tied to certification or recertification. Professional societies, government agencies, and other organizations are moving toward certification as a way to verify that they are serious about their commitment to professionalism and quality. As an integral part of the workforce, OWLS will need to obtain and upgrade the necessary certifications to make their organizations credible competitors. In an article on the myths of certification, Mulkey and Naughton (2005) quote Jim Olsen, vice president and chief measurement scientist for Alpine Media: "Certification programs are a standard way of distinguishing between qualified and unqualified individuals, companies, and institutions" (p. 21).

Certification and standards go hand in hand. As the world flattens, standards are becoming an important enabler: they can level the playing field and make it possible for more and more companies to compete in the global marketplace. Companies will need to make sure that their OWLS are certified standard bearers who can stand up to the scrutiny of quality audits and government or industry audits. Certification offers OWLS a balance between prestige and protection. It adds to professional credibility and provides opportunities for employment, promotion, and earning potential (Mulkey & Naughton, 2005; Biech, 2005).

Technology Interface Training Will Increase

Technology is an integral, inevitable component of the twenty-first-century workplace. Older OWLS often find this daunting; even some younger OWLS may fight the need to interface with technology or begrudgingly consent to use it only "if necessary." Some OWLS are willing, but find that age-related changes make it difficult or uncomfortable for them to master or use technology. Others cannot use technology without support from assistive technologies. The sidebar describes the challenge faced by one chief learning officer (CLO).

WORKPLACE APPLICATION

In Chapter One we used the Library of Congress staff as an example of a mature workforce. When Terry Bickham became first CLO for the Library of Congress, he was faced with a multifaceted challenge typical in today's aging workplace: he was to design and develop an online learning program to help the library's four thousand employees of all ages "to work in the world of digital information, and then to prepare those who are rapidly moving toward retirement to pass on their skills, knowledge, and vast experience to new employees" (Joyce, 2005). Bickham accepted the challenge to adapt new technology to meet the needs of both young and not-so-young, experienced and inexperienced workers and to build content that captured the knowledge power of the OWLS in his workforce.

OWLS need real-time or simulated, hands-on, on-the-job, just-in-time training to learn how to use technology for working, learning, and communicating. Training, supported by electronic performance support systems (EPSS) or print performance support tools (PST); online or real-time tutors; and the appropriate assistive technology will play a critical role in preventing and resolving problems with the OWL-technology interface.

Communication Training Goes High Tech

More and more, workplace communication and interaction are going high tech. OWLS and others are expected to communicate by email, instant messaging, texting, and voice mail; it's becoming the rule rather than the exception. The OWL in Figure 15.2 is faced with a number of telecommunication options.

Digital communication is both an art and a skill. Many organizations have found that they need to train employees not only to use telecommunication devices and computer communication programs, but also how to say what

Figure 15.2. Communication Options in the Twenty-First-Century Workplace.

they mean and mean what they say when they are not communicating face to face. According to Ron McMillan, author and founder of a communications firm, "For sharing information, asking questions, alerting people—modern technology is a marvel"; however, McMillan warns that the remaining 10 to 30 percent of business communication is "high stakes" crucial conversation or confrontation, and electronic means are "inadequate" and may even "magnify the problem" (in Summerfield, 2005, n.p.).

Many Mid-Old to Oldest OWLS are the newcomers on the block in terms of their experience with electronic communication. Most Gen X and Gen Y workers grew up with virtual communication. Mid-Old to Oldest OWLS may need to be convinced that virtual is okay, and maybe even better than okay. These OWLS need to learn how to let their fingers and thumbs do the talking, through email, chat rooms, text messaging, and so forth. Older OWLS, many of whom grew up with radio, so talking and listening are familiar waves of communication, may feel more comfortable with voice mail; younger OWLS may prefer text messaging.

Leadership Training Is Multigenerational

OWL leaders will both generate a need for leadership training and help provide leadership training to younger leaders. OWL leaders will need to learn new knowledge and skills to function in the new connected and collaborative workplace.

Feld (1999) suggests that the ever-changing global workplace requires special leadership skills: "The traits most commonly desired for the new world of work are flexibility, acceptance of change, and the ability to solve problems independently" (n.p.). Companies also seek energy and new ideas. Even OWLS who are experienced leaders will need training in the new skills, but many OWLS can solve problems independently, and many accept change and are flexible.

Today's OWL leaders need to be more independent. They have increased demands on their time and talent but cannot always count on support from above or below. Some OWL leaders must learn how to report to younger superiors, who expect them to be independent, entrepreneurial, connected, and collaborative. Many OWL leaders will find that a computer comes with the title and they are expected to be online—that's the "connected" part—as well as do their own memos, spreadsheets, reports, research, and so forth—that's the communication and collaboration part.

OWL leaders today must also learn to manage or supervise the most diverse, multigenerational group of workers in the history of the workplace. Workers may hold multiple jobs, speak multiple languages, and come from multiple cultures. Young workers will want work to be fun and will want to balance work and life outside of work. Other workers may be uncommitted, cynical, burned out, or angry. OWL leaders will need to add multitasking, sensitivity, adaptability, and technical know-how to their leadership repertoire. They may also need to learn how to be both connected and collaborative.

The situation may also arise in which younger leaders are supervising OWLS or training OWL leaders to use new technologies. OWLS may have to "learn how to take supervision from younger workers" (Beigel, 2001). This is an opportunity for WLP practitioners to use communication, team building, or interpersonal relationships training to help both OWLS and younger workers discover ways to understand and work with each other.

Workplace learning and performance opportunities for OWL leaders will be just-in-time, on-the-job, and personal. The opportunities will change with the job and the times, build on past experience, and allow OWL leaders to deal with current realities before or as they happen.

OWLS Can Train, Coach, Mentor New Leaders

OWLS also need to help their organizations train new leaders to fill the gap when they retire. Training alone can help new supervisors learn leadership skills; however, "[r]apid workplace changes often thrust brand new supervisors and managers into positions of pivotal importance without allowing them time to get acclimated" ("AchieveGlobal," 2005). Coaching and mentoring are two ways to acclimate new leaders.

Some companies are willing to invest in developing new talent through coaching and mentoring; for example, Dell offers pay incentives to managers who "nurture other people" at work. It is not unusual for Dell managers to have their own coaches and also to spend 30 to 35 percent of their time coaching and mentoring others (Byrnes, 2005).

When OWLS are called upon to train new supervisors and managers or coach and mentor newcomers as they transfer knowledge and skill to the real world of work, the OWLS themselves often need train-the-trainer sessions as well as training in coaching and mentoring skills.

Leadership is not the only area in which OWLS are useful as trainers, coaches, or mentors. Procter & Gamble and other manufacturing companies often use OWLS as turnkey trainers for new process or product start-ups. Prior to the start-up, the OWLS collaborate with the instructional designers to prepare the training and undergo an extensive train-the-trainer program in which they also learn coaching and mentoring skills. The OWLS then become the trainers, coaches, and mentors for other worker-trainers on the job and just in time to ensure a smooth start-up.

OWLS Need Health and Wellness Training

When you scan the training offerings of all types of organizations, there are always programs that relate to the well-being of OWLS in particular—health prevention and control, weight management counseling, nutrition and fitness, financial and retirement planning, stress control, and so forth.

Wellness programs pay off handsomely. DuPont, for example, substantially reduced absenteeism, and The Travelers Corporation and the Union Pacific Railroad report high returns for the dollars they invest in company-wide wellness (Greenberg & Baron, 2003). Wellness demands individual responsibility for maintaining optimal health. The reader is encouraged to review the dimensions of wellness previously discussed in Chapter Nine. Balance and maintenance of these essential components will help an organization's employees achieve high-level wellness.

Ask an OWL

How do learning and performance improvement professionals discover the specific OWL-driven training needs for their organization? Asking the organization or benchmarking the industry or other organizations is a start; however, the best way is to go directly to the source and ask an OWL, or OWLS, as the case may be. Figure 15.3 illustrates what happens when you collaborate with an OWL to analyze training needs.

Figure 15.3. Ask an OWL: A Collaborative Training Needs Analysis.

Collaborate to Design and Develop

Once learning and performance professionals discover the OWL-driven training needs, they can continue their collaboration with OWLS through the design and development phases. OWLS can be subject matter experts (SMEs) on how to design and develop OWL-friendly learning experiences. Here is an example: one guide for designing OWL-friendly learning is the "industrial gerontology model" (Callahan, Kiker, & Cross, 2003). The model focuses on the following design issues: motivation, structure, familiarity, organization, and time from the perspective of OWLS. Collaborating with OWLS is one way to determine just what that perspective might be—see Figure 15.4.

Figure 15.4. Ask An OWL: Collaborative Training Design and Development.

Here are some examples of questions to ask an OWL during a collaborative design session:

1. Motivation—What content and materials will be relevant to OWLS?

2. Structure—What do we need to do to meet the cognitive needs of OWLS? For example, does memory building instruction precede content instruction? Should we teach technology before using technology?

3. Organization—How should we sequence the content; for example, simple to complex, familiar to unfamiliar, general to particular?

4. Breaks—How are we going to schedule the activities so there is time for comfort breaks?

5. Time—How much time should we allow for OWLS to master the learning and performance tasks successfully?

Of course, the next logical step is to involve OWLS in the implementation and evaluation phases as well. We have already discussed how OWLS can train, coach, and mentor other OWLS and other worker-learners. Learning and performance professionals can also ask OWLS to help establish criteria or provide feedback for evaluating OWL-driven training programs.

Friedman (2005) discusses the importance of collaborating or partnering with customers; he even presents the concept of a "buffet" where customers can "serve themselves in their own way, at their own pace, in their own time, according to their own tastes" (p. 350) and extends the concept to the ideal of a "self-directed consumer" (p. 351). Although Friedman is talking about how companies can use collaboration to cope with a flat world, his analogy fits perfectly into our discussion of how companies can collaborate with OWLS to design, develop, implement, and evaluate OWL-friendly training. When learning and performance professionals view OWLS as customers or consumers, the idea of collaboration is one step closer to possible.

But we should not get ahead of ourselves. There is one more collaborative effort: deciding how to evaluate whether training policies, procedures, practices, and programs really are OWL-friendly. The sidebar shows that even OWLS consider evaluation an important part of workplace learning and performance.

EVALUATION CREATES WINNERS

It's important to evaluate what's happening in the workplace . . . Too often HRD departments only evaluate personnel functions . . . Organizations should evaluate the core of what we do to see what needs to be changed, adapted, modified or tweaked. Both the organization and the individual are winners when evaluation efforts are planned. Lots of learning takes place too.

Sally, age sixty-two, health care program specialist

Collaborate to Evaluate

Organizations support policies, procedures, practices, and programs to accomplish their mission and goals and remain competitive entities. When evaluation is woven into the fabric of the organization, it plays an integral part in guaranteeing success and everyone wins. This final section considers how to collaborate with OWLS and use evaluation protocol and opportunities to determine whether an organization's policies, procedures, practices, or programs are OWL-friendly. Figure 15. 5 illustrates a collaborative evaluation session between OWLS and others in the organization.

Figure 15.5. Ask an OWL: Collaborative Training Evaluation.

Evaluation Establishes Value

The term *evaluation* means establishing the merit or worth of something. It is decision 'making, and it leads to judgments. Evaluation is also used to value, to describe, and to measure (Margolis & Bell, 1989). Table 15.1 gives examples of using evaluation to value, describe, or measure workplace learning and performance efforts that involve OWLS.

Table 15.1. Examples of Evaluations That Value, Describe, or Measure.

Use	Examples
Value	• A trainer tells a team of OWLS, "Four of the last six networking luncheons have been rated 'excellent.'" • An OWL manager says to her immediate supervisor, "We figure the dispute resolution workshop has saved us $25,000."
Describe	• An OWL tells the trainer, "This workshop has taught me a variety of solid approaches in understanding generational differences." • A trainer instructs OWL participants at the end of the workshop: "Use two descriptive words to characterize the experience we shared."
Measure	• An OWL trainer says to his boss, "Eighty-two percent of the workshop participants scored ninety-two or better on the posttest." • An OWL participant says to the trainer, "This program would be better if the case studies were geared to our workplace issues."

Evaluation Provides Feedback

The purpose of evaluation is to provide feedback to individuals who have a need to know. These people are stakeholders, clients, sponsors, or general audiences. Biech (2005) suggests that evaluation serves:

- Employees who are mastering new knowledge, skills, and attitudes
- Employees who want to be reinforced and motivated regarding work-related issues

- Trainers who are addressing program needs or modifications in training efforts

- Supervisors who want to see if skills learned in training get transferred to the job

- Organizations who want to justify return on investment in workplace learning and performance (p. 252)

Evaluation Is Proactive

Why should we be concerned about evaluating organizational policies, procedures, practices, and programs? Phillips (1997) offers reasons that encourage us to be proactive:

- Accountability to stakeholders, sponsors, and clients

- Decreased spending budgets

- Mushrooming information technology

- Roles that evaluation and measurement play in professionalism

- Bottom-line contributions

- Competitive survival (pp. 11–12)

Successful evaluation of workplace learning and performance confirms whether or not what we've done has worked; whether improvements in individual and team learning have been successful; whether training goals and objectives have been met; whether the commitment of time and resources were justified; whether the organization's effort as a learning organization was realized; and whether continuous improvement at all levels was more than lip service (Goleman, 2002).

WLP Program Evaluation Is Systematic

Program evaluation is a systematic set of data collection and analysis activities undertaken to determine a program's characteristics, merits, or value. The process provides information on the effectiveness of programs to optimize their outcomes, efficiency, and quality (Fink, 2005; Fitzpatrick, Sanders, & Worthen, 2004; Boulmetis & Dutwin, 2006). Organizations conduct evaluations of their programs to prove that they make a difference and contribute to the client's success. In addition, program evaluations improve speed, determine costs and benefits, and help organizations make decisions for marketing future programs (Hale, 2002; Phillips, 1997).

Organizations can provide many kinds of programs to support their OWLS' needs and cater to their differences. These programs vary from living options to physical health and nutrition; from chemical dependency to financial planning; from retirement, leisure, and recreation to awareness about long-term care; the list is endless (Moseley & Dessinger, 1994). Whoever is charged with evaluating the organization's learning programs will find the checklist suggested in PST 15.1 a useful tool for evaluating whether the programs are OWL-friendly.

PST 15.1. Checklist for Evaluating WLP Programs for OWLS.

Purpose: To help WLP practitioners evaluate the effectiveness of training programs for OWLS

Instructions:

a. Place a check (✓) mark next to the criteria that apply to the program you are evaluating.

b. If the criteria are met, circle the check mark.

c. If at least 80 percent of the checked criteria for each element are met, the program will be OWL-driven or the elements will be effective for OWLS.

Collaboration with OWLS:

1. ☐ OWLS were involved in the needs analysis for the program.

2. ☐ OWLS were involved in the design of the program.

3. ☐ OWLS were involved in the development of the program.

4. ☐ OWLS were included in the pilot-test of the program.

5. ☐ OWLS were involved in planning the evaluation for the program.

6. ☐ OWLS evaluated the program.

Visual Elements: (illustrations, transparencies, slides, video, etc.)

1. ☐ The various visual elements do not require frequent changes in the level of lighting.

2. ☐ The visual aids will project clearly using the available equipment (VCR, slide projector, overhead projector, etc.).

3. ☐ The type size and amount of detail in the visual elements will project clearly in the environment (room, auditorium, etc.).

4. ☐ The environment will allow everyone in the group to see the visuals clearly.

5. ☐ The color in the visuals is predominantly black, nonglare white, red, yellow, and orange (as opposed to blue, green and violet).

6. ☐ Language clarity and presentation speed are addressed if required.

PST 15.1. Checklist for Evaluating WLP Programs for OWLS, *Continued*.

Text Elements: (books, worksheets, handouts, text on visuals, etc.)

1. ☐ The text is printed on nonglossy paper.

2. ☐ Color used in the printed material is predominantly red, yellow, and orange (as opposed to blue, green and violet).

3. ☐ Type size for all printed material is 12–14 point minimum.

4. ☐ There is high contrast between the paper and the ink.

5. ☐ The layout is "uncluttered."

6. ☐ There is an appropriate amount of white space.

7. ☐ Frequently used polysyllabic words are changed to their more simple synonyms.

Auditory Elements:

1. ☐ The voices on the sound track are loud enough to be heard without turning the volume to maximum.

2. ☐ Diction on the sound track is clear.

3. ☐ The face of the speaker (video) is clearly visible at all times so that the OWL can lip-read if necessary.

4. ☐ The gestures, expressions, and motion of the speaker enhance the meaning of the spoken word.

5. ☐ The tone of the voices on the sound track is low to medium.

6. ☐ The equipment you will use to produce the auditory track will be able to reproduce the sound without distortion.

7. ☐ The environment will reduce or eliminate interfering noise.

8. ☐ The presentation rate allows the OWL to take in the information and review it before retrieval.

9. ☐ Background music is appropriate for the program.

Instructional Strategies:

1. ☐ The program secures the OWL's attention before providing information.

2. ☐ The program provides sufficient practice for mastery.

3. ☐ The program provides constructive feedback.

4. ☐ The material is broken into units or modules of 10–20 minutes each.

5. ☐ Total time for each session is 2 hours or less.

6. ☐ There are frequent breaks and opportunities for walking, talking, and sharing.

7. ☐ The program works into physical activities gradually, rather than plunging into them.

8. ☐ Activities, including writing assignments, do not involve prolonged physical exertion.

9. ☐ Directions for the physical activities are flexible and can adapt to any perceived changes in the energy or the enthusiasm level of learners.

10. ☐ OWLS have time to review, reflect, and apply a new task before introducing another task.

11. ☐ A supportive, nonthreatening climate is provided.

12. ☐ The instruction minimizes conflict with previous knowledge by gradually introducing new concepts and allowing time for discussion and reflection.

13. ☐ The instruction allows OWLS to control time (self-paced).

14. ☐ The instruction minimizes the fear of failure.

15. ☐ The reward for participation is clear and constant.

16. ☐ The instruction combines auditory and visual modalities for most learning.

17. ☐ The instruction stresses auditory modality for information that must be stored in the short-term memory.

18. ☐ It stresses visual modality for information that must be stored in and later retrieved from long-term memory.

19. ☐ It allows OWLS to take an active part in the learning process.

20. ☐ The program stresses positive over negative feedback.

21. ☐ The feedback provided is constant.

22. ☐ Support mechanisms are built in to help OWLS avoid error.

PST 15.1. Checklist for Evaluating WLP Programs for OWLS, *Continued.*

Instructional Content:

1. ☐ The program emphasizes new knowledge that is consistent with previous knowledge.

2. ☐ The instruction is organized into categories and sequences.

3. ☐ The instruction contains visual and/or mnemonic clues to aid memory.

4. ☐ It reflects the context in which it will be used.

5. ☐ Instruction is concrete rather than abstract.

6. ☐ Instruction is of direct and immediate usefulness to the OWL.

Culturally Sensitive Awareness:

1. ☐ The program does not favor one group over another (e.g., more males than females, no minorities).

2. ☐ The program can be used by an OWL who is physically challenged.

3. ☐ The program does not reflect or support stereotypes (e.g., female secretary to white, male manager; minorities in subservient roles).

4. ☐ The program does not threaten an OWL's values and self-interest.

5. ☐ The program can be understood by its intended audience (e.g., reading level is appropriate for the audience).

Special Considerations and Recommendations:

_____

_____

_____

_____

Source: Moseley, J. L., & Dessinger, J. C. (1994, March). Criteria for evaluating instructional products and programs for older adult learners. *Performance and Instruction, 33*(3), pp. 39–45. Reproduced with permission.

And Finally . . .

All employees deserve the benefits derived from solid, systematic, and purposeful evaluation. OWLS—especially because of who they are, where they are, and what they bring to the learning organization—deserve policies, procedures, practices, and programs that are well evaluated and capitalize on their qualities of wisdom, balance, punctuality, vision, and caring (Edmondson, 2005). The organization also needs to view OWLS as customers and collaborators in all phases of workplace learning and performance—including evaluation.

ADDITIONAL RESOURCES

Davidson, E. J. (2005). *Evaluation methodology basics: The nuts and bolts of sound evaluation.* Thousand Oaks, CA: Sage.

Dessinger, J. C., & Moseley, J. L. (2004). *Confirmative evaluation: Practical strategies for valuing continuous improvement.* San Francisco: Pfeiffer.

Hodges, T. K. (2002). *Linking learning and performance: A practical guide to measuring learning and on-the-job application.* Boston: Butterworth Heinemann.

Preskill, H., & Russ-Eft, D. (2005). *Building evaluation capacity: 72 activities for teaching and training.* Thousand Oaks, CA: Sage.

Epilogue

The workplace is aging, and workplace learning and performance (WLP) practitioners are taking a closer look at how to train older worker-learners (OWLS). WLP practitioners need new knowledge and skills to maximize the learning and performance of OWLS and their organizations. For years, adult educators have recognized that older learners may require learning events that are different in design and content from those provided for younger adult learners. In the workplace, OWLS may also need some assistance and accommodation to capitalize on their potential for amplifying the successful performance of their companies and organizations.

Our chief goal was to help WLP practitioners maximize the workplace learning and performance of OWLS based on sound theory and best practice. We have accomplished that. We hope that you have learned about the many characteristics that make OWLS unique workplace inhabitants. We also hope that you have expanded your repertoire of OWL-friendly learning interventions and have used a set of performance support tools (PST) for analyzing, designing, developing, implementing, and evaluating WLP interventions for and with OWLS.

Consider the many strengths that OWLS bring to the workplace, and use their talents to make the workplace better, happier, and more productive. Here are some suggestions for involving OWLS:

- Capitalize on the wisdom and tremendous knowledge and skills OWLS bring to organizational dynamics. The attitudes they have about their work ethic, their approaches to handling difficult cases, and their definite sense of self-assurance that all is right with the world is helpful in workplace learning and performance.

- Capitalize on the punctuality of OWLS in working with their peers and team members. View their generational differences as positive forces in planning policies, following through with procedures, and carrying out the practices that give organizations cohesiveness. They model dependency.

- Capitalize on the vision OWLS bring to WLP. They usually think clearly when policies are planned or discussed and they are quick to identify problems, opportunities, and challenges and offer potential solutions.

- Capitalize on the OWLS' abilities to achieve appropriate balance in their work. They are well motivated, and they are flexible when policies are reviewed, when procedures are challenged, and when practices are implemented.

- Capitalize on OWLS' abilities to care. Caring about their work and about the people with whom they interact is an extension of their work ethic, and it shows their colleagues they are committed to the organization.

- Finally, capitalize on the OWLS' sense of fun, firmness, and fair play. As a group, they are happy folk, and they have great, detailed stories—and sometimes tall tales—to tell anyone willing to listen. They stand up for their beliefs, and they have the ability to laugh at themselves.

We have made way for OWLS in the workplace. We have seen them in transition. We have suggested ways for WLP practitioners to transform them. We have strongly urged WLP practitioners to collaborate with them. A bouquet of possibilities lies before us. Let us answer the call to fully integrate OWLS into our workplaces.

GLOSSARY

accessible technology: Computer technology that enables individuals to adjust a computer to meet their visual, hearing, dexterity, cognitive, and speech needs.

accuracy standards: Standards intended to ensure that an evaluation will provide technically accurate information.

age bias/discrimination: Decisions against OWLS based solely on age; usually triggered by perceptions of the negative effects of aging on workplace learning and performance.

aging workforce: A global trend toward an increase in OWLS and a decrease in younger workers.

analytical problem-solving: A sequential, systematic process that (1) consists of identifying the problem, selecting and implementing the solution, and evaluating the results; and (2) encourages convergent thinking and tends to focus on one solution rather than multiple or blended options. See also *creative problem-solving* and *problem-solving*.

andragogy: A theory of adult learning developed by Malcolm Knowles, which postulates that adults are self-directed in their learning.

assistive technology: Products specially designed to provide additional accessibility to individuals with physical or cognitive difficulties, impairments, and disabilities.

attention: The ability to mentally focus on an object or task. See also *selective attention* and *sustained attention.*

Attention Deficit Disorder (ADD): A neurobiological disorder characterized by exaggerated levels of inattention and distractibility, without the extreme behaviors related to hyperactivity.

Attention Deficit Hyperactivity Disorder (ADHD): A neurobiological disability characterized by exaggerated levels of any or all of the following: inattention, distractibility, impulsivity, and over- or under-activity.

automaticity: Repeating knowledge and skills until they can be repeated automatically.

baby boomer: Belonging to the generation born between 1946 and 1964.

BOP, The Big: Acronym for three common on-the-job issues faced by OWLS—*burnout* or a feeling of being used up, exhausted; *obsolescence* or a feeling of being replaced by technology or someone new and more up to date; and *plateauing* or coming to the end of a career with no possibility of an increase in rank or remittance.

brain drain: A popular term that refers to the movement of highly knowledgeable and skilled workers out of their current organization or out of the workplace entirely, and the difficulty of replacing their knowledge and skills.

capital: Legitimate asset or resource that can generate economic wealth. See also *knowledge capital* and *people capital.*

champion: As commonly used in the quality field, a person who is a strong advocate or supporter of a quality initiative.

chunking: Transforming information into smaller parts that are more easily remembered.

cognitive: An adjective used to describe mental activities, such as reasoning, intuition, or perception, that are related to the acquisition of knowledge.

cognitive abilities: Mental processing aptitudes, such as attending, remembering, communicating, and understanding thought sequences, and visual, auditory, or kinesthetic perception.

cognitive load theory: An instructional design theory that suggests chunking information to avoid cognitive overload.

cohort: A sociological term used to describe a "group of people who will always share a common location in history" (Sheehy, 1995, p. 23).

color sensitivity: Ability to differentiate between various colors and hues; affects the legibility and readability of printed materials.

contrast sensitivity: Ability to detect slight changes in brightness between areas that have no sharp lines around them; affects the legibility and readability of printed materials.

creative problem-solving: A process for solving problems that encourages divergent thinking; participants consider solutions that are novel, inconsistent, or never considered before to produce many different solutions to a single problem. See also *problem-solving.*

creative thinking: Use of the mind to consider original and imaginative ideas and make judgments that are original or new. See also *think.*

creativity: A universal ability to use the imagination to develop new and original ideas or things; an output of creative thinking.

crystallized intelligence: Intelligence that is affected by culture and experience. See also *fluid intelligence, intelligence,* and *multiple intelligence.*

culture of retention: Values, norms, and practices that focus on keeping and maintaining both knowledge and people capital within an organization.

decode: To transform an encoded message into a usable form; to interpret or make sense of sensory data.

demographer: A person who studies and analyzes statistics related to the size, growth, density, distribution, and other characteristics of human populations.

demographic shift: Movement away from the traditional workplace in which there is a balance between young workers entering the workforce and older workers leaving the workplace.

demographics: Statistics related to the size, growth, density, distribution, and other characteristics of human populations.

developmental task: A task, arising during a period in the lifespan of an individual, whose successful achievement will result in happiness and success in later tasks; each developmental task generates a readiness to learn and a teachable moment.

dialogue: Team learning or action learning strategy that asks learners to put away their assumptions and build connections by "thinking together."

dual processing: The use of both auditory and visual cues to process memory.

dyscalculia: A learning disability that makes it difficult to perform basic mathematical functions and/or solve mathematical problems.

dysgraphia: A learning disability that impairs writing ability and makes it difficult to communicate clearly in handwriting.

dyslexia: A learning disability marked by severe difficulty in recognizing and understanding written or printed language; may be caused by problems with the visual or phonological processing of letters and words; also known as "word blindness."

educational gerontology: The study of how and why older adults learn; an interface between adult education and social gerontology.

electronic performance support system: Software that provides information on-demand and just-in-time to support human performance.

encode: A cognitive process that brings meaning to sensory data and connects or associates it with other data already stored in long-term memory.

evaluation standards: See *program evaluation standards.*

executive control or function: A complex set of cognitive abilities that includes cognitive flexibility or concurrent manipulation of information, concept formation, and cue-driven behavior; sometimes referred to as part of attention, and sometimes as a separate cognitive domain.

experience: The sum total of an individual's repertoire of knowledge and skills derived from past actions and perceptions.

explicit memory: Information that a person consciously learns and retains; declarative knowledge such as facts, rules, and definitions is an example of an explicit memory. See also *implicit memory* and *memory.*

feasibility standards: Standards intended to ensure that an evaluation will be prudent, cost effective, and realistic.

fluid intelligence: Intelligence that is determined by genetics and physiology. See also *crystallized intelligence* and *intelligence.*

formal OJT: Planned on-the-job training that may include a combination of classroom, follow Harry around, practice, feedback, and testing.

generations: All of the people who were born at approximately the same time and are considered as a group or cohort, who share the same values, interests, and attitudes.

global workplace: Concept that workers conduct work-related duties or activities within a worldwide system with fewer and fewer boundaries.

health: State of complete physical, mental, and social well-being and not merely the absence of disease.

hue: The property of light by which an object is classified on the color spectrum as red, blue, green, yellow, and so forth.

implicit memory: A category of informal learning and a by-product of some other activity such as task accomplishment, interpersonal activity, and so forth.

informal learning: Learning that originates in everyday activities; intentional but not highly structured.

informal OJT: Practice of asking an experienced employee to teach a new employee the knowledge *and* skills required to perform a job; the process includes show-and-tell, practice, and test.

intelligence: An individual's inherited or genetic ability for acquiring new knowledge and skill. See also *crystallized, fluid,* and *multiple intelligence.*

intervention: An action taken to change what is happening or what might happen. See also *performance interventions.*

just-in-time training (JITT): Real-time learning that delivers the right information to the right person at the right time using the right delivery method. See also *learning continuum.*

knowledge capital: View of knowledge as a legitimate asset or resource that can generate economic wealth.

knowledge worker: White-collar or blue-collar workers with specialized knowledge, skills, and/or responsibilities.

learning continuum: A continuous, seamless series of learning opportunities that blend into each other so that it is difficult to say where one learning opportunity ends and the next learning opportunity begins.

legibility: The speed with which each letter or word in a printed document can be recognized.

life expectancy: The average number of years that an individual of a given age can expect to live, based on the longevity experience of the person's population.

lifespan: A biological estimate of the maximum number of years a species is expected to live, based on the longest living cases observed and inherited characteristics.

lifetime employability: A policy in which governments partner with companies to give employees the resources they need to remain employable.

lifetime employment: A policy in which organizations guaranteed a job for life.

longevity: The expected duration of life, based on life table analyses of age-specific death rates.

long-term memory: That part of memory where data are cataloged and stored so that they can be recognized and recalled immediately or at a later time.

memory: A cognitive function that allows the mind to retain learned information and knowledge of past events and experiences and to retrieve it. See also *explicit, implicit, long-term, short-term, primary, secondary,* and *sensory memory; memory cues.*

memory cues: Something said or done that provides a signal to prompt or trigger a memory of something; a response-producing stimulus that results in the recall of a specific memory.

meta skills: Higher-level thinking skills such as metacognition, metamemory, and so forth, that help adults think about and use abstract concepts, and gain insights from self-analysis and experience.

mnemonics: Tools or systems used to improve or help the memory, that is, the ability of the mind to retain learned information and knowledge of past events and experiences and to retrieve it.

multigenerational workplace: A term used to describe the broad age-range of workers in a given workplace.

multiple intelligence: Theory by Gardner (1983) that intelligence is composed of eight separate and distinct dimensions: verbal, logical-mathematical, visual-spatial, musical-rhythmic, bodily-kinesthetic, interpersonal, intrapersonal, and naturalist.

noncognitive factors: Variables such as motivation, education level, health and wellness, sensory status, functionality, and experience that have an effect on the learner's ability to transfer learning into performance.

nonphysical job demands: Work that does not require strenuous physical activity; may be stressful if the job does require intense concentration, intense contact with coworkers or customers, and so forth.

on-the-job-training (OJT): A seamless, on-the-job learning continuum for workers. See *learning continuum, formal OJT,* and *informal OJT.*

OWLS: Acronym for older worker-learners—men and women age 40+ who actively participate in the workplace as workers and learners.

OWL-centric training: Training that is focused on the audience—OWLS—rather than on the content or format.

people capital: View of employees as a legitimate asset or resource that can generate economic wealth.

perception: An attitude or understanding based on what is observed, felt, or thought.

performance: The action of a person and the result of the action.

performance intervention: Training or nontraining action taken to change, improve, or maintain individual or organizational performance.

physical job demands: Work that requires strenuous physical activity.

presbyopia: Medical term for a progressive reduction in the eye's ability to focus on close material such as reading matter, which occurs naturally with aging.

primary memory: Another phrase for short-term memory.

problem-solving: A process used to resolve or find a solution for a difficult situation, matter, or person.

program evaluation: A systematic way of collecting and analyzing data to determine the value of a program.

program evaluation standards: Standards for evaluating education programs established by the Joint Committee on Standards for Educational Evaluation (1994) and applicable to both education and training programs. See also *accuracy, feasibility, propriety,* and *utility standards.*

propriety standards: Standards intended to ensure that an evaluation will be conducted ethically, legally, and with consideration of all the people involved. See also *feasibility, utility standards.*

readability: Ease of reading a page of text.

real-time training: Face-to-face, concurrent individual or group training; trainer or coach and learner(s) are together in time and space.

rehearsal: The process of repeating the input data over and over again without changing it; drill-and-practice.

reinforcement: A technique used to increase or improve a desired behavioral outcome by rewarding positive performance and/or punishing negative performance.

retention: The ability to keep ideas or information in mind or memory.

retirement: The act of leaving a job or career at or near the traditional age for doing so.

reverse coaching or mentoring: A term used to describe a situation where the coach or mentor is younger than the person being coached or mentored.

secondary memory: Another phrase for long-term memory.

selective attention: Cognitive ability to identify and focus on relevant information.

self-directed learning: The ability of learners to proactively diagnose their learning needs and plan and implement their own learning.

sensory memory: The mind's ability to use the visual, auditory, and/or tactile senses to process sensory information in the environment.

short-term memory: Working memory; can store up to seven items or process 2–3 items; has a maximum duration of ten to twenty seconds.

simulation: Replication of the essential features of a real-life situation or object.

stereotype: To assign characteristics to an individual or group based on an oversimplified, standardized image or idea held by one person or a group of people.

structured OJT: See *formal OJT.*

sustained attention: Cognitive ability to focus on and perform a task without losing track of the task objective; usually "well preserved" over the lifespan.

teachable moment: Window of opportunity for learning a new concept or skill based on a real or perceived need for that concept or skill.

think: Use the mind to consider ideas and make judgments. See also *creative thinking*.

transformational learning: A theory and a process; Meizrow, Freire, and others postulate that given new information, past experience, and a period of critical reflection, the learner can be empowered or self-directed to transform or change learning into performance.

unstructured OJT: See *informal OJT*.

utility standards: Standards intended to ensure that the evaluation serves the needs of its users.

values: The accepted principles or standards of an individual or a group. See *workplace values*.

virtual learning: Trainer or coach and student(s) are separated by time, space, or both.

visuospatial functions: The cognitive function that allows a person to visually perceive spatial relationships among objects.

volunteering: The act of donating individual time and talents to a community or an organization.

well-being: A state of comfort that affects how a person copes with change and transitions.

wellness: Mental and physical soundness that is achieved and maintained through good nutrition, exercise, and so forth.

wisdom: Ability to perceive and explain the meaning or the intrinsic character of somebody or something.

WLP: Acronym for workplace learning and performance.

WLP roles: Functions that WLP practitioners perform in the workplace; the roles include Manager, Analyst, Intervention Selector, Intervention Designer and Developer, Intervention Implementer, Change Leader, and Evaluator.

work: The duties or activities that are part of a job or occupation; "one version of performance" (Langdon, 1995, p. 12)

worker: A person who performs the duties or activities that are part of a job or occupation.

workflow learning: Learning that takes place on-the-job and/or just-in-time; learning that is part of the natural progress of work; a fusion of learning and doing. See *learning continuum.*

workforce: The total group of people who work in a specific workplace, or a group of people who work together for a specific purpose.

workplace: The general location—U.S., global, and so forth—or specific location—factory, office, and so forth—where workers conduct work-related duties or activities. See also *multigenerational workplace* and *workplace values.*

workplace values: The accepted principles or standards of an individual or a group that relate to and are reflected in workplace behavior.

workspan: An estimate of the maximum number of years a worker can remain in the workforce.

REFERENCES

Preface

Hutchinson, C. S., & Stein, E. S. (1997). A whole new world of interventions: The PT practitioner as integrating generalist. *Performance Improvement, 36*(10), 28–35.

Rothwell, W. J. (1999). *Beyond training and development: State-of-the-art strategies for enhancing human performance.* NY: American Management Association (AMACOM).

Rothwell, W. J., Sanders, E., & Soper, J. G. (1999). *ASTD models for workplace learning and performance: Roles, competencies, and outputs.* Alexandria, VA: American Society for Training and Development (ASTD).

Spitzer, D. (1992). The design and development of effective interventions. In H. D. Stolovitch & E. J. Keeps (Eds.), *Handbook of human performance technology: A comprehensive guide for analyzing and solving performance problems in organizations* (pp. 114–129). San Francisco: Jossey-Bass.

Chapter One

Aaron, H. J., Bosworth, B. P., & Burtless, G. (1989). Can America afford to grow old? Paying for social security. Washington, DC: Brookings Institution Press.

Age: The position of older workers. Retrieved January 8, 2006, from http://www.diversityatwork.net/EN/en_theme_age.htm

Allier, J. J., & Kolosh, K. (2005, June). Preparing for baby boomer retirement. *Chief Learning Officer 4*(6), 42–44; 49.

Arrowsmith, J., & McGoldrick, A. (1996). *Breaking the barriers.* London, England: Institute of Management Studies (IMS).

Atchley, R. C. (1991*). Social forces and aging* (6th ed.). Belmont, CA: Wadsworth.

Briefing sheet: Older people and learning—Some key statistics. (2005). Retrieved May 5, 2005, from http://www.niace.org.uk/information/Briefing_sheets/Older_Learners_Stats.htm

Callahan, J. S., Kiker, D. S., & Cross, T. (2003). Does method matter? A meta-analysis of the effects of training method on older learner training performance. *Journal of Management 29*(5), 663–680.

Fullerton, H., Jr. (1999, December). Labor force participation: 75 years of change, 1950–98 and 1998–2025. *Monthly Labor Review,* 3–12.

Hale, N. (1990). *The older worker.* San Francisco: Jossey-Bass.

Hall, B. (2005). The top training priorities for 2005: The third annual leaders of learning survey. *Training, 42*(2), 22–29.

Johnson, R. W. (2004, July). Trends in job demands among older workers, 1992–2002. *Monthly Labor Review, 127*(7), 48–56. Retrieved February 22, 2005, from http://www.bls.gov/opub/mlr/2004/07/art4full.pdf

Joyce, A. (2005, May 29). Easier lessons to take: Best training systems are mindful of matching employees' needs. *Washington Post,* p. F04. Retrieved June 1, 2005 from www.washingtonpost.com

Kraut, A. I. (Ed.). (1996). *Organizational surveys: Tools for assessment and change.* San Francisco: Jossey-Bass.

Labor force predictions to 2012: The graying of the U.S. workforce. (2004, February). *Monthly Labor Review.* Washington, DC: U.S. Department of Labor.

Lesser, E., Farrell, B., & Payne, M. (2004, October 21). *Addressing the challenges of an aging workforce: A human capital perspective for firms operating in Asia Pacific.* Somers, NY: IBM Business Consulting Services. Retrieved from www.ibm.com/bus

Lesser, E., Hausmann, C., & Feuerpeil, S. (2005, March 16). *Addressing the challenges of an aging workforce: A human capital perspective for companies operating in Europe.* IBM Institute for Business Value study. Somers, NY: IBM Global Services. Retrieved from www.ibm.com/bcs

Leven, C. (2004, September). Older workers: Opportunity at our doorstep. Speech presented at Nikkei Senior Work-life Forum, Tokyo, Japan.

Maher, K. (2005, May 3). Skills shortage gives training programs new life. *Wall Street Journal,* A2.

McIntire, M. B. (2005, March). The aging workforce: Helping older workers remain productive. *The Journal of Employee Assistance, 35*(1), 26.

Metcalf, H., & Thompson, M. (1990). Older workers: Employers' attitudes and practices. London: Institute of Management Studies (IMS).

Neikrug, S. M., Ronen, M., & Glanz, D. (1995). A special case of the very old lifelong learners. *Educational Gerontology, 21,* 345–355.

Neugarten, B. L. (1936). *Middle age and aging: A reader in social psychology.* Chicago: University of Chicago Press.

O'Toole, J., & Lawler, E. E., III. (2006). *The new American workplace.* New York: Palgrave Macmillan.

Reimagining America: AARP's blueprint for the future. (n.d.) Washington, DC: American Association for Retired Persons (AARP). Hard copy received August 31, 2005, from AARP.

Roberson, D. N. (2003). Education and today's older worker. ERIC Document Reproduction Service No. EDU 480 721.

Rothwell, W. J., Sanders, E. S., & Soper, J. G. (1999). *ASTD models for workplace learning and performance: Roles, competencies, and outputs.* Alexandria, VA: ASTD.

The search is on for America's oldest worker for 2006. (2006, February 4). *Experience Works News.* Retrieved February 4, 2006, from www.experienceworks.org

SHRM Trends. (2003, January 27). Retrieved February 4, 2006, from www.shrm.org/trends/visions/aging.asp

Staying ahead of the curve: The AARP Work and Career Study. (2002). Washington, DC: AARP.

Stein, D., & Rocco, T.S. (2001). *The older worker: Myths and realities.* Columbus, OH: ERIC Clearinghouse on Adult, Career, and Vocational Education. ED99CO0013.

Turning boomers into boomerangs. (2006, February 18). *The Economist, 378*(8465), 65.

The U.S. Bureau of Labor Statistics. (2002). Report on the civilian labor force. Washington, DC: U.S. Government Printing Office.

Van Tiem, D.M., Moseley, J. L., & Dessinger, J.C. (2001). *Performance improvement interventions: Enhancing people, process and organizations through performance technology.* Silver Spring, MD: International Society for Performance Improvement (ISPI).

Watanabe, C. (2005, March 21). Centenarians leave their mark on Japan. *Detroit News*, Metro Edition, p. 10A.

Wellner, A. (2002, March). Tapping a silver mine. *HR Magazine, 47*(3), 26–32.

Woodwell, W., Jr. (2004). Demography is destiny: Population shifts will transform the 21st century workplace. *The ASTD trend watch: The forces that shape workplace performance and improvement.* Alexandria, VA: ASTD. Retrieved June 11, 2005 at www.astd.org

Chapter Two

Age: The position of older workers. Retrieved January 8, 2006, from http://www.diversityatwork.net/EN/en_theme_age.htm

Allen, A. Z. (1993). *Training an aging workforce: Overcoming myths. Training Manual for McDonald's McMasters Program,* ERIC Document Reproduction Service No. EDU 362 662.

America's changing workforce. (2003). Washington, DC: American Association of Retired Persons (AARP).

Atchley, R. C. (1991*). Social forces and aging* (6th ed.). Belmont, CA: Wadsworth.

Baltes, P. B. (1993). The aging mind: Potential and limits. *The Gerontologist 33*(5), 580–594.

Beigel, J. (2001, July/August). Business and aging: Business, labor explore growing need for older workers. *Aging Today, xxii*(4), 13.

Bolch, M. (2000, December). The changing face of the workforce. *Training 37*(12), 72–78.

Crimmins, E. M., Reynolds, S. L., & Saito, Y. (1999, January). Trends in health and ability to work among the older working age population. *Journal of Gerontology: Social Sciences,* 531–540.

Findsen, B. (2005). *Learning later.* Malabar, FL: Krieger.

Friedman, T. L. (2005). *The world is flat: A brief history of the twenty-first century.* New York: Farrar, Straus & Giroux.

Grossman, R. J. (2003, August). Are you ignoring older workers? *HR Magazine, 48*(8). Retrieved March 3, 2005, from www.shrm.org/hrmagazine/articles/0803/0803covstory.asp

Hodson, R., & Sullivan, T. A. (2002). *The social organization of work* (3rd ed.). Belmont, CA: Wadsworth/Thomson Learning.

Hooyman, N., & Kiyak, H. A. (1999). *Social gerontology: An interdisciplinary perspective* (5th ed.). Boston: Allyn and Bacon.

Johnson, R. W. (2004, July). Trends in job demands among older workers, 1992–2002. *Monthly Labor Review, 127*(7), 48–56. Retrieved February 22, 2005, from http://www.bls.gov/opub/mlr/2004/07/art4full.pdf

Lesser, E., Farrell, B., & Payne, M. (2004, October 21). *Addressing the challenges of an aging workforce: The graying of Asia Pacific's workforce: A human capital perspective for firms operating in Asia Pacific.* Somers, NY: IBM Business Consulting Services. Retrieved from www.ibm.com/bus

Odums, G. (2006, January). A new year's resolution: Optimize older workers. *Training + Development, 60*(1), 34–36.

Older worker adjustment programs. (1999, March). *Lessons Learned Series.* Canada: Human Resources Development Canada (HRDC). Retrieved February 2, 2006, from http://www11.hrsdc.gc.ca/en/cs/sp/hrsdc/edd/brief/1999–000578/owap.shtml

Ramsey, R. D. (June, 2003). Tapping the strengths of older workers. *Supervision, 64*(6), 9–11.

Roberson, D. N. (2003). *Education and today's older worker.* ERIC Document Reproduction Service No. EDU 480 721.

Self-employment and the 50+ population: Self-employed tend to be older. (2004, May). AARP Bulletin. Retrieved from www.research.aarp.org/econ/2004_03_self_employ.html

Sicker, M. (1993). The future of mid life and older workers: The question of social responsibility and a national employment policy. *The 35th Annual Haak-Lilliefors Memorial Lecture.* Flint: Michigan Society of Gerontology Conference.

Staying ahead of the curve: The AARP Work and Career Study. (2002). Washington, DC: AARP.

Test your attitudes about older workers. (n.d.). *The Pfizer Journal.* Retrieved February 9, 2006, from http://www.thepfizerjournal.com/default.asp?a=article&j=tpj42&t=Test%20Your%20Attitudes%20About%20Older%20Workers

Watanabe, C. (2005, March 21). Centenarians leave their mark on Japan. *Detroit News Metro Edition,* 10A.

Wild, R. (July & August 2004). Older workers, big returns. *AARP The Magazine, 47*(4B), 16.

The wonder years. (2004, May & June). *AARP The Magazine,* 18.

Chapter Three

AARP/Home Depot: Thousands answer call for jobs at Home Depot. (2004, May). *AARP Bulletin 45*(5), 30.

Allier, J. J., & Kolosh, K. (2005, June). Preparing for baby boomer retirement. *Chief Learning Officer 4*(6), 42–44; 49.

Best practices: Flexible work. (2004). Retrieved June 20, 2005, from http://www.aarp.org/money/employerresourcecenter/bestpractices/Articles/a2004-12-17-flexiblework.html

Blank, R., & Slipp, S. (1994). *Voices of diversity: Real people talk about problems and solutions in a workplace where everyone is not alike.* New York: AMACOM.

Concelman, J., & Burns, J. (2006, March). The perfect storm or just a shower? *Training + Development 60*(3), 51–54.

Cross, J., & O'Driscoll, T. (2005, February). Workflow learning gets real. *Training 42*(2), 30–35.

Davenport, T. H. (2005). *Thinking for a living: How to get better performance and results from knowledge workers.* Boston: Harvard Business School Press.

DeLong, D. W. (2004). *Lost knowledge: Confronting the threat of an aging workforce.* New York: Oxford University Press.

Dychtwald, K., Erikson, T. J., & Morison, R. (2006). *Workforce crisis: How to beat the coming shortage of skills and talent.* Boston: Harvard Business School Press.

Dychtwald, K., & Flower, J. (1989). *Age wave: The challenges and opportunities of an aging America.* Los Angeles: Tarcher.

The Global Human Capital Study 2002. Retrieved May 9, 2005, from http://www.1. http://www.ibm.com/services or contact IBM Business Global Consulting Services 1-800-IBM-7080.

The Global Human Capital Study 2005. Retrieved May 9, 2005, from http://www.ibm.com/services or contact IBM Business Global Consulting Services 1-800-IBM-7080.

Gomez-Mejia, L. R., Balkin, D. B., & Cardy, R. L. (2001). *Managing human resources* (3rd ed.). Upper Saddle River, NJ: Prentice Hall.

Grossman, R. J. (2003, August). Are you ignoring older workers? *HR Magazine, 48*(8). Retrieved March 3, 2005, from www.shrm.org/hrmagazine/articles/0803/0803covstory.asp

Hardy, M. A. (2002, Summer). The transformation of retirement in twentieth-century America: From discontent to satisfaction. *Generations Journal, 26*(2), n.p. Retrieved August 18, 2005, from http://www.generationsjournal.org/generations/gen26–2/article.html

Harris, P. (May, 2005). Boomer vs. echo boomer: The work war? *Training + Development,* 44–50.

Hodson, R., & Sullivan, T. A. (2002). *The social organization of work* (3rd ed.). Belmont, CA: Wadsworth/Thomson Learning.

Jarvis, P. (2001). *Learning in later life: An introduction for educators and caregivers.* London: Kogan Page.

Johnson, R. W. (2004, July). Trends in job demands among older workers, 1992–2002. *Monthly Labor Review, 127*(7), 48–56. Retrieved February 22, 2005, from http://www.bls.gov/opub/mlr/2004/07/art4full.pdf

Kaplan-Leiserson, E. (2005, April). Mind the (talent) gap. *Training + Development, 59*(4), 12–13.

Kramer, L. (2004, June 7). Firms try to defuse massive boomer exit. *Crain's New York Business, 20*(23), 20.

Kroll, K. You can't fire me now: There's no business like your own business. (2004, July/August). *AARP: The Magazine, 47*(4B), 18.

Lesser, E., Hausmann, C., & Feuerpeil, S. (2005, March 16). *Addressing the challenges of an aging workforce: A human capital perspective for companies operating in Europe.* IBM Institute for Business Value study. Somers, NY: IBM Global Services. Retrieved from www.ibm.com/bcs

Peterson, D. S. (1985). A history of education for older learners. In D. B. Lumsden (Ed.), *The older adult as learner: Aspects of educational gerontology* (pp. 1–23). New York: Hemisphere.

The Perfect Storm. (2005, June 8). *CLO Executive Briefings,* online newsletter.

Self-employment and the 50+ population: Self-employed tend to be older. (2004, May). AARP Bulletin. Retrieved from www.research.aarp.org/econ/2004_03_self_employ.html

Sheppard, N. A., & Fisher, G. S. (1985). Career education for older learners. In D. B. Lumsden (Ed.), *The older adult as learner: Aspects of educational gerontology.* (pp. 197–226). New York: Hemisphere.

Stetson, S. (2006, July). Boomers fill gap. *Training + Development, 60*(7), 12.

Time to start focusing on attracting older workers. (2004, February). *HR Focus, 81*(2), 13–14.

Tiwana, A. (2002). *The knowledge management toolkit: Orchestrating IT, strategy, and knowledge platforms* (2nd ed.). Upper Saddle River, NJ: Prentice Hall PTR.

Van Tiem, D. M., Moseley, J. L., & Dessinger, J. C. (2001). *Performance improvement interventions: Enhancing people, processes, and organizations through performance technology.* Silver Spring, MD: International Society for Performance Improvement.

Woodwell, W., Jr. (2004). Demography is destiny: Population shifts will transform the 21st century workplace. *The ASTD trends watch: The forces that shape workplace performance and improvement.* Washington, DC: ASTD. Retrieved June 11, 2005 at www.astd.org

Chapter Four

Age Concern: Welcome to the cyber senior web site. Retrieved March 3, 2006, from http://www.cyberseniorsgroup.co.uk/facts.html

Baumgartner, L. M. (2001). An update on transformational learning. In S. B. Merriam (Ed.), *New directions for adult and continuing education: The new update on adult learning theory* (pp. 15–24). San Francisco: Jossey-Bass.

Binstock, R. H., & George, L. K. (Eds.). (1996). Handbook of aging and the social sciences (4th ed.). San Diego: Academic Press.

Briefing sheet: Older people and learning—Some key statistics. (2005). Retrieved May 5, 2005, from http://www.niace.org.uk/information/Briefing_sheets/Older_Learners_Stats.htm

Brockett, R. G. (1997). Humanism as an instructional paradigm. In C. Dills & A. J. Romiszowski (Eds.), *Instructional development paradigms.* Englewood Cliffs, NJ: Educational Technology Publications.

Brookfield, S. D. (1991). *The skillful teacher: On technique, trust, and responsiveness in the classroom.* San Francisco: Jossey-Bass.

Cross, J., & O'Driscoll, T. (2005, February). Workflow learning gets real. *Training 42*(2), 30–35.

Cross, K. P. (1981). *Adults as learners.* San Francisco: Jossey-Bass.

Findsen, B. (2005). *Learning later.* Malabar, FL: Krieger.

Freire, P. (1970). *Pedagogy of the oppressed* (revised 20th anniversary ed.). New York: Continuum.

Hayslip, B., Jr., & Kennelly, K. J. (1985). Cognitive and non-cognitive factors affecting learning among older adults. In D. B. Lumsden (Ed.), *The older adult as learner: Aspects of educational gerontology.* New York: Hemisphere.

Houle, C. (1961). *The inquiring mind.* Norman: Oklahoma Research Center for Continuing Professional and Higher Education.

International Symposium on Self Directed Learning. (n.d.). Retrieved May 31, 2005, from http://sdlglobal.com

Jarvis, P. (2001). *Learning in later life: An introduction for educators and caregivers.* London: Kogan Page.

Joyce, A. (2005, May 29). Easier lessons to take: Best training systems are mindful of matching employees' needs. *Washington Post,* p. F04. Retrieved June 1, 2005, from http://www.washingtonpost.com/wp-dyn/content/article/2005/05/27/AR2005052700527.html?referrer=emailarticlepg

Kaeter, M. (1995, January). Age-old myths. *Training, 32*(1), 61–66.

Kidd, J. R. (1973). *How adults learn.* New York: Cambridge.

Knowles, M. S. (1975). *Self-directed learning: A guide for learners and teachers.* Upper Saddle River, NJ: Prentice Hall/Cambridge.

Knowles, M. S. (1980). *The modern practice of adult education: From pedagogy to andragogy* (2nd ed.). New York: Cambridge.

Knox, A. B. (1981). *Adult development and learning.* San Francisco: Jossey-Bass.

Longworth, N. (2003). *Lifelong learning in action: Transforming education in the 21st century.* London: Kogan Page.

Marsick, V., & Watkins, K. (1990). *Informal and incidental learning in the workplace.* London: Routledge.

Merriam, S. B. (Ed.) (2001). *New directions for adult and continuing education: The new update on adult learning theory.* San Francisco: Jossey-Bass.

Merriam, S., & Caffarella, R. S. (1999). *Learning in adulthood* (2nd ed.). San Francisco: Jossey-Bass.

Mezirow, J., & associates (2000). *Transformative dimensions of adult learning.* San Francisco: Jossey-Bass.

Moody, H. R. (1985). Philosophy of education for older adults. In D. B. Lumsden (Ed.), *The older adult as learner: Aspects of educational gerontology* (pp. 25–49). New York: Hemisphere.

National Coalition of Independent Scholars (NCIS). (2000–2001; 2004).

Neikrug, S. M., Ronen, M., & Glanz, D. (1995). A special case of the very old lifelong learners. *Educational Gerontology 21,* 345–355.

Peterson, D. A. (1983). *Facilitating education for older learners.* San Francisco: Jossey-Bass.

Older worker adjustment programs. (1999, March). *Lessons Learned Series.* Canada: Human Resources Development Canada (HRDC). Retrieved February 2, 2006, from http://www11.hrsdc.gc.ca/en/cs/sp/hrsdc/edd/brief/1999–000578/owap.shtml

Schaie, K. W., & Willis, S. L. (2002). *Adult development and aging* (5th ed.). Upper Saddle River, NJ: Prentice Hall.

Sherron, R. H., & Lumsden, D. B. (1990). *Introduction to educational gerontology* (3rd ed.). New York: Hemisphere

Stein, D., & Rocco, T. S. (2001). *The older worker: Myths and realities.* Columbus, OH: ERIC Clearinghouse on Adult, Career, and Vocational Education. ED 99CO0013.

Stolovitch, H. D., & Keeps, E. K. (2004). Key ingredients for learning. *HSA e-Xpress:* http://www.hsa-lps.com/E_News/ENews_Jan04/HSA_e-Xpress_Jan04.htm

Tough, A. (1979). *The adult's learning projects: A fresh approach to theory and practice in adult learning* (2nd ed.). Toronto: Ontario Institute for Studies in Education.

Zemke, R., & Zemke, S. (1995, June). Adult learning: what do we know for sure? *Training, 32*(6), 31–37.

Appendix 4.1

Bernthal, P., Colteryahn, K., Davis, P., Naughton, J., Rothwell, W., & Wellins, R. (2004). *Mapping the future: Shaping new workplace learning and performance competencies.* Alexandria, VA: ASTD.

Lombardo, M., & Eichinger, R. (2000). High potentials as high learners. *Human Resource Management, 39*(4), 321.

McLagan, P. (1989). *Models for HRD practice.* 4 vols. Alexandria, VA: ASTD Press.

Rothwell, W. (2002). *The workplace learner: How to align training initiatives with individual learning competencies.* New York: AMACOM.

Rothwell, W., Sanders, E., & Soper, J. (1999). *ASTD models for workplace learning and performance: Roles, competencies, work outputs.* Alexandria, VA: ASTD.

Toffler, A. (1994). *Powershift: Knowledge, wealth, and violence at the edge of the 21st century.* New York: Bantam Books.

Chapter Five

Aging Quiz. (2004, September 17). Mayo Foundation for Medical Education and Research. Retrieved July 8, 2005, from www.mayoclinic.com

Albert, M. S., & Moss, M. B. (1997). Neuropsychology of aging: Findings in humans and monkeys. In E. L. Schneider & J. W. Rowe (Eds.), *Handbook of the biology of aging* (4th ed., pp. 217–233). San Diego: Academic Press.

Albrecht, K. (2006). *Social intelligence: The new science of success.* San Francisco: Jossey-Bass.

Begley, S. (2006, March, 3). Old brains don't work that badly after all, especially trained ones. *Wall Street Journal,* ccxlvii (51).

Callahan, J. S., Kiker, D. S., & Cross, T. (2003). Does method matter? A meta-analysis of the effects of training method on older learner training performance. *Journal of Management, 29*(5), 663–680.

Eggen, P., & Kauchak, D. (2001). *Educational psychology: Windows on classrooms* (5th ed.). Upper Saddle River, NJ: Merrill Prentice Hall.

Gagne, R. M. (1985). *The conditions of learning.* New York: Holt, Rinehart and Winston.

Gardner, H. (1983). *Frames of mind: The theory of multiple intelligences.* New York: Basic Books.

Gardner, H. (1998, Winter). A multiplicity of intelligences. *Scientific American, 9*(4), 19–23.

Hayslip, B., Jr., & Kennelly, K. J. (1985). Cognitive and non-cognitive factors affecting learning among older adults. In D. B. Lumsden (Ed.), *The older adult as learner: Aspects of educational gerontology.* New York: Hemisphere.

Jacoby, S. (2005). Mind aerobics: 10 ways to get your memory in shape. *AARP Bulletin, 46*(2), 22–24.

Jarvis, P. (2001). *Learning in later life: An introduction for educators and caregivers.* London: Kogan Page.

Jonassen, D. H. (2004). *Learning to solve problems: An instructional design guide.* San Francisco: Pfeiffer.

Lowenstein, D. (2005, May 16). *Neuropsychological assessment of MCI and early dementia.* Presentation at the 18th Annual Continuing Education Program on Issues in Aging, Wayne State University Institute of Gerontology. Troy, MI: Management Education Center.

Miller, G. A. (1956). The magical number seven, plus or minus two. *Psychological Review, 63,* 81–97.

Papalia, D. E., Camp, C. J., & Feldman, R. D. (1996). *Adult development and aging*. New York: McGraw-Hill.

Perlmutter, M., & Hall, E. (1985). *Adult development and aging*. Hoboken, NJ: Wiley.

Plutowski, S. (2005, November). Better with age: Still sharp at 90 and up. *NWA World Traveler, 36*(11), 22.

Roth, C. L. (2005, February 18). How to protect the aging workforce. *Occupational Hazards, 67*(2). 52–53. Retrieved July 5, 2005, from http://www.occupationalhazards.com/articles/13012

Stolovitch, H. D., & Keeps, E. K. (2004). Key ingredients for learning. *HSA e-Xpress*. Retrieved August 30, 2005, from http://www.hsa-lps.com/E_News/ENews_Jan04/HSA_e-Xpress_Jan04.htm

Sweller, J., van Merrienboer, J., & Paas, F. (1998) Cognitive architecture and instructional design. *Educational Psychology Review, 10*(3), 251–296.

Tracey, M. W. (2001). *The construction and validation of an instructional systems design model incorporating multiple intelligences*. Unpublished doctoral dissertation, Wayne State University, Detroit, MI.

Weil, A., M.D. (2005). *Healthy aging: A lifelong guide to your physical and spiritual well-being*. New York: Knopf.

Chapter Six

Bond, K. (1994, May 15). *Priming your workplace puzzlers for success: Reaching employees with learning disabilities (LD), Attention Deficit Disorder (ADD), or both*. Presentation at the ASTD International Conference and Exhibition.

Byrnes, G., & Watkins, C. (2005). Advertisement. Retrieved August 7, 2005, from http://www.nepamd.com/adultadd.htm

Clark, D. (2000). *Learning styles or how we go from the unknown to the known*. Retrieved March 17, 2006, from http://www.nwlink.com/~donclark/hrd/learning/styles.htm

Dunn, R., & Dunn, K. (1972). *Educator's self-teaching guide to individualizing instructional programs*. Upper Saddle River, NJ: Prentice Hall.

Gregorc, A. F. (1982). *An adult's guide to style*. Maynard, MA: Gabriel Systems.

Hartmann, T. (1997). *Attention deficit disorder: A different perception* (revised ed.). Nevada City, CA: Underwood Books.

Kolb, D. A. (1984). *Experiential learning: Experience as the source of learning and development.* Upper Saddle River, NJ: Prentice Hall.

Merriam, S., & Lumsden, B. (1985). Educational needs and interests of older adults. In D. B. Lumsden (Ed.), *The older adult as learner: Aspects of educational gerontology* (pp. 51–71). New York: Hemisphere.

Read, M. (2005, May 10). ADHD drugs not just for children anymore. Associated Press. Retrieved May 10, 2005, from http://portal.wowway.com/news/read.php?id=13163697&ps=1019

Rose, C. (1985). *Accelerated Learning.* New York: Dell.

Santo, S. (n.d.). *About learning styles.* Retrieved March 13, 2006, from http://www.usd.edu/~ssanto/styles.html

Shapiro, J., & Rich, R. (1999). *Facing learning disabilities in the adult years.* New York: Oxford University Press.

Wallis, C. (1994, July 18). Life in overdrive. *Time,* 43–50.

Chapter Seven

Beigel, J. (2001, July/August). Business and aging: Business, labor explore growing need for older workers. *Aging Today, xxii*(4), 13.

Blank, R., & Slipp, S. (1994). *Voices of diversity: Real people talk about problems and solutions in a workplace where everyone is not alike.* New York: AMACOM.

Erikson, E. H. (1963). *Childhood and society* (2nd ed.). New York: Norton.

Fisher, J. C. (1993, Winter). A framework for describing developmental change among older adults. *Adult Education Quarterly, 43*(2), 76–89.

Harris, P. (May, 2005). Boomer vs. echo boomer: The work war? *Training + Development,* 44–50.

Havighurst, R. J. (1972). *Developmental tasks and education* (3rd ed.). New York: McKay.

Kaplan-Leiserson, E. (2005, February). The changing workforce. *Training + Development, 59*(2), 10–11.

Lesser, E., Farrell, B., & Payne, M. (2004, October 21). *Addressing the challenges of an aging workforce: A human capital perspective for firms operating in Asia Pacific.* Somers, NY: IBM Business Consulting Services. Retrieved from www.ibm.com/bus

Lesser, E., Hausmann, C., & Feuerpeil, S. (2005, March 16). *Addressing the challenges of an aging workforce: A human capital perspective for companies operating in Europe.* IBM Institute for Business Value study. Somers, NY: IBM Global Services. Retrieved from www.ibm.com/bcs

Merriam, S., & Caffarella, R. S. (1999). *Learning in adulthood* (2nd ed.). San Francisco: Jossey-Bass.

Merriam, S., & Lumsden, B. (1985). Educational needs and interests of older adults. In D. B. Lumsden (Ed.), *The older adult as learner: Aspects of educational gerontology.* New York: Hemisphere.

Santrock, J. (1985). *Adult development and aging.* Dubuque, IA: William C. Brown.

Schaie, K. W., & Willis, S. L. (2002). *Adult development and aging* (5th ed.). Upper Saddle River, NJ: Prentice Hall.

Sheehy, G. (1976). *Passages.* New York: NAL/Dutton.

Sheehy, G. (1995). *New passages.* New York: Random House.

Smola, K. W., & Sutton, C. D. (2002). Generational differences: Revisiting generational work values for the new millennium. *Journal of Organizational Development, 23,* 363–382.

Stepanek, M. (September 17, 2003). The generation gap at work. *CIO Insight.* Transcript of roundtable discussion conducted July 24, 2003. Retrieved March 30, 2005, from http://www.cioinsight.com/article2/0,1397,1272084,00.asp

Woodwell, W., Jr. (2004). Demography is destiny: Population shifts will transform the 21st century workplace. *The ASTD trends watch: The forces that shape workplace performance and improvement.* Retrieved June 11, 2005, from www.astd.org

Zemke, R., Raines, C., & Filipczak, B. (2000). *Generations at work: Managing the clash of veterans, boomers, xers, and nexters in your workplace.* New York: American Management Association.

Chapter Eight

Aging Quiz. (2004, September 17). Mayo Foundation for Medical Education and Research. Retrieved July 8, 2005, from www.mayoclinic.com

Aging: What to expect as you get older. (2004, August 13). Mayo Foundation for Medical Education and Research (MFMER). Retrieved July 7, 2005, from www.mayoclinic.com

Albert, M. S., & Moss, M. B. (1997). Neuropsychology of aging: Findings in humans and monkeys. In E. L. Schneider & J. W. Rowe (Eds.), *Handbook of the biology of aging* (4th ed., pp. 217–233). San Diego: Academic Press.

Begley, S. (2006, March 3). Old brains don't work that badly after all, especially trained ones. *Wall Street Journal, ccxlvii* (51).

Bellantoni, M. J., & Blackman, M. R. (1997). Menopause and its consequences. In E. L. Schneider & J. W. Rowe (Eds.), *Handbook of the biology of aging* (4th ed., pp. 393–414). San Diego: Academic Press.

Blumberg, J. B. (1997). Status and functional impact of nutrition in older adults. In E. L. Schneider & J. W. Rowe (Eds.), *Handbook of the biology of aging* (4th ed., pp. 393–414). San Diego: Academic Press.

Cotman, C. W., & Neeper, S. (1997). Activity-dependent plasticity and the aging brain. In E. L. Schneider & J. W. Rowe (Eds.), *Handbook of the biology of aging* (4th ed., pp. 283–299). San Diego: Academic Press.

Denying, defying limits of age. (2004, March). *AARP Bulletin, 45*(3), 2.

Ekstrom, I. (1997). *An investigation of age related relationships between reading speed and paper color intensity.* Unpublished doctoral dissertation, Wayne State University, Detroit, MI.

Ferrini, A. F., & Ferrini, R. L. (2000). *Health in the later years* (3rd ed.) Boston: McGraw-Hill.

Goldberg, A. P., Dengel, D. R., & Hagberg, J. M. (1997). Exercise physiology and aging. In E. L. Schneider & J. W. Rowe (Eds.), *Handbook of the biology of aging* (4th ed., pp. 331–354). San Diego: Academic Press.

Hayslip, B., Jr., & Kennelly, K. J. (1985). Cognitive and non-cognitive factors affecting learning among older adults. In D. B. Lumsden (Ed.), *The older adult as learner: Aspects of educational gerontology.* New York: Hemisphere.

Hiatt, L. G. (1981). The color and use of color in environments for older people. *Nursing Home, 3,* 18–22.

Human intelligence determined by volume, location of gray matter tissue in brain. (2004). *Ascribe Newswire Health News Service Report.* Irvine: University of California.

McIntire, M. B. (2005, March). The aging workforce. *The Journal of Employee Assistance, 35,* (i1), 26. Retrieved April 20, 2005, from Infotrac database.

Medsker, K.L. (2006). Workplace design. In J.E. Pershing (Ed.). *The handbook of human performance technology: Principles, practices, potential* (3rd ed.) San Francisco: Pfeiffer/International Society for Performance Improvement..

Moody, H. R. (1985). Philosophy of education for older adults. In D. B. Lumsden (Ed.), *The older adult as learner: Aspects of educational gerontology* (pp. 25–49), New York: Hemisphere.

Roth, C. L. (2005, February 18). How to protect the aging workforce. *Occupational Hazards, 67*(2), 52–53. Retrieved July 5, 2005, from http://www.occupationalhazards.com/articles/13012

Troll, L. E. (1982). *Continuations: Adult development and aging.* Monterey, CA: Brooks/Cole.

Whitbourne, S. K. (1985). *The aging body.* New York: Springer-Verlag.

Chapter Nine

Aging Quiz. (2004, September 17). Mayo Foundation for Medical Education and Research. Retrieved July 8, 2005, from www.mayoclinic.com

Anspaugh, D. J., Hamrick, M. H., & Rosata, F. D. (1994). *Wellness: Concepts and applications* (2nd ed.). St. Louis, MO: Mosby-Yearbook.

Bradford, M. (2005, June 27). On-the-job safety concerns increase as numbers of senior workers rise. *Business Insurance, 39,* 4.

A close-up look at 50+ America. (2004). Washington, DC: American Association of Retired Persons (AARP).

Conlin, M. (2004a, August 30). Meditation: New research shows that it changes the brain in ways that alleviate stress. *Business Week,* 136–137.

Conlin, M. (2004b, December 20). Take a vacation from your BlackBerry. *Business Week,* 56.

Constitution of the World Health Organization (WHO). (1947). *Chronicle WHO 1,* 29–43.

Costa, P. T., Jr., & McCrae, R. R. (1996). Mood and personality in adulthood. In C. Magai & S. H. McFadden (Eds.), *Handbook of emotion, adult development, and aging* (pp. 369–383). San Diego: Academic Press.

Crimmins, E. M., Reynolds, S. L., & Saito, Y. (1999, January). Trends in health and ability to work among the older working age population. *Journal of Gerontology: Social Sciences,* 531–540.

Edlin, G., Golanty, E., & McCormack Brown, K. (2002). *Health and wellness* (7th ed.). Sudbury, MA: Jones & Bartlett.

Gatz, M., Kasl-Godley, J. E., & Karel, M. J. (1996). Aging and mental disorders. In J. E. Birren & K. Warner Schaie (Eds.), *Handbook of the psychology of aging* (4th ed., pp. 365–382). San Diego: Academic Press.

Lamdin, L., & Fugate, M. (1997). *Elderlearning: New frontier in an aging society.* Phoenix, AZ: American Council on Education and The Oryx Press.

Magai, C., & Nusbaum, B. (1996). Personality change in adulthood. In C. Magai & S. H. McFadden (Eds.), *Handbook of emotion, adult development, and aging* (pp. 403–420). San Diego: Academic Press.

Manheimer, R. J., Snodgrass, D. D., & Moskow-McKenzie, D. (1995). *Older adult education: A guide to research, programs, and policies.* Westport, CT: Greenwood Press.

Mobbs, C. V. (1997). Neuroendocrinology of aging. In E. L. Schneider & J. W. Rowe (Eds.), *Handbook of the biology of aging* (4th ed., p. 234–282). San Diego: Academic Press.

Payne, W. A., & Hahn, D.B. (2000). *Understanding your health* (6th ed.). Boston: McGraw-Hill.

Roth, C. L. (2005, February 18). How to protect the aging workforce. *Occupational Hazards, 67*(2). 52–53. Retrieved July 5, 2005, from http://www.occupationalhazards.com/articles/13012

Summerfield, B. (2005, June 28). Get physical: Healthy lifestyles lead to higher performance. *Workplace Performance Solutions.* Retrieved July 7, 2005, from http://www.wpsmag.com/content/templates/wps_article.asp?articleid=251&zoneid=48

Teaff, J. D. (1985). *Leisure services with the elderly.* St. Louis, MO: Times Mirror/Mosby.

Tucker, J. S., & Friedman, H. S. (1996). Emotion, personality, and health. In Magai, C., & McFadden, S. H. (Eds.), *Handbook of emotion, adult development, and aging* (pp. 307–326). San Diego: Academic Press.

Vojta, C. (2003, April 28). Covering the gray: Benefit programs that address an aging workforce. *National Underwriter: Life & Health/Financial Services Edition, 107,* 17–25. Retrieved March 14, 2005, from First Search database.

Part Three

European Union. (1995, November 21). *Teaching and Learning: Towards the learning society.* White Paper on education and training. Brussels: European Union.

Jarvis, P. (2001). *Learning in later life: An introduction for educators and caregivers.* London: Kogan Page.

Chapter Ten

Dick, B. (1997). *Action learning and action research.* Retrieved March 24, 2006, from http://www.scu.edu.au/schools/gcm/ar/arp/actlearn.html

Dilworth, R. I. (1998). Action learning in a nutshell. *Performance Improvement Quarterly, 11*(1), 28–43.

Dixon, N. M. (1998). Action learning. More than just a task force. *Performance Improvement Quarterly, 11*(1), 44–58.

Gomez-Mejia, L. R., Balkin, D. B., & Cardy, R. L. (2001). *Managing human resources* (3rd ed.). Upper Saddle River, NJ: Prentice Hall.

Marquardt, M. J. (1999). *Action learning in action: Transforming problems and people for world-class organizational learning.* Palo Alto, CA: Davies-Black.

Marquardt, M. J. (2004, June). Harnessing the power of action learning. *Training + Development, 58*(6), 4, 26–32.

Rothwell. W. J. (1999). *The action learning guidebook: A real-time strategy for problem solving, training, design, and employee development.* San Francisco: Pfeiffer.

Salopek, J. J., & Kesting, B. (1999, February). Stop playing games. *Training + Development, 53*(2), 32–33.

Silberman, M. (1998). *Active training: A handbook of techniques, designs, case examples, and tips* (2nd ed.). San Francisco: Pfeiffer.

Van Tiem, D. M., Moseley, J. L., & Dessinger, J. C. (2001). *Performance improvement interventions: Enhancing people, processes, and organizations through performance technology.* Silver Spring, MD: International Society for Performance Improvement.

Chapter Eleven

Clark, R. E. (2006). Motivating individuals, teams, and organizations. In J.E. Pershing (Ed.), *The handbook of human performance technology: Principles, practices, potential* (3rd ed.). (pp. 478–497). San Francisco: Pfeiffer/International Society for Performance Improvement.

Gagne, R. M., & Medsker, K. L. (1996). *The conditions of learning: Training applications.* Alexandria, VA: American Society for Training and Development (ASTD).

Goldin, D.S., Venneri, S. L., & Noor, A.K. (n.d.). *Ready for the future? NASA explores virtual environments.* Retrieved July 13, 2006 from http://nasa.gov/archives

Houle, C. (1996). *The design of education* (2nd ed.). San Francisco: Jossey-Bass.

Kayes, A. B., Kayes, D. C., & Kolb, D. A. (2004, December 13). *Experiential learning in teams.* Cleveland, OH: Department of Organizational Behavior, Weatherhead School of Management, Case Reserve Western University. Working Paper ORBH. Retrieved July 7, 2006, from http://www.learningfromexperience.com/images/uploads/experiential-learning-in-teams.pdf

McDonnell, S. (2005, August 23). Team-building with a twist. *New York Times,* p. C7. Retrieved August 29, 2005, from www.nytimes.com

Martin, C.A. & Tulgan, B. (2001).*Managing Generation Y.* Amherst, MA: HRD Press.

Novicevic, M. M., & Buckley, M. R. (2001). How to manage the emerging generational divide in the contemporary knowledge-rich workplace. *Performance Improvement Quarterly, 14*(2), 125–144.

Rothwell, W. J. (2002). *The workplace learner: How to align training initiatives with individual learning competencies.* New York: AMACOM.

Senge, P. M. (1990). *The fifth discipline: The art and practice of the learning organization.* New York: Currency Doubleday.

Thiagarajan, S. (1999). Team activities for learning and performance. In H. D. Stolovitch & E. J. Keeps (Eds.), *Handbook of human performance technology: Improving individual and organizational performance worldwide* (2nd ed., pp. 518–544). San Francisco: Pfeiffer.

Tough, A. (1979). *The adult's learning projects: A fresh approach to theory and practice in adult learning* (2nd ed.). Toronto: Ontario Institute for Studies in Education.

Zemke, R., Raines, C., & Filipczak, B. (2000). *Generations at work: Managing the clash of veterans, boomers, xers, and nexters in your workplace.* New York: American Management Association.

Chapter Twelve

Boehle, S. (2005, January). Simulations: The next generation of e-learning. *Training, 42*(1), 22–31.

Chang, C. C. (2003, July-August). An electronic performance support system for learning and doing instructional design tasks. *Educational Technology, 43*(4), 46–51.

Coutu, D. (2000, November-December). Too old to learn? *Harvard Business Review,* 37–52.

Cross, J., & O'Driscoll, T. (2005, February). Workflow learning gets real. *Training, 42*(2), 30–35.

Ford, R. (1999). Traditional vs. real-time training. *Performance Improvement, 38*(1), 25–29.

Gery, G., & Jezsik, L. (1999). Electronic performance support system (EPSS). In D. G. Langdon, K. S. Whiteside, & M. M. McKenna (Eds.), *Intervention resource guide: 50 performance improvement tools* (pp. 142–148). San Francisco: Pfeiffer.

Mondy, R. W., Noe, R. M., & Premeaux, S. R. (2002). *Human resource management* (8th ed.). Upper Saddle River, NJ: Prentice Hall.

Nguyen, F., Klein, J. D., & Sullivan, H. (2005). A comparative study of electronic support systems. *Performance Improvement Quarterly, 18*(4), 71–86.

O'Driscoll, T., & Cross, J. (2005, September). In her own words: Gloria Gery on performance. *Performance and Instruction, 44* (8), n.p. Retrieved March 29, 2006, from http://www.workflowlearning.com/

Rossett, A., & Gautier-Downes, J. (1991). *A handbook of job aids.* San Francisco: Pfeiffer.

Rothwell, W. J., & Kazanas, H. C. (1994). *Improving on-the-job training: How to establish and operate a comprehensive OJT program.* San Francisco: Jossey-Bass.

Solano, K. (2005, October). Training turns exciting. *Training + Development, 59*(10), 38–40.

Van Tiem, D. M., Moseley, J. L., & Dessinger, J. C. (2001). *Performance improvement interventions: Enhancing people, processes, and organizations through performance technology.* Silver Spring, MD: International Society for Performance Improvement.

Zarrabian, M. (2004, December). The learning matrix—Just-in-time learning. *Chief Learning Officer Magazine.* Retrieved from http://www.clomedia.com/

Chapter Thirteen

Dessinger, J. C., & Moseley, J. L. (2006). The full scoop on full scope evaluation. In J. E. Pershing (Ed.), *The handbook of human performance technology: Principles, practices, potential* (3rd ed.). San Francisco: Pfeiffer/International Society for Performance Improvement.

House, R. S. (1996). Classroom instruction. In Craig, R. L. (Ed.), *The ASTD training & development handbook: A guide to human resource development* (4th ed., pp. 437–452.). New York: McGraw-Hill.

Joint Committee on Standards for Educational Evaluation. (1994). *The program evaluation standards: How to assess evaluations of educational programs* (2nd ed.). Thousand Oaks, CA: Sage.

Knowles, M. S. (1980). *The modern practice of adult education: From pedagogy to andragogy* (2nd ed.). New York: Cambridge.

Moody, H. R. (2004, August/September). PowerPoint: The hidden curriculum. *Newsletter of the Association for Gerontology, 14.*

Skills for tomorrow's leaders. (2005, August 3). *CLO Executive Briefings 3*(31), n.p. Online newsletter received August 5, 2005.

Stolovitch, H. D., & Keeps, E. K. (2004). Key ingredients for learning. *HSA e-Xpress.* Retrieved August 30, 2005, from http://www.hsa-lps.com/E_News/ENews_Jan04/HSA_e-Xpress_Jan04.htm

Sugrue, B., & Kim, K. H. (2004). *State of the industry: ASTD's annual review of trends in workplace learning and performance.* Alexandria, VA: ASTD.

Van Tiem, D. M., Moseley, J. L., & Dessinger, J. C. (2001). *Performance improvement interventions: Enhancing people, processes, and organizations through performance technology.* Silver Spring, MD: International Society for Performance Improvement.

Whitney, K. (2005, October 19). Tips for virtual management: Maximize learning effectiveness. *CLO Executive Briefings, 3*(42), n.p. Online newsletter received October 19, 2005, from www.clomedia.com

Yelon, S. (1999). Live classroom instruction. In H. D. Stolovitch & E. J. Keeps (Eds.), *Handbook of human performance technology: Improving individual and organizational performance worldwide* (2nd ed., pp. 485–517). San Francisco: Pfeiffer.

Chapter Fourteen

ASTD The Buzz. (2005a, May 5). Online newsletter, n.p. *ASTD The Buzz.* (2005b, October 3). Online newsletter, n.p. *ASTD The Buzz.* (2005c, October 3), n.p. Online newsletter retrieved October 14, 2005, n.p.

Cross, J., & O'Driscoll, T. (2005, February). Workflow learning gets real. *Training, 42*(2), 30–35.

Dessinger, J. C., Brown, K. G., Reesman, M. N., & Elliott, L. E. (1998). Measuring attitudes to assess training: The interactive distance learning group looks at learning and transfer from satellite training. In D. A. Schreiber & Z. L. Berge (Eds.), *Distance training: How innovative organizations are using technology to maximize learning and meet business objectives* (pp. 328–350). San Francisco: Jossey-Bass.

Dessinger, J. C., & Conley, L. (2001). Beyond the sizzle: Sustaining distance training for Ford Motor Company dealerships. In Z. L. Berge (Ed.), *Sustaining distance learning: Integrating learning technologies into the fabric of the enterprise* (pp. 178–198). San Francisco: Jossey-Bass.

Michalski, G. V. (2001). Learning to work in web time. In Z. L. Berge (Ed.), *Sustaining distance learning: Integrating learning technologies into the fabric of the enterprise* (pp. 199–217). San Francisco: Jossey-Bass.

MP3s and iPods aren't just for music these days. (2005, July 6). *CLO Executive Briefings,* online newsletter received July 10, 2005.

Rosenberg, M. J. (2001). *E-learning: Strategies for delivering knowledge in the digital age.* New York: McGraw-Hill.

Rossett, A. (2005, February). Moving online. *Training + Development, 59*(2), 14–15.

Sales, G. C. (2002). *A quick guide to e-learning.* Andover, MN: Expert.

Sloman, M. (2002). *The e-learning revolution: How technology is driving a new training paradigm.* New York: AMACOM.

Sugrue, B., & Kim, K. H. (2004). *State of the industry: ASTD's annual review of trends in workplace learning and performance.* Alexandria, VA: ASTD.

Van Tiem, D. M., Moseley, J. L., & Dessinger, J. C. (2001). *Performance improvement interventions: Enhancing people, processes, and organizations through performance technology.* Silver Spring, MD: International Society for Performance Improvement.

Verduin, J. R., Jr., & Clark, T. A. (1991). *Distance education: Foundations of the practice.* San Francisco: Jossey-Bass.

Whitney, K. (2005, October 19). Tips for virtual management: Maximize learning effectiveness. *CLO Executive Briefings, 3*(42), n.p. Online newsletter received October 19, 2005, from www.clomedia.com

Chapter Fifteen

AchieveGlobal report: New supervisors face greater challenges. (2005, September 14). *CLO Industry News 3*(37). Online newsletter received September 16, 2005, www.clomedia.com

Beigel, J. (2001, July/August). Business and aging: Business, labor explore growing need for older workers. *Aging Today, xxii*(4), 13.

Biech, E. (2005). *Training for dummies.* Hoboken, NJ: Wiley.

Boulmetis, J., & Dutwin, P. (2006). *The ABCs of evaluation: Timeless techniques for program and project managers* (2nd ed.). San Francisco: Jossey-Bass.

Byrnes, N. (2005, October 10). Home schooled by the brass. *Business Week,* 71.

Callahan, J. S., Kiker, D. S., & Cross, T. (2003). Does method matter? A meta-analysis of the effects of training method on older learner training performance. *Journal of Management, 29*(5), 663–680.

Edmondson, B. (2005, November/December). Working wonders. Washington, DC: *AARP Magazine, 48*(6B), 58–66.

European Union. (1995, November 21). *Teaching and learning: Towards the learning society.* White Paper on education and training. Brussels: European Union.

Feld, J. (1999, January). Eye on the future: Can you "age proof" your career? SOHO, online newsletter, retrieved January 1999.

Fink, A. (2005). *Evaluation fundamentals: Insights into the outcomes, effectiveness, and quality of health programs* (2nd ed.). Thousand Oaks, CA: Sage.

Fitzpatrick, G. L., Sanders, J. R., & Worthen, B. R. (2004). *Program evaluation: Alternative approaches and practical guidelines* (3rd ed.). Boston: Pearson Education.

Friedman, T. L. (2005). *The world is flat: A brief history of the twenty-first century.* New York: Farrar, Straus & Giroux.

Goleman, D. P. (2002). *Business: The ultimate resource.* Cambridge, MA: Perseus.

Greenberg, J., & Baron, R. A. (2003). *Behavior in organizations: Understanding and managing the human side of work* (8th ed.). Upper Saddle River, NJ: Prentice Hall.

Hale, J. (2002). *Performance-based evaluation: Tools and techniques to measure the impact of training.* San Francisco: Pfeiffer.

Joyce, A. (2005, May 29). Easier lessons to take: Best training systems are mindful of matching employees' needs. *Washington Post,* p. F04.

Lumsden, D. B. (Ed.). (1985). *The older adult as learner: Aspects of educational gerontology.* New York: Hemisphere.

Margolis, F. H., & Bell, C. R. (1989). *Understanding training: Perspectives and practices.* San Diego: University Associates, and Minneapolis: Lakewood.

Moseley, J. L., & Dessinger, J. C. (1994, March). Criteria for evaluating instructional products and programs for older adult learners. *Performance and Instruction, 33*(3), 39–45.

Mulkey, J., & Naughton, J. (2005, January). 10 myths of certification. *Training + Development, 59*(1), 20–29.

Phillips, J. J. (1997). *Handbook of training evaluation and measurement methods* (3rd ed.). Houston: Gulf.

Richey, R. (1992). *Designing instruction for the adult learner: Systemic training theory and practice.* London: Kogan Page.

Summerfield, B. (2005, August 11). A time and place for technology. *Workplace Performance Solutions: Performance Perspectives, 1*(7), n.p. Online newsletter

received August 11, 2005, from http://www.wpsmag.com/content/templates/
wps_article.asp?articleid=316&zoneid=48

VanTiem, D.M., Moseley, J.L., & Dessinger, J.C. (2004). *Fundamentals of performance technology: A guide to improving people, process, and performance* (2nd ed.). Silver Springs, MD: International Society for Performance Improvement (ISPI).

Whitney, K. (2005, October 19). Tips for virtual management: Maximize learning effectiveness. *CLO Executive Briefings, 3*(42), n.p. Online newsletter received October 19, 2005, from www.clomedia.com

Woodwell, W., Jr. (2004). Demography is destiny: Population shifts will transform the 21st century workplace. *The ASTD trends watch: The forces that shape workplace performance and improvement.* Retrieved June 11, 2005, from www.astd.org

Glossary

Gardner, H. (1983). *Frames of mind: The theory of multiple intelligences.* New York: Basic Books.

Joint Committee on Standards for Educational Evaluation. (1994). *The program evaluation standards: How to assess evaluations of educational programs* (2nd ed.). Thousand Oaks, CA: Sage.

Langdon, D. (1995). *The new language of work.* Amherst, MA: Human Resource Development Press.

Sheehy, G. (1995). *New passages.* New York: Random House.

James L. Moseley is associate professor of instructional technology at Wayne State University College of Education. He teaches program evaluation and human performance technology courses and advises graduate students at the dissertation level. He transferred to the College from the School of Medicine after thirty-one years of administrative and teaching service both as an OWL and as a WLP practitioner. In a previous life he was a successful secondary English teacher, a director of guidance, and a principal of two high schools.

In addition to *Training Older Workers and Learners,* Moseley has coauthored four books, of which two—*Fundamentals of Performance Technology: A Guide to Improving People, Process, and Performance* (2000 and 2004, ISPI) and *Performance Improvement Interventions: Enhancing People, Process, and Organizations through Performance Technology* (2001, ISPI)—have received the ISPI Award of Excellence for Outstanding Instructional Communication. The fourth book is *Confirmative Evaluation: Practical Strategies for Valuing Continuous Improvement* (2004, Pfeiffer). In addition, he has coauthored a chapter on evaluation for the *Performance Improvement Series Volume Two: Performance Improvement Interventions*; evaluation instruments for the Pfeiffer *Training and Consulting Annuals*; and two chapters on evaluation and Six Sigma for the 2006 third edition of *Handbook of Human Performance Technology: Principles, Practices, Potential.* Moseley has published journal articles and conducted numerous workshops at professional national and international meetings. He is a member of ISPI and the American Society for Training and Development (ASTD) and a former president of the Michigan Society of Gerontology. He holds numerous graduate degrees, licenses, and certificates, including licensed professional counselor (LPC), certified health education specialist (CHES), and certified performance technologist (CPT).

Moseley has won four School of Medicine Teaching awards; the Outstanding Graduate Mentor Award in the Social Sciences and the Alumni Association Faculty Service Award from Wayne State University; the Everett J. Soop Outstanding Educator of the Year Award for dedication, creativity, and foresight in gerontology; and a Distinguished Alumnus Award. He is most proud, however, of the North Star Award and the Rock Star Award presented by residence hall students for his work with them as Faculty Associate for the Pre-Med Living Learning Community at Wayne State University.

Dr. Joan Conway Dessinger is a senior consultant with and founder of The Lake Group, a consulting firm that specializes in analyzing, designing, developing, and evaluating workplace learning and performance interventions. She has consulted with national and international education, business and industry, health, and service organizations. Dr. Dessinger also teaches graduate courses in instructional design, instructional systems planning and management, needs analysis, program evaluation, and adult learning in the Instructional Technology Department at Wayne State University, Detroit, and for Oakland University's Human Resource Development graduate program in Rochester, Michigan.

In addition to *Training Older Workers and Learners,* Dr. Dessinger has coauthored four books: *Confirmative Evaluation: Practical Strategies for Valuing Continuous Improvement* (2004, Pfeiffer); *Fundamentals of Performance Technology: A Guide to Improving People, Process, and Performance* (2000 and 2004, ISPI); and *Performance Improvement Interventions: Enhancing People, Process, and Organizations through Performance Technology* (2001, ISPI). Both *Fundamentals* and *Interventions* received ISPI Awards of Excellence for Communication.

Recently Dr. Dessinger coauthored two chapters for the third edition of *The Handbook of Performance Technology* (2006, Pfeiffer/ISPI)—a chapter on full-scope evaluation and a chapter on Six Sigma applications in HPT. She has also coauthored a chapter on full scope evaluation for the *Performance Improvement Series Volume Two* (1998, ISPI), a chapter on evaluating satellite-based distance training for *Distance Training* (1998, Jossey-Bass), and a chapter on the FORDSTAR distance learning program at Ford Motor Company for *Sustaining Distance Training* (2001, Jossey-Bass).

Dr. Dessinger is a member of the International Society for Performance Improvement (ISPI) and the American Society for Training and Development (ASTD). She is frequently invited to present at state, national, and international conferences as well as local professional meetings.

INDEX

Rita C. Richey is professor and program coordinator of instructional technology at Wayne State University. She has been at Wayne State for over thirty years and is experienced in not only program development, but also in education and training research. She has published widely in the areas of instructional design theory, including such books as *The Theoretical and Conceptual Bases of Instructional Design, Designing Instruction for the Adult Learner,* and *The Legacy of Robert M. Gagne.* Rita is coauthor of the third edition of *Instructional Design Competencies: The Standards* and the third edition of *Training Manager Competencies: The Standards.* She is also coauthor of *Instructional Technology: The Definition and Domains of the Field,* a book that received the 1995 Outstanding Book Award and the 1996 Brown Publication Award, both from the Association of Educational Communications and Technology. She has also received four major awards from Wayne State University: the President's Award for Excellence in Teaching, the Outstanding Graduate Mentor's Award, a Distinguished Faculty Fellowship, and an award for Outstanding Scholarly Achievement by Women Faculty. In addition, she has been elected to the Wayne State University Academy of Scholars. In recognition of her career's work, she received the AECT Distinguished Service Award in 2000.

William J. Rothwell, Ph.D., SPHR certification, is professor in charge of the workforce education and development program in the Department of Learning and Performance Systems at Pennsylvania State University. He is also president of Rothwell and Associates, Inc., an independent consulting firm. He has been a training director in a government agency and a large insurance company, a consultant to many organizations, and a college professor.

William is the author and coauthor of many books. His most recent publications include *Mastering the Instructional Design Process: A Systematic Approach,* 3rd edition (with H.C. Kazanas, 2004), *The Strategic Development of Talent* (with H.C. Kazanas, 2003), *What CEOs Expect from Corporate Training: Building Workplace Learning and Performance Initiatives That Advance Organizational Goals* (with J. Lindholm and W. Wallick, 2003), *Planning and Managing Human Resources,* 2nd edition (with H.C. Kazanas, 2003), *Creating Sales Training and Development Programs: A Competency-Based Approach to Building Sales Ability* (with W. Donahue and J. Park, 2002), *The Workplace Learner: How to Align Training Initiatives with Individual Learning Competencies* (2002), and *Building Effective Technical Training: How to Develop Hard Skills Within Organizations* (with J. Benkowski, 2002).

In his consulting work, William specializes in human resources practices—particularly in competency modeling and succession planning and management.

Timothy W. Spannaus, Ph.D., is senior lecturer in instructional technology and research fellow with the Institute for Learning and Performance Improvement, at Wayne State University. He is also chief learning architect at The Emdicium Group, Inc., in Southfield, Michigan.

Tim is president of the International Board of Standards for Training, Performance, and Instruction and was previously president of the Association for Development of Computer-Based Instructional Systems. He is active in the International Society for Performance Improvement and the American Society for Training and Development.

His teaching, research, and development focus on interactive technologies for learning and performance improvement. Recent projects include the creation of a training vision for a major municipal utility, the design and development of web-based learning courses, and a knowledge management plan for a Fortune 500 manufacturer. Recent publications include *Training Manager Competencies: The Standards,* two chapters in the *ID Casebook*—a forthcoming book on development of web-based learning—and numerous papers and presentations.

GAME A group activity that has the purpose of fostering team spirit and togetherness in addition to the achievement of a pre-stated goal. Usually contrived—undertaking a desert expedition, for example—this type of learning method offers an engaging means for participants to demonstrate and practice business and interpersonal skills. Games are effective for team building and personal development mainly because the goal is subordinate to the process—the means through which participants reach decisions, collaborate, communicate, and generate trust and understanding. Games often engage teams in "friendly" competition.

ICEBREAKER A (usually) short activity designed to help participants overcome initial anxiety in a training session and/or to acquaint the participants with one another. An icebreaker can be a fun activity or can be tied to specific topics or training goals. While a useful tool in itself, the icebreaker comes into its own in situations where tension or resistance exists within a group.

INSTRUMENT A device used to assess, appraise, evaluate, describe, classify, and summarize various aspects of human behavior. The term used to describe an instrument depends primarily on its format and purpose. These terms include survey, questionnaire, inventory, diagnostic, survey, and poll. Some uses of instruments include providing instrumental feedback to group members, studying here-and-now processes or functioning within a group, manipulating group composition, and evaluating outcomes of training and other interventions.

Instruments are popular in the training and HR field because, in general, more growth can occur if an individual is provided with a method for focusing specifically on his or her own behavior. Instruments also are used to obtain information that will serve as a basis for change and to assist in workforce planning efforts.

Paper-and-pencil tests still dominate the instrument landscape with a typical package comprising a facilitator's guide, which offers advice on administering the instrument and interpreting the collected data, and an initial set of instruments. Additional instruments are available separately. Pfeiffer, though, is investing heavily in e-instruments. Electronic instrumentation provides effortless distribution and, for larger groups particularly, offers advantages over paper-and-pencil tests in the time it takes to analyze data and provide feedback.

LECTURETTE A short talk that provides an explanation of a principle, model, or process that is pertinent to the participants' current learning needs. A lecturette is intended to establish a common language bond between the trainer and the participants by providing a mutual frame of reference. Use a lecturette as an introduction to a group activity or event, as an interjection during an event, or as a handout.

MODEL A graphic depiction of a system or process and the relationship among its elements. Models provide a frame of reference and something more tangible, and more easily remembered, than a verbal explanation. They also give participants something to "go on," enabling them to track their own progress as they experience the dynamics, processes, and relationships being depicted in the model.

ROLE PLAY A technique in which people assume a role in a situation/scenario: a customer service rep in an angry-customer exchange, for example. The way in which the role is approached is then discussed and feedback is offered. The role play is often repeated using a different approach and/or incorporating changes made based on feedback received. In other words, role playing is a spontaneous interaction involving realistic behavior under artificial (and safe) conditions.

SIMULATION A methodology for understanding the interrelationships among components of a system or process. Simulations differ from games in that they test or use a model that depicts or mirrors some aspect of reality in form, if not necessarily in content. Learning occurs by studying the effects of change on one or more factors of the model. Simulations are commonly used to test hypotheses about what happens in a system—often referred to as "what if?" analysis—or to examine best-case/worst-case scenarios.

THEORY A presentation of an idea from a conjectural perspective. Theories are useful because they encourage us to examine behavior and phenomena through a different lens.

TOPICS

The twin goals of providing effective and practical solutions for workforce training and organization development and meeting the educational needs of training and human resource professionals shape Pfeiffer's publishing program. Core topics include the following:

Leadership & Management

Communication & Presentation

Coaching & Mentoring

Training & Development

e-Learning

Teams & Collaboration

OD & Strategic Planning

Human Resources

Consulting

What will you find on pfeiffer.com?

- The best in workplace performance solutions for training and HR professionals

- Downloadable training tools, exercises, and content

- Web-exclusive offers

- Training tips, articles, and news

- Seamless online ordering

- Author guidelines, information on becoming a Pfeiffer Affiliate, and much more

Discover more at www.pfeiffer.com